The
BUSH TRAGEDY

BY THE SAME AUTHOR

In an Uncertain World
(with Robert E. Rubin)

In Defense of Government

George W. Bushisms

The BUSH TRAGEDY

JACOB WEISBERG

BLOOMSBURY

First published in Great Britain 2008

Bloomsbury Publishing Plc,
36 Soho Square,
London W1D 3QY

A CIP catalogue record for this book is available from the British Library

ISBN 978 0 7475 9394 2

10 9 8 7 6 5 4 3 2 1

Printed in Great Britain by Clays Ltd, St Ives plc

Bloomsbury Publishing, London, New York and Berlin

The paper this book is printed on is certified by the © 1996 Forest Stweardship Council A.C. (FSC). It is ancient-forest friendly. The printer holds FSC chain of custody SGS-COC-2061

To Deborah,
with love and gratitude

See, sons, what things you are!
How quickly nature falls into revolt
When gold becomes her object!
For this the foolish over-careful fathers
Have broke their sleep with thoughts, their brains with care,
Their bones with industry;
For this they have engrossed and piled up
The canker'd heaps of strange-achieved gold;
For this they have been thoughtful to invest
Their sons with arts and martial exercises:
When, like the bee, culling from every flower
The virtuous sweets,
Our thighs pack'd with wax, our mouths with honey,
We bring it to the hive, and, like the bees,
Are murdered for our pains.

—HENRY IV, PART 2

Contents

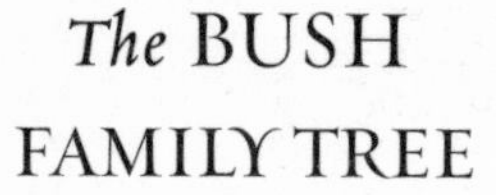

The BUSH FAMILY TREE

James Smith Bush
JUNE 15, 1825–
NOVEMBER 11, 1889

m.

Harriet Eleanor Fay
OCTOBER 29, 1829–
FEBRUARY 27, 1924

Samuel Prescott Bush
OCTOBER 4, 1863–
FEBRUARY 8, 1948

m.

Flora Sheldon
MARCH 17, 1872–
SEPTEMBER 4, 1920

Prescott Sheldon Bush
MAY 15, 1895–
OCTOBER 8, 1972

m.

Dorothy Wear Walker
JULY 1, 1901–
NOVEMBER 19, 1992

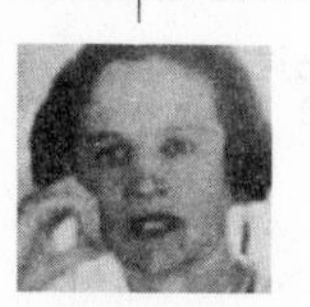

Nancy Walker
OCTOBER 24, 1899–
MAY 7, 1997

Prescott "Pressie" Bush
AUGUST 10, 1922–

Nancy Bush
FEBRUARY 4, 1926–

Jonathan James Bush
MAY 6, 1931–

Pauline "Robin" Bush
DECEMBER 20, 1949–
OCTOBER 11, 1953

John Ellis "Jeb" Bush
FEBRUARY 11, 1953–

Neil Mallon Bush
JANUARY 22, 1955–

Marvin Pierce Bush
OCTOBER 22, 1956–

David Davis "D.D." Walker *m.* Martha Adela Beaky
JANUARY 19, 1840–OCTOBER 4, 1918 | JUNE 1, 1841–JULY 17, 1917

George Herbert "Bert" Walker *m.* Lucretia "Loulie" Wear
JUNE 11, 1875–JUNE 24, 1953 | SEPTEMBER 17, 1874–AUGUST 28, 1961

George Herbert "Herbie" Walker, Jr.
NOVEMBER 24, 1905–NOVEMBER 29, 1977

James Walker
MARCH 25, 1907–AUGUST 30, 1997

John Walker
DECEMBER 15, 1909–AUGUST 16, 1990

Louis Walker
APRIL 14, 1912–NOVEMBER 17, 2001

William "Bucky" Bush
JULY 14, 1938–

George Herbert Walker Bush *m.* Barbara Pierce
JUNE 12, 1924– | JUNE 8, 1925–

Dorothy Walker Bush
AUGUST 18, 1959–

George Walker Bush *m.* Laura Lane Welch
JULY 6, 1946– | NOVEMBER 4, 1946–

Barbara Pierce Bush
NOVEMBER 25, 1981–

Jenna Welch Bush
NOVEMBER 25, 1981–

Introduction

PRINCE HAL IN HOUSTON

—

The commonwealth is sick of their own choice.

—HENRY IV, PART 2

IF YOU HAD TO EXPLAIN THE SECOND BUSH PRESIDENCY THROUGH the lens of a single day, the day to choose would be May 1, 2003, when George W. arrived by fighter jet on the deck of the USS *Abraham Lincoln*. Pulling off his white aviator's helmet and hopping down onto the deck of the aircraft carrier, he embraced cheering sailors just returned from Afghanistan and the Persian Gulf. Removing his parachute harness, Bush exchanged a few surly words with the pool reporters covering the event. Had the president taken the controls of the plane from the co-pilot seat? *Yes, I flew it!* Did he enjoy it? *Of course I liked it!*

Those who criticized Bush for playing soldier that day missed the way in which he was playing a specific soldier: his dad, circa 1944. After twice zipping past the aircraft carrier, the president's Navy S-3B Viking executed a perfect tailhook landing. Hitting the deck at 150 mph, the fighter plane caught the steel wires stretched across the flight deck and screeched to a halt in less than four hundred feet. This was the dangerous maneuver his father executed more than a hundred times as the pilot of a Grumman TBM Avenger, over the same ocean, in World War II.

Back when he applied to the Texas Air National Guard in 1968, George W. had a simple explanation for an officer he hoped would help him get in. "I want to be a fighter pilot because my father was," he said. Like most other members of his social class, Bush was of course eager to avoid Vietnam. He didn't volunteer for the air force or navy, where he could have flown real combat missions. But that doesn't mean his cover story wasn't also true. Nearly everything he did in his youth represented an attempt to emulate his beloved, successful father—with unimpressive and sometimes farcical results. Only following a midlife crisis at forty did he begin to succeed. The triumphant arrival was an apt metaphor for George W. Bush's life and career to that moment. After years of trying to be like his father and failing, as a student, athlete, businessman, and politician, George Junior had finally gotten it right. On the third pass, his plane safely executed the difficult landing.

Lest anyone miss it, the message of the day was spelled out on a giant banner stretched across the ship's tower: MISSION ACCOMPLISHED. Bush patted backs, posed for pictures, and shook hands with the ship's crew members, who surely would have borne him aloft if not for the presence of the Secret Service. As the sailors cheered from the observation deck, Bush looked up and raised both arms over his head, the body language of triumph. Every gesture of the president's that day spoke to his feelings of personal as well as national vindication. The mission he thought he had accomplished was not just vanquishing Saddam Hussein, but overcoming his father's shadow. For that brief, shining moment, righteous purpose and psychological need were fully joined.

That evening, the president appeared live from the deck of the ship to announce the end of major combat operations in Iraq. "In the battle of Iraq, the United States and our allies have prevailed," he declared. The invasion had been "carried out with a combination of precision, speed and boldness the enemy did not expect—and the world had not seen before." Bush then spoke directly to the men and women on the ship: "Your courage—your willingness to face danger for your country and for each other—made this day possible." His exultant declarations built to a stern warning to other dictators not to defy his will. "Let tyrants fear," Bush proclaimed.

A little over a year later, this dramatization of the son's pride was followed by a vignette of his father's pain. Bush Senior has always made a point of not taking criticism from his children personally. In 1998, he wrote an affecting letter to his two sons in politics, telling them to feel free to challenge his views, and not to worry about people drawing contrasts unflattering to their father. But by mid-2004, Bush Senior couldn't help feeling wounded by some of his oldest son's comments. During the 2004 Republican convention in New York City, the former president appeared on Don Imus's show, where the host asked about George W.'s statement in an interview with *The Washington Times* that he didn't intend to send mixed signals to the Iraqi people or to "cut and run early, like what happened in '91."

"I didn't like that much," George H. W. Bush told Imus. "Frankly, it hurt a little bit." The elder Bush usually kept such thoughts to himself. This was the first time he had publicly disagreed with his son, and he quickly backtracked. After saying that he was proud of what his own administration had done during the first Gulf War, the former president minimized what might have appeared as criticism by adding, in a classic bit of Bushese, that he didn't want to sound like "the nutty father unleashed out there. We don't need that. I had my chance."

But Bush couldn't resist saying a few words more. The Bush presidents, father and son, are not introspective men and they fiercely resist any form of psychological explanation. "I don't think he personally felt that 'I have to compete with my dad,'" the elder Bush went on. "You read all this psychobabble stuff and I know that it's not true. . . . These damn issues now for me, they don't matter. What does matter to me, though, is if they have assigned things to him in some salon in the Upper East Side of New York that he is trying to get out from under some shadow to escape his father and to have his own legacy and not his dad [sic]. Maybe there were people around him four years ago who felt that way."

Read this answer closely, and you can track the father's surrender to the reality of his son's challenge: *It's not true. It's psychobabble. It bothers me that elitist snobs say it. My son's political advisers are responsible for it.*

The father-son relationship lies at the very core of the second Bush presidency and its spectacular, avoidable flame-out. All sons compete with their fathers. But the term *competition* doesn't begin to do justice to the Oedipal complexities of this particular relationship. George W. Bush has been driven since childhood by a need to differentiate himself from his father, to challenge, surpass, and overcome him. Accompanying those motives have been their precise opposites, expressed through a lifelong effort to follow, copy, and honor his father. These contradictory impulses have no psychological novelty beyond the degree to which the parties involved repress and deny them. Neither does George W. Bush's long-running battle with his younger brother Jeb, whose relationship with both parents is less tormented and more straightforwardly devoted. What makes the family drama unusual—and important to outsiders—is the way it played out on a national and world stage.

George W.'s leadership of the Bush family implicates not just his father, mother, and siblings, but cousins, uncles, aunts, ancestors, and descendants. When 41 gave 43 his chair at the head of the table at the family compound in Kennebunkport over Christmas in 2002, the younger Bush disparaged the gesture, brushing it off in a way that family friends report injured his dad's feelings. But the head-of-family role is real. George W. Bush has understood since deciding to run for president that he was assuming leadership of a political clan, and that the Bush past as well as the Bush future rested on his shoulders. Part of what the second Bush presidency represented from the start was an effort at vindication, not just for a father turned out of office by people the Bushes detest at a glandular level, but for the family and its multigenerational political venture as a whole.

Emphasizing that Bushes work collectively to advance the family's reputation points toward a dynastic interpretation they like even less than they do being put on the couch, as both 41 and 43 call it. Where "psychobabble" suggests that they have invisible motivations and buried differences, "dynasty" implies for them something even worse, that the House of Bush is an enterprise based on class rule and economic interest. To the Bushes, a quasi-Marxist reading is even worse than a pop Freudian one.

It is not up to the Bushes to decide how we understand them. But they're right in the sense that both the psychological and the economic readings, in the forms we usually get them, are too schematic, too pat. The reason we need a more nuanced understanding at the end of the second Bush presidency is the magnitude of the Bush failure. In one sense, George W. Bush's two terms in office have merely been lost years, a period of ineptitude, neglect, and falling behind on a variety of domestic and international problems. But the Bush period also looks like something worse, a moment in which the power and prestige of the United States diminished in relation to the rest of the world. George W. Bush bears direct and personal responsibility for the fiasco in Iraq, which looks increasingly like a national disaster on the order of Vietnam or Watergate. Because of his decisions, America has squandered much of its global leadership role, making itself weaker diplomatically, militarily, and economically. After its victory in the Cold War, the United States lost respect, support, and influence. This may take a generation to fix, or it may never be fully fixed, in which case the second Bush presidency will mark the beginning of a long-term decline in American status. This didn't have to happen. We need to make some sense of how it did.

This book isn't intended as an indictment. It is an attempt at explanation. I don't want to add to the long shelf of books arguing that Bush has fallen short—of his own aims in education, energy independence, and spending restraint, and by declining to address major problems like health care, global poverty, and climate change. Instead, I'm going to skip ahead to the next stage by *assuming* he has failed as president—something that few people without a financial stake in defending him still dispute with much conviction. As with the post-Watergate period, what comes next is a reckoning with the long national nightmare from which we will soon emerge. After a presidency that resembles a plane crash, we need to examine the political wreckage around us to try to understand what went wrong. I believe that there is a black box when it comes to the Bush presidency, and that it is filled with a series of relationships—familial, personal, religious, and historical. Only by examining the president in these contexts can we understand how the country finds itself in its current predicament.

Of course, all presidents have relationships that influence the course of their presidencies—think of Franklin Roosevelt's with Harry Hopkins, or Bill Clinton's with Hillary Clinton, or Richard Nixon's with Henry Kissinger, or Lyndon Johnson's with the Kennedy brothers. But with none of these presidents do even the closest relationships explain ultimate success or failure. Nearly all of Bush's predecessors, including his father, have been understood to be autonomous actors. They pursued politics, developed ideas about the world, and reacted to historical events. None appears today as a subsidiary or a function of anyone else. But looking at George W. Bush as the sum of his views or a product of his times doesn't get you very far. For most of his life, George W. Bush did not engage with public affairs. Bush basically blew off the 1960s, the Vietnam War, and Watergate. Ideas have never interested him except as tools. He didn't tune in to domestic policy in any serious way until he was in his forties or into foreign policy until his fifties. History had little impact on him until he became a shaper of it. For this reason, a study of George W. Bush's character is unavoidably a study of the people closest to him. Without them, his story would not be about politics at all.

The story begins and ends with his family drama. Like no president since John F. Kennedy, George W. Bush came to us as part of a pre-established dynasty. He pursued a political career because of the expectations and pressures that came from being an heir apparent in the House of Bush. But unlike Kennedy, Bush has always been a prickly nepotist. He accepted the leg up, but bristled at the stigma and rejected the very notion of self-doubt. Bush showed his dependency even in the context of asserting his independence. Rather than play the role desired by his parents, he commandeered the stage and rewrote the drama himself, casting his relations in the parts he chose for them.

He cast others in the roles of his relatives. There is a reason that Karl Rove has been the most influential political adviser of the modern era; that Dick Cheney has been the most powerful vice president; and that Condoleezza Rice has been personally closer to Bush than any other national security adviser or secretary of state to any other president. These have been not just Bush's aides, but an idealized, alternative family he has constructed around himself. This family has its own chosen ancestors—Winston Churchill and Ronald Reagan. It has its own form of worship, recovery movement evangelicalism. It has its own imaginary homestead, in Crawford, Texas. Being caught in two family webs—the one of his birth and the one of his devising—makes George W. Bush no less responsible for his actions than any of his predecessors. But it does frame his choices and actions in an essential way. Every one of his politically important relationships has served to mislead him, or if you prefer, played a part in the way Bush has misled the country.

I've structured my account around these relationships. The first chapter explores Bush's connection to the ancestors on his father's side of the family and dwells on his curious affinity for one he knew only as a child, his great-grandfather George Herbert Walker. Chapter 2 focuses on the relationships within Bush's nuclear family and tries to explain his complicated pattern of emulation and repudiation of his father, as well as his long-standing rivalry with his younger brother Jeb. Chapter 3 looks at Bush's relationship with God. It reexamines, with some skepticism, the familiar story of Bush's midlife crisis and concludes that faith is far less significant to him and his choices than he has led people to believe. Chapter 4 revisits Bush's political rise through the lens of his involvement with Karl Rove, which I argue set his presidency on a wrong track from the beginning. Chapter 5 is about how Bush's relationship with Dick Cheney led him to misconceive his war presidency after September 11. Chapter 6 proposes a way of looking at how all of these relationships—with his father, Cheney, and God (as well as Rice and Donald Rumsfeld)—misguided George W. Bush's foreign policy, and provoked his fateful decision to go to war with Iraq. Chapter 7 delves into Bush's relationships with a series of ancestors he has chosen at various moments: Theodore Roosevelt, Abraham Lincoln, Winston Churchill, Harry Truman, and Ronald Reagan, and the way that thinking by historical analogy has sustained his delusions.

My approach to politics is a kind of close reading: to look again at what's already known, and sometimes well known. It is a prejudice of journalism to privilege the classified and the withheld above the open public record. I believe the opposite: that our inability to understand decisions and deciders stems less from any lack of information than from a failure of examination and imagination. In pursuit of leaks and scoops, we journalists often miss what's hiding in plain sight. The key that unlocks the mystery of political motivation is seldom hidden in a locked vault. It's usually right in front of us, in the words of decision-makers, who even when they are trying to dissemble and conceal, end up revealing far more than they intend.

Accordingly, this is principally a work of analysis and interpretation, not news reporting or historical narrative. I have no personal dislike for George W. Bush and never have. When I first covered Bush, as a reporter for *Slate* during the 2000 presidential campaign, I got a sense of his twitchy, aggressive charm during off-the-record conversations on his campaign plane. One evening, he interrupted the conversation he was having with some Texas reporters about baseball to raise his bottle of O'Doul's and shout to the cameramen getting trashed at the back of the plane, "I love drunk people! I used to be one of 'em!" He would be a great guy to have a (nonalcoholic) beer with, something his Democratic opponent surely wasn't. He was comfortable in his skin and fun to be around, which is why after he beat John McCain in the primaries, I spent more time reporting from the Bush bubble than from Al Gore's.

But while I appreciated Bush's gift for filling up a room, I can't claim ever to have been an admirer. I came away from the 2000 campaign unimpressed by what he had to say on every subject other than baseball. Though smarter than he sounds in the selective quotations I've collected in several volumes of *Bushisms*, Bush appeared to lack any real engagement with the serious work of government or the compelling questions about policy. Whenever anyone pressed him on issues, he played back the same tape of calculated bromides. I found him incurious and intellectually lazy.

That view evolved as I wrote this book, but only somewhat. Bush is more intelligent than I thought he was in 2000 and, after seven years in office, he is considerably more knowledgeable. What strikes people as a lack of smarts is attributable in part to a language problem, and in part to his peculiar brand of anti-intellectualism. Bush is a man who would rather be underestimated than esteemed, who would rather have everyone think he's thick than have anyone think he's trying to look sophisticated. But despite his hidden layers, Bush remains a fundamentally limited person. As I've tried to understand more deeply who he is, what he thinks, and why he does what he does, the question of blame has become less interesting to me. Driven by family demons, overflowing with confidence, and lacking any capacity for self-knowledge, Bush seems to me to have done precisely what we should have expected of him. My feelings follow the sympathy Sigmund Freud expresses in the study of Woodrow Wilson he wrote with the American diplomat William C. Bullitt. Freud and Bullitt argue that Wilson's inability to process aggressive feelings toward the man he called his "incomparable father" left him increasingly messianic and detached from reality. "And finally, when one compared the strength of the man to the greatness of the task he had taken upon himself, this pity was so overwhelming that it conquered every emotion," Freud writes in his introduction. I was originally going to call this book "The Bush Detour," thinking of the Bush presidency simply as lost time for the country. But as I studied George W. Bush, I came to think of the story as a tragedy because of the way the president's inability to master his feelings toward his parents drove decisions with terrible consequences not just for him, but also for America and the world. To state it simply, the Bush Tragedy is that the son's ungovernable relationship with his father ended up governing all of us.

Bush's is an Icarus story—the crash to earth of someone who does not comprehend his limits or his motives. Being president was something beyond Bush's capacities in a way he didn't recognize. It is something he should never have been given a chance to do, and I continue to fault those who gave him the opportunity to fail more than I fault him for trying. With Bush's approval rating dipping into the 20s, we can safely say that the commonwealth is sick of its own choice, not just in the sense of the country being disillusioned with Bush, but in the sense of the country having brought the malady upon itself. The commonwealth had every reason to know better before and not just after, and especially the second time around.

For help in understanding the Bush family, I would like to thank the above-quoted William Shakespeare. As a guide for political reporters, Shakespeare remains underrated. Political science and a lot of political journalism explain the behavior of politicians mostly in terms of interest and ideology. Shakespeare reminds us that their motives tend to be more complicated than that, and that however much they may try to obscure them, politicians do in fact have inner lives. If sometimes used to turn rascals into cartoons—think LBJ as Macbeth or Nixon as Richard III—Shakespearean analogies can also remind us to look harder at family, religion, national myth, at character. When we are confronted with a political breakdown, Shakespeare advises us to look deeper and judge less.

With the Bushes, father and son, we have the benefit of an archetype that fits so well it's uncanny: the story of Prince Hal. I'm not the first to employ this conceit—it came up often after September 11 and in the immediate aftermath of the invasion of Iraq, when the prevailing wisdom held Bush to be a heroic wartime president. Conservatives back then often compared George W. to Henry V, the swaggering monarch Hal became. But I think there's much more in the comparison—and much more in *Henry IV, Parts 1* and *2,* than in *Henry V*. The chief themes of these plays are the hidden themes of our nation's political life for the past seven years: the complications of the father-son relationship, the awkwardness of dynastic power, and the issues around a willful leader's underlying motives.

You may know these plays and you may not. To outline the story in brief, the intensely ambitious King Henry IV deposes Richard II and causes him to be murdered. But like George H. W. Bush, Henry IV is a conscientious politician without much greatness about him. He keeps talking about his big plans for a crusade to Jerusalem, but gets diverted by various domestic rebellions. He also spends a lot of time worrying about his son Hal, also known as Harry, the royal ne'er-do-well who fritters away his evenings wenching and robbing pilgrims with his friend Falstaff instead of helping out around the castle.

Hal—like George W. Bush at forty—gets his act together and accepts the obligations of his breeding. He repents, brushes off Falstaff, and becomes a warrior for his father. The pivotal moment in Prince Hal's transformation is his defeating his rival, Hotspur, in single combat at the Battle of Shrewsbury. Hotspur is the more driven, diligent, and focused of the two—Henry IV admits to wishing that Hotspur were his son and heir, instead of the dissolute Hal. The joyless Hotspur reminds me of somber, single-minded Jeb. Until 1994, Jeb thought he had taken George's W.'s place—and so did everyone else in the family. Their parents expected that George W. would lose his race for governor of Texas and that Jeb would win his for governor of Florida, and thereby become the leader of the family.

After his father dies, Prince Hal becomes King Henry V, the most warlike (and religious) of English kings. In *Henry V*, the last play of what scholars call the Henriad, the new monarch confounds the expectations of family, friend, and foe alike by leading an invasion of France. Only his closest advisers and the audience understand that Henry's rationales for war are not the same as his reasons. These he, unlike Bush, admits—but only to himself. He is trying to atone for his father's wrongs, and disprove a lifetime of doubts—his own and everyone else's. The play culminates with his astounding victory at Agincourt, where the greatly outnumbered English triumph over the haughty French. King Henry believes that the miraculous victory of his band of brothers shows the hand of God at work.

Shakespeare's Elizabethan audience knew these early-fifteenth-century characters, but didn't know much about them, so the playwright could tinker with the facts. He infused the medieval chronicles with the plot structure of a narrative his audience knew much better, the parable of the Prodigal Son. In the fable from the Gospel of Luke, the son squanders his patrimony on prostitutes and reckless living, but when he returns home and repents his sin, his father welcomes him back. This is a story with a happy ending, which is how most stage and screen versions, including Kenneth Branagh's film—a favorite in the Bush family—have interpreted *Henry V*.

But at the end of the play, a great question remains, one that has divided readers and scholars for centuries. Did Shakespeare truly admire Henry V, or does the last play in the sequence reveal, in ways subtle enough to miss, how cruel, narcissistic, and careless he remained even after becoming a heroic military leader? The more closely you read these plays, the more you suspect Hal's miraculous conversion. The brutality and calculation in Henry V's makeup were there all along. Hal's immaturity and selfishness remain as aspects of Henry V's personality. His ostentatious piety is at least in part an act. The question at the center of the Henriad begs the one at the heart of George W. Bush's narrative. Did he really change in the middle of life, when he found God, sobriety, and success? Is such a transformation of character even possible?

The *Henry* plays are Shakespeare's greatest histories because they are also great tragedies. What makes them so powerful is the way Hal's drive for family vindication, personal legitimacy, and political power crushes his friend and surrogate father, Falstaff, the character whom the literary critic Harold Bloom equates with humanity itself. "Banish Plump Jack, and banish all the world," Falstaff pleads with his friend as they role-play the prince's anticipated ascent to the throne in a tavern. "I do, I will," Hal says. His only true loyalty is to his political ambition. Bush too thought he was prepared to accept the consequences of taking his place in the family business. But lacking a tragic sense, he seems never to have considered the cost of his choices.

The

BUSH TRAGEDY

CHAPTER ONE

The Bushes and the Walkers

O, had thy grandsire with a prophet's eye
Seen how his son's son should destroy his sons,
From forth thy reach he would have laid thy shame,
Deposing thee before thou wert possess'd
Which art possess'd now to depose thyself.

—RICHARD II

—

GEORGE WALKER BUSH IS THE PRODUCT OF TWO FAMILY TRADITIONS, the Bushes and the Walkers. On one side is the familiar patriarch Prescott Bush (1895–1972), the decorous Republican senator from Connecticut, the New England WASP, the pennant-waving Yale man. On the other side of his father's family stands a lesser-known patriarch, George Herbert Walker (1875–1953), the St. Louis buccaneer and raucous playboy.

The Bushes as we know them today are the product of a combination of—one might say the combustion between—the two very different families arrayed around these two dominant men. Because the family is private to the point of being obsessively secretive, its basic internal struggle has been largely obscured in favor of a familiar cliché: the old American upper class. But this isn't the story of a happy, unified family. Drilling into the history of the Walkers and the Bushes, one hits layer upon sedimentary layer of conflict among brothers, cousins, uncles, and grandparents. The buried drama and forgotten ancestors are the beginning point for understanding George W. Bush, the roots of whose temperament are not as shallow as they appear.

Superficially, the Walkers and Bushes had much in common when they came together just after the First World War. Both families represented industrial fortunes from the Midwest transplanted into East Coast finance. Both were fanatical about sports and ferociously competitive, sharing a passion for baseball, golf, and tennis. Both came to worship side by side at Christ Church in Greenwich, Connecticut, and at St. Ann's in Kennebunkport, Maine, where George H. W. Bush's parents, Prescott Bush and Dorothy Walker (1901–1992), were married in 1921. Endless connections to Yale, Skull and Bones, and the Harriman banking enterprises run through both families.

Yet an enormous amount is papered over by the simplification that George H. W. Bush was raised a Connecticut Yankee. The union of Prescott Bush and Dorothy Walker represented less a merger of equals than a crossing of lines: old fortune and new, Protestant and Catholic, Republican and Democrat. Prescott Bush descended from New England abolitionists. Dorothy Walker came from a Maryland family that owned slaves—a family secret that has been previously reported only in a small paper published in Springfield, Illinois. The more noticeable differences were resolved with relative ease. Both families soon became thoroughly Episcopal and Republican, and money ages quickly in America. But there endured a less visible conflict over attitudes, beliefs, and principles.

To put it simply, the value system of the original patriarch, George W.'s great-grandfather George Herbert Walker, was based on the pursuit of wealth. The one embodied by George W.'s grandfather Prescott Bush was an ethical ideal. The ramifications of this divergence were infinite and insurmountable. The Walkers behaved like the worst nouveaux riches: they were grand, greedy, extravagant, and focused on class distinctions. Prescott Bush's clan was pointedly modest, frugal, and egalitarian. George Herbert Walker's world was one of yachts, racehorses, estates, and servants. Prescott Bush couldn't abide a yacht, was uncomfortable at clubs, and hated formal dinners, preferring the modestly genteel lifestyle of a suburban commuter. His social life was the Whiffenpoofs, the Greenwich town council, and golf.

The Walkers were gamblers; the Bushes conservators. The Walkers pursued winning and success; the Bushes sought to serve and lead. The Walkers viewed wealth as an end; the Bushes as a means. The Bushes embodied the old WASP embarrassment about being rich; they pretended they really weren't, and treated the help as "family." As Richard Ben Cramer puts it in *What It Takes*, whose early chapters contain the most insightful writing about them, the Bushes were known in Greenwich as being "not like that"—not the sort of people who lorded their wealth or station over their social and economic inferiors. Biographers find no shortage of tales of the early George H. W. Bush's egalitarian decency; how he stood up for a Jewish kid being bullied at Andover, how he bonded with the enlisted men on his boat during World War II, how in Congress he wrote personal letters to crotchety constituents, turning them into devoted friends.

Counter-snobbery can be a more highly evolved snobbery. In the Bush family, downplaying social superiority is a subtle way to hold it over those who advertise their class—people like the boorish George Herbert Walker and his sons. George H. W. Bush's exaggeratedly considerate and self-effacing behavior is typically attributed to his mother, Dorothy, who was George Herbert Walker's daughter. But in this, Dotty Walker was a defector from her father's family to her husband's. She rejected the egoistic, mercantile values of George Herbert Walker and absorbed her husband, Prescott's, asceticism, rectitude, and sense of duty. The admirable, sometimes hyperbolic selflessness she passed on to her children represented a transfer of loyalties and ultimately a shift in the Walker-Bush balance of power.

In the battle of the two patriarchs, Prescott might, until fairly recently, have been thought the winner. The first Bush presidency expressed Prescott's ethic of self-restraint and public service, not the

Walker ethic of masculine risk-taking, conquest, and domination. The Bush name became famous around the world; the Walker name was absorbed. Even Walker's Point, George Herbert Walker's summer haven in Kennebunkport, and a place that Prescott Bush found too unpleasant to visit in the 1950s because of his feelings toward his in-laws, was assumed to be the ancestral manse of George H. W. Bush's Yankee ancestors. But the struggle in which the Bush victory was achieved left some rogue DNA. George W. Bush's likeness to some of his Walker ancestors offers a conspicuous display of the phenomenon sociologists call intergenerational rootedness—the curious persistence of family patterns over long spans of time. While George H. W. Bush is Prescott's son, George W. Bush is in many respects his great-grandfather's. He is more Walker than Bush.

BUSH PARSIMONY MEETS WALKER egotism in the practice of recycling an insufficient number of names among an excessive number of male heirs. The result is a profusion of Samuels, Georges, Herberts, Johns, Walkers, and Prescotts, applied as first, second, third, and fourth names—an exploding blob of WASP nomenclature that deters comprehension. The older George Bush, the forty-first president, had always been known growing up as "Poppy" or "Pop," a diminutive of "little Pop," to distinguish him from what the family called his namesake and grandfather, George Herbert Walker. Bush avoided this preppie moniker in the Navy, where his nickname became his actual name, "George Herbert Walker Bush," played out to mock his upper-class breeding and manners. At Yale he reverted to Poppy, which he remained to his family. On oil rigs, he was just plain George. When Poppy named his first son after himself but not quite, he compounded the confusion. Growing up, his son was known as Little George, Georgie, George Junior, and Junior, which was how he was known to friends at college. As his political career took form in Texas, he eschewed all versions of Junior, embracing "George W." or merely "W" (pronounced "Dubya"). Only when he became president did he reclaim the name "George Bush," relegating his father to the status of

"41," "George H. W. Bush," or "Bush Senior." Given how confusing the men's names are, one can only be thankful that W. had daughters.

Having an ordinary three names instead of a pretentious four helps to answer the implication George W. Bush most resents, that he arrived in the White House with the help of such un-American principles as primogeniture, dynasty, and aristocracy. Though he can hardly cultivate a log cabin myth, this Bush has long thought of himself as a Texan rather than a New Englander, an entrepreneur rather than a beneficiary of inherited wealth, and the opposite of any kind of snob. Distinctions he draws with his preppie father are central to his personal and political identity.

George H. W. Bush struck a Texan pose as well, with far less success. Former President Bush mainly set himself up for ridicule when he professed a love for country music and pork rinds or when he claimed that he didn't know what the word "patrician" meant. In truth, Bush embodied the easily parodied but much admired WASP type as thoroughly as any man of his generation, not just its taste and manners, but the ideals and moral vision of the old New England upper class. He wore Brooks Brothers and believed in duty to country. He was a skinflint who wrestled with his conscience. He personified good sportsmanship and drizzled thank-you notes. These preppie folkways made George H. W. Bush's Texan mask comically transparent.

Not so his son, on whom Kennebunkport, Andover, Yale, and Harvard left few visible traces. Through his manners, tastes, and beliefs, George W. Bush places himself about as far as it is possible to get from his New England patrimony. He shows no sign of thinking or caring much about his ancestry, never discusses it in public, and seems not even to know much about it. He displays a brash informality and sometimes outright rudeness, kicking his cowboy boots up on the desk, swearing lustily, and holding garrulous phone conversations while visitors sit awkwardly in his office. His idea of relaxation is clearing brush in sweltering, landlocked Midland; fine dining a hamburger and a Coke. George W. seems entirely genuine when he explains in his West Texan twang that his values were formed in forthright (and never mind segregated) Midland, and that his relationship with God is expressive, not Episcopalian. To call this persona a conscious construction is not to say it is artificial. The president's Texan identity was forged in necessary opposition; it represents his attempt to assert himself as an original theme and not a familial variation.

George W. Bush's middle name comes from a large Catholic family resident in Maryland from the early nineteenth century. The family of George E. Walker (1797–1864) was poor, but not so poor that it didn't have a couple of slaves on its 321-acre farm in Cecil County, Maryland, according to an 1830 census—a female between the ages of ten and twenty-four, and a male between the ages of twenty-four and thirty-six. After they fell on hard times and lost their land, the Walkers traveled by wagon to southern Illinois, where they homesteaded a few miles from Bloomington.

The youngest of their eight sons, David Davis Walker (1840–1918), moved to St. Louis where he made his fortune as a dry goods wholesaler. In the Midwest, David Walker maintained the Southern attitude about race, though with a contemporary overlay of social Darwinism. He was a believer in eugenics and the "unwritten law" of lynching. In a letter to the editor of the *St. Louis Republic* published in 1914, David Walker described Negroes as a greater menace than prostitution and "all the other evils combined."

David Walker's son George Herbert Walker, born in St. Louis in 1875, was raised like a Midwestern prince. Bert Walker, as he was known, had both a nurse and his own valet. In the summer, the family would travel by private train car to the coast of Maine. The valet went with Bert to Stonyhurst, the Jesuit boarding school in England, where his mother sent him, out of concern that Catholic education in St. Louis was too dominated by ill-bred German immigrants.

In England, Bert Walker developed into a physically powerful young man, excelling at boxing, polo, and golf. He would later win the amateur title as Missouri heavyweight champion in the days when boxers wore no gloves. Much of his overflowing aggression was directed at his father. Rather than join the family business or the priesthood as his parents hoped, he returned to St. Louis to make his own fortune. Though he stayed in the same city, he broke with his parents in every other way, rejecting his father's Republican politics and his Catholic faith. This rupture came when he decided to marry a girl from a higher-class Presbyterian family, a society beauty named Lucretia "Loulie" Wear (1874–1961). Bert's parents told him he would be disinherited and boycotted the wedding. Though father and son were later partners in investments, including the house in Kennebunkport, the breach between them was never fully mended. Years later, Bert sued to have his father declared mentally unfit when David Walker really did attempt to disinherit his son by giving all his money to the Catholic Church. The two were battling in court when David Walker died in Kennebunkport in 1918.

When he was still in his early twenties, Bert Walker set up G. H. Walker and Company, one of the first investment banking firms in the Midwest. He flourished as a speculator, losing several fortunes, but winning several more, and helping to finance the St. Louis World's Fair in 1904. Bert was rowdy, profane, and generally obnoxious. Even an approved family history describes him as "coarse." At a friend's boisterous birthday party, he grabbed a bass drum from the orchestra and led a drunken parade through the St. Louis Club. Rather than apologize to the board, he resigned to form the Racquet Club, whose motto was "Youth Will Be Served." Bert liked to plaster his name around—on his companies, his houses, and his children. As president of the U.S. Golfing Association, he founded an Anglo-American tournament known, of course, as the Walker Cup.

In the family, Bert Walker is described as a bully and a boor, or worse—a violent tyrant who pummeled his sons in a boxing ring set up in his house in hopes of toughening them into professional athletes. When his son Lou embarrassed him by showing up tipsy on the tennis court after lunch one day in Maine, his father told him he was too stupid for college and sent him to work the next morning in a steel mill in Bradford, Pennsylvania. "I was always scared as hell of him," Lou said. One of George Herbert Walker's grandchildren, Elsie Walker Kilbourne, was quoted in a newspaper story describing the conflict between father and sons even more bluntly. Bert Walker, she said, was a "tough old bastard." As she put it, "there really wasn't a lot of love on the part of the boys for their father." Bert Walker's relationships with his daughters were more pleasant, though he refused to send them to college because he didn't believe in educating women.

As the leading investment banker in the Midwest, Bert Walker got to know the Harriman family. The young Harriman brothers, Averell and Roland, had inherited their father's railroad fortune after graduating from Yale, and in 1919 found themselves needing an experienced man to head their Wall Street firm. Bert Walker readily agreed to relocate east and take charge of the Harriman enterprises. Unlike the Smith family in *Meet Me in St. Louis,* who can't bear to abandon their friendly hometown, the Walkers couldn't wait to move to New York City. After arriving in 1920, they lived far more luxuriously than they had in St. Louis, in a mansion on Madison Avenue, and later in a grand apartment at One Sutton Place. The Walker weekend home on the north shore of Long Island was a Gatsby palace with marble floors, a swimming pool, and a lawn sloping down to the sound. Bert Walker appeared at dinner in white tie, to be served by liveried butlers. He had another grand estate in Santa Barbara, California.

With the money they made financing Soviet oil drilling in the Caucasus, Bert Walker and Averell Harriman bought a stable of racing horses. But after a time, they couldn't agree about how to handle their best horse, Chance Play. Walker, who loved to gamble, wanted to race him as often as possible. Harriman wanted to hold out for a few important races and a long career of stud fees. So they divvied up the horses and instead bought a 150-foot yacht together. Bert Walker's success on Wall Street also supported a small army of Negro servants at the ten-thousand-acre hunting lodge he bought in South Carolina and named Duncannon. The current owners have preserved the bullet holes left in the dining room ceiling when Bert fired at a wasp that stung him.

The Great Depression spelled the end of Bert Walker's career at Harriman; he wanted to take on levels of risk that the brothers considered dangerous at a time when the firm was operating in the red. He was pushed out at the time of the merger that his son-in-law Prescott Bush helped to engineer with the firm of Brown Brothers. But Bert Walker had liquidated his portfolio near the top, and the Walkers were untouched by the stock-market crash. In the 1930s, he and his wife each had their own chauffeured Rolls-Royce. "Gampy" Walker, as his grandchildren called him, gave them $500 each for their birthdays—a sum so enormous that it directly threatened Prescott's ethos of an honest day's work for a day's pay.

THE BUSH HERITAGE is something closer to the Puritan stereotype. The presidential line descends from James Smith Bush (1825–1889), whose connection to Yale and the Episcopal clergy dates from the 1840s, and who married into a distinguished Concord, Massachusetts, family. James Bush left the law for the ministry, which he served in Orange, New Jersey, San Francisco, and Staten Island.

It is with J. S. Bush that we first spot the intensity of duty and principle that is one powerful strain in the Bush ethos. This struggle comes through in the two books of sermons he published, *More Words About the Bible* (1883) and *Evidence of Faith* (1885). As the second title suggests, the Reverend Bush was divided between reason and belief. He thought that Christianity needed a rational basis, not an appeal to miracles, and he lost his respect for an Episcopal hierarchy he thought detached from the use of intellect and true spirituality. Under the influence of Ralph Waldo Emerson, James Bush resigned his parish in Staten Island and moved to Concord in 1883. He was on his way to leaving the Episcopal Church and becoming a Unitarian. According to his Yale obituary, it was anguish over this decision that killed him at the age of sixty-five.

From J. S. Bush on, father-son relationships on the Bush side of the family follow a distinct pattern of rebellious emulation. Sons seek their own paths to the paternal destinations of financial independence and political accomplishment. Unlike Walker men, Bush men never simply join the family firm. Walker sons tend to succumb in a contest of wills with their fathers. Bush sons follow their fathers while convincing themselves they are starting from scratch. As Jeb once put it, the Bush kids grew up believing they "weren't crap" (meaning that they *were* crap) until they'd gone out and done something on their own. The Walker kids were raised to believe they were crap in any case, and would have a chair waiting for them at the G. H. Walker & Co. office in St. Louis. Running through the conjoined family is a confusion between high personal accomplishment, which both Bushes and Walkers expect, and hereditary privilege, which both sides assume, but the Bushes disclaim.

Rather than follow his father to Yale and into the ministry, Samuel Prescott Bush (1863–1948) studied business at Stevens College and in the 1890s went to work for the Pennsylvania Railroad in Columbus, Ohio. But Samuel P. Bush embodies the family type as much as the seeking transcendentalist he rebelled against: he is described as austere and frugal, a rather cold man, but with a powerful sense of social obligation. He went on to pursue a successful career in the railroad equipment business, eventually running a Rockefeller-backed company called Buckeye Steel, where he was known for his community-mindedness and benevolent paternalism toward his workers, many of whom were African-American.

Samuel's oldest son, Prescott Bush, followed the family pattern in rejecting his father's chosen home (the Midwest), his calling (manufacturing), and his politics (Democratic). Later in life, after he had achieved his own financial independence and political success as a two-term senator from Connecticut, Prescott often said—and seemed actually to believe—that he had been required to make his own way in the world because his father couldn't afford to support him. Though Prescott returned to work briefly for his father after college, the two were never close, and according to his own children, Prescott never spoke about him. When Samuel P. Bush died in 1948, Prescott turned down his share of the inheritance. Temperamentally, father and son seem to have been very much alike.

Sent to St. George's, an elite boarding school on the East Coast, Prescott was elected head prefect his final year and contemplated a career in the ministry. After he arrived at Yale in 1913, he epitomized the college career depicted in *Stover at Yale*, the 1912 novel that F. Scott Fitzgerald called a "textbook" for his generation. Like Stover, Prescott came from the Midwest, learned to navigate a social system revolving around sports and secret societies, and triumphed by being tapped for Skull and Bones. At a time when Ivy League sports were treated as having national significance, he collected varsity letters in baseball, hockey, and golf. A powerful bass, he was a fixture of the Yale Men's Choir, the Glee Club, and the Whiffenpoofs. As for Stover, his college years paved his path to business success and defined the rest of his life.

In Fort Sill, Oklahoma, Prescott and fellow members of the Yale Battalion "crooked" a skull they claimed was Geronimo's from an Apache cemetery for the Bones temple—a prank that would have repercussions for his son and grandson when the tribe sought to have it returned. From there, Prescott shipped out to France, where he served in the trenches near Verdun for the last ten weeks of the First World War. The key episode in his military career—and perhaps in his entire early life—was a missed joke that embarrassed the family. Prescott wrote a satiric letter home about his Davy Crockett–like exploits; he spun a satiric yarn about saving the lives of the Allies' three most famous generals, Foch, Haig, and Pershing, by batting away a German shell with his service knife. Prescott went on to humorously describe being covered with ribbons and medals by the grateful French, British, and Americans. Prescott's mother, Flora, missing her son's Yale-inflected irony and taking the facetious account literally, proudly sent the letter off to her local newspaper, the *Ohio State Journal*. Also missing the joke, the paper ran an account on its front page ("3 High Military Honors Conferred on Capt. Bush"), which was then picked up by the *New Haven Journal-Courier* ("Triple Honor to P.S. Bush, Yale '17"). Parents and son alike felt deep shame when the local paper had to publish a letter from his mother as a front-page retraction. In this episode, Prescott inadvertently transgressed every Bush family value—modesty, honesty, and propriety.

After Prescott returned home in 1919, he moved to St. Louis to take a job selling hardware for Walter Simmons, whom he met at a Yale reunion. There he began courting the eighteen-year-old Dorothy Walker. If Bert Walker had a touch of Gatsby, Prescott Bush was at that stage the ingenuous Nick Carraway. Bert was impressed by Prescott's physical presence and athletic ability, and even more that he'd been a member of the right secret society at Yale. Prescott always tried to downplay his father-in-law's role in bringing him to Harriman Brothers a few years later. As he often noted, he had his own connections there: fellow Bonesmen Roland Harriman, Bob Lovett, and Knight Woolley. In reality, Prescott had considerable help from his father-in-law but resented anyone thinking he had.

Despite the chumminess of his Wall Street world, Prescott could not have flourished on the basis of relationships alone. He thrived because of his business sense. After the financial crash in 1929, he helped save Harriman by pushing the spendthrift Averell to close offices in Paris and Warsaw and cut costs in the one remaining European outpost in Berlin. It was Prescott who initiated a pivotal merger with his fellow Bonesmen at the more solvent Brown Brothers, which had the further advantage of pushing his father-in-law out. Prescott had a nose for deals, including one to buy a quarter-interest in CBS for $2.5 million in 1932. At one point, Prescott served on seventeen corporate boards, not counting the Yale Corporation.

As he achieved his own success, Prescott pulled his wife away from her father and his avaricious values. Indeed, it was Dotty Bush who became known as the guardian of the family's Puritan ethic because of the way she inculcated their five children with the wisdom that intense competitiveness was compatible with severe modesty. Dotty was known in the family for slapping down anyone caught bragging, and is probably responsible for her son the forty-first president's nonsense-generating aversion to the first-person pronoun (and sometimes to pronouns altogether). Dotty's version of this ethic came originally from her long-suffering mother, Loulie Walker, but was powerfully reinforced by Prescott. At Prescott's funeral in 1972,

Dorothy gave a eulogy in which she thanked her late husband for teaching her a "lack of pride in material possessions."

Prescott was a huge man—six foot four and 250 pounds, a giant to his children, with a gravelly baritone voice and formal bearing. He wore a coat and tie to dinner, even during summer vacations at Kennebunkport. His children feared and admired him; it's not clear that anyone other than Dorothy ever felt much affection for him. He comes across in family descriptions as gloomy and distant, a "scary man" to his son Jonathan, "stern" and "righteous" in his grandson Jeb's description. Prescott never spoke to his children about the sudden death of his mother, Flora, who was killed by a car while strolling on vacation, in 1920. In later life, after retiring from public office, he demanded that the grandchildren call him "Senator." In various accounts, Prescott is a curiously blank figure—an upright man, expressing little emotion other than irritability, which was exacerbated when he drank. He liked playing golf, but his only apparent joy was music, and in particular the Ivy League style of a cappella singing. Never happier than when harmonizing in a straw boater, he performed "I'm Going to Raise the Deuce When I Get Loose in Town" with his barbershop quartet of Yale Glee Club alumni at a Connecticut Republican convention. He was extremely proud of the comic speech he delivered at the Alfalfa Club's 1959 dinner, which he naturally concluded with a solo performance of "The Whiffenpoof Song."

The only attempt to write Prescott Bush's biography, by the Houston sportswriter Mickey Herskowitz, resulted in vivid sketches of everyone around him, with a void at the center of the canvas.* Pres-

* That this book exists is the result of a conflict among Bush men. In 1999, Herskowitz, a well-regarded Texas ghostwriter, was hired to draft George W. Bush's presidential campaign autobiography, the book published in 2000 as *A Charge to Keep*. But the early chapters Herskowitz submitted were judged to overemphasize W.'s early difficulties, describing him, for instance, as having been unsuccessful in the oil business. As a result, Herskowitz was fired in favor of George W.'s dauntless propagandist, Karen Hughes. But George H. W. Bush, who was friendly with Herskowitz, felt bad about this harsh treatment, and so gave Herskowitz the consolation prize of burnishing his late father's image. This assignment reflected not just George H.W. Bush's dismay at the mistreatment of a loyal family courtier, but his effort to posthumously ensure that his father would replace the rapacious Bert Walker as the family's official founder.

cott's own autobiographical account, a 454-page oral history he deposited at Columbia University, is singularly lacking in color, passion, or emotion. What does come through is his sense of propriety and obligation—to community, country, and family. The Bush patriarch operated according to a code typical of his era and social class, but with a particular emphasis on the repression of selfish desire. Bush played golf well enough to pursue a professional career, but never seems to have considered it—though he later rendered "service" to the sport as president of the U.S. Golf Association. In his family, one pursued one's passions as hobbies, not vocations. He both envied and disapproved of his third son, Johnny Bush, who pursued a career in musical theater before settling down to work for G. H. Walker. Prescott's code also involved strict rules about how to live, dress, and comport oneself. "I never heard him fart," Johnny once said of his father. As a senator, Prescott introduced a rule change forbidding his colleagues to wave to guests in the gallery.

At the Round Hill Country Club in Greenwich, Prescott stormed out of the locker room when a friend told a mildly dirty joke in front of his fourteen-year-old son. "I don't ever want to hear that kind of language in here again," he harrumphed. Prescott was struck dumb by the vamping and flirting of Clare Boothe Luce, a sometime rival in Connecticut Republican politics. He broke off relations with his younger brother James, when James left his first wife in 1946. Years later, he pulled his support from Nelson Rockefeller on the same grounds. "Have we come to the point in our life as a nation when the governor of a great state—one who perhaps aspires to be nominated for President of the United States—can desert a good wife, divorce her, then persuade a young mother of four youngsters to abandon her husband and their four children and marry the governor?" he asked the 1963 graduating class at the girls' prep school Rosemary Hall in a commencement address. This survives as Senator Bush's only memorable speech.

Prescott had definite ideas about money, one of which was that men shouldn't live off their wives. That his home in Greenwich was purchased by his father-in-law and remained in Dorothy's name was a contradiction he had to live with. Prescott was perpetually distinguishing himself from both the kind of people who inherited wealth and those who pursued money for its own sake—namely the Walkers. The cheapness of the Bush men isn't just an endearing comic trait. It reflects the reality that there has never been any large pool of capital on the Bush side of the family. Though he poor-mouthed preposterously, Prescott actually accumulated fairly little, and didn't leave much behind. When George H. W. Bush set up his first oil business in 1950, he got his seed capital from his Uncle Herbie Walker, who was by then running G. H. Walker. When George W. Bush did the same thing twenty-five years later, it was with money from a Walker trust fund.

Wealth for Prescott Bush was a lever rather than a yardstick. He deplored people who took their servants for granted or used them as markers of status. The Bush servants were auxiliary semifamily—the not-really-a-chauffeur Alec who drove him to the station in his secondhand car, the-sort-of-a-housekeeper Alice—as opposed to the cowed, uniformed cadres at the Walker mansions. For Prescott, the point of money was the freedom to perform service, or "giving back to the community" as his son Poppy called it. Prescott idealized the role his partner Averell Harriman played for FDR and Truman. Short of opportunities at that level, he was willing to put in decades of drudgery at the Greenwich Representative Town Meeting. Campaigning for office was a necessary evil, a debasing impediment on the path to public service and ultimately becoming a Harriman-type wise man.

PRESCOTT BUSH ESTABLISHED three essential myths that Bush men live by. The first is: *I made it on my own*. The second is: *I'm not really rich*. The third is: *I'm running to serve my country*. Not until 1950, when he was in his mid-fifties and nearly done paying private school bills did Prescott feel financially secure enough to try for a U.S. Senate seat left open by a retirement. This was the first of four campaigns that remain significant because of the way they forged the Bushes as a political force, and because of the lessons the family developed from them. Though Poppy, unlike his siblings, worked on none of his father's campaigns, he watched closely and took in the implications. His sons George and Jeb would do the same with his, fostering the conundrum of independence as a family tradition. Bush men try to be different by doing essentially the same thing.

On top of these three myths were the seven lessons that Prescott's Senate losses and eventual victories imparted to the family. The first lesson was the treachery of the press. In 1950, Bush was running even with William Benton, the Democratic nominee. But on the Sunday before the election, the muckraking columnist Drew Pearson asserted on his radio show that Prescott was treasurer of the Birth Control League. In the days before *Griswold v. Connecticut*, birth control remained illegal in the majority-Catholic state. While the family has long decried this as a smear, it was in fact a minor distortion—carefully orchestrated for maximum harm. Prescott was listed as treasurer on a letterhead for Planned Parenthood, a successor organization to the Birth Control League, which had closed up shop in 1942. Though he denied the charge, Prescott lost by 1,102 votes.

Lesson #2 from Prescott's early campaigns was the importance of moment. Bush tried again in 1952, but this time lost the Republican primary. He thought his final shot had passed. Then he got a third chance when Connecticut's other sitting senator died and he was handed the Republican nomination for an open seat. Prescott got the Whiffs out on the trail again and, wearing a raccoon coat, introduced Dwight Eisenhower at a rally in New Haven. With the wind of Ike's 1952 landslide at his back, Prescott won. In future campaigns, family members would ponder obsessively whether conditions were ripe.

Lesson #3 was money before politics. Prescott thought only someone who was financially secure could resist the corrupting pressures of politics. In 1956, he was pleased to tell President Eisenhower that he had brushed off threats to run Poppy out of the oil business if Prescott voted against legislation to deregulate natural gas. Prescott opposed increasing the salary of senators from $12,500 to $22,500, arguing that the job was "service" like the ministry or teaching. In this vision, either an independent income or a monastic lifestyle was required for elected officials. Like Prescott, Poppy and his sons would seek wealth before aiming for office.

Lesson #4 was the primacy of connections and manners. Politics for the "modern Republican" Prescott Bush was not principally about ideology or a set of beliefs. It was an establishment responsibility pursued on the basis of relationships cultivated through sports, business, and the Ivy League. The best golfer in the Senate, Prescott played often with Eisenhower at the Burning Tree Country Club. But Prescott also shared Yale and Ohio bonds with Robert Taft, who led the antediluvian wing of the GOP. Prescott helped Taft's son become ambassador to Ireland as a way to arbitrate between the president and the party leader. In an act of some courage, he introduced Joe McCarthy at a rally in Bridgeport in 1952 while expressing "reservations" about McCarthy's methods. But he took greatest pride in being one of the only colleagues to visit McCarthy on his deathbed at Walter Reed Hospital.

Lesson #5 was that Northeastern moderates were becoming an endangered species. In office, Prescott Bush supported civil rights legislation, larger immigration quotas, and higher taxes. Conservatives classified him alongside Clifford Case of New Jersey, Leverett Saltonstall of Massachusetts, and Nelson Rockefeller of New York. Liberal Republicanism was his son Poppy's natural political tendency as well. But it wouldn't last and couldn't travel. An international investment banker trailing Whiffenpoofs, Prescott was easily caricatured as a softheaded patrician. His son Poppy's decision to pursue politics from Texas rather than Connecticut—and his early efforts to appease the most noxious elements on the right, including the John Birch Society—reflected his understanding of what sort of Republican would predominate in the future. Prescott's Texas-bred grandsons George W. and Jeb would shed the taint of moderation altogether and hide their establishment trappings more convincingly.

Lesson #6 was to not give up. Prescott Bush got elected to the Senate only on his third try, thanks to an opportunity that arose unexpectedly after he had seemingly failed for good. Beset by dizzy spells and stomach pains—and facing what would have been a tough campaign—

Prescott did not run for reelection in 1962. This was a decision he came to regret as soon as he took a rest and felt better. He returned to Brown Brothers Harriman, where he had little to do, and lived for another ten years, lamenting his mistake until the end.

The most important lesson of all, #7, was to trust only the family. Prescott's Democratic partners, Averell Harriman and Bob Lovett, supported his opponent Abraham Ribicoff in the 1952 election. At the state Democratic convention, Harriman gave a rousing speech attacking Prescott. Prescott, who had helped save the firm during the Depression, took this as an enormous betrayal and the two men didn't speak to each other for more than a decade. This is the trust-only-blood mind-set that led Howard Fineman of *Newsweek* to dub the Bushes "the WASP Corleones." George H. W. Bush's longtime spokesman Marlin Fitzwater once described a meeting that took place in 1985 at Camp David, to organize Poppy's upcoming presidential run. Poppy's brothers and sons were on one side of a long table, the advisers on the other. "It struck me then and there that the Bushes were very different from the Kennedys in that they would never have their Ted Sorensen," Fitzwater said. "No one outside the family would ever enter the inner circle."

THERE'S A USEFUL COMPARISON here to the tribe the Bushes have always regarded as their antithesis. Joe Kennedy was Prescott Bush's contemporary, just six years older, and bore a striking physical resemblance to him. Like Prescott, he did not found a dynasty so much as he took one over in a merger and made it a success, displacing his father-in-law as patriarch of the family. Joe Kennedy's father-in-law, John Fitzgerald, was the first Irish mayor of Boston and one of its famous citizens, while his own father, Patrick Joseph Kennedy, was merely a prosperous bar owner and minor politician. Through sheer force of will—and because his children got his last name rather than his wife's—Joe Kennedy was able to dominate the family, mold it in his image, and direct its fortunes.

Prescott Bush never liked what he saw reflected in the Kennedy mirror. Part of this was old-fashioned social snobbery; Prescott was a member of all the clubs that wouldn't let in Joe Kennedy because he was Irish and Catholic. And part of the complaint was political. The Democratic Kennedys were on the other side of presidential campaigns in which Prescott and his sons supported Eisenhower and Nixon. But the real reason Prescott Bush found the Kennedys so distasteful is that he identified them with the hubristic wealth and entitlement of his father-in-law, George Herbert Walker's, large Catholic family. Joe Kennedy was too greedy, too flashy, and insufficiently devoted to the community. With their well-known infidelities, reckless risk-taking, and scandals, the Kennedys, like the Walkers, were morally deficient. Prescott also objected to Joe Kennedy's effort to direct and finance the political careers of his sons, which violated his family's precept of making it on your own (with help). Prescott took what he considered a more proper route of giving his sons a good start in life and setting an example for them to follow.

Poppy later channeled his father's view of the Kennedy clan in relation to his son George W.'s presidential campaign. Now he was Joseph Kennedy, the father of the candidate, in the imputed analogy. Poppy emphasized that the Bushes didn't have anything to prove, that they didn't need to win the way the Kennedys did. "It's not that this is John F. Kennedy's father driving his sons to do something," George H. W. Bush told Hugh Sidey of *Time* during the post-election limbo in November 2000. "We are not that way in this family. This is not about vindication or legacy or entitlement." In Poppy's mind as in his father's, the decent and sincere Bushes seek office as individuals. The corrupt and decadent Kennedys run as representatives of the family conglomerate. The Bush boys got to choose their paths in life. The Kennedys had theirs chosen for them. George W. Bush perpetuated the family prejudice, "They never had to work," he commented about the Kennedys in 1989, "They never had to have a job."

Perhaps it was the parallels in his own generation that prompted Poppy to disown the natural comparison so strenuously. In Prescott Bush's as in Joe Kennedy's household, the second son took his older brother's place as the vehicle for the family's ambitions as a result of

what happened in the Second World War. John F. Kennedy, who suffered from chronic health problems, was given a battlefield promotion by his father only after his older and more beloved brother Joseph Kennedy Jr. was killed in the defense of Britain. Jack's wartime heroism in rescuing the survivors of *PT-109* strengthened his father's confidence in his political prospects. After JFK was assassinated, the family elevated Robert F. Kennedy to the leadership position. After Robert was killed, it focused on the youngest of the four brothers, Ted.

In the Bush family, Poppy overtook his older brother, Prescott Jr. (b. 1922), in a similar way during World War II, but without anyone getting killed. Pressie, two years older than Poppy, wanted to enlist in the armed forces as well, but was rejected for service because of near-blindness in one eye. While Poppy flew bombing missions over the Pacific, Pressie whiled away his days at a tennis club in Rio. Poppy's wartime heroics fixed his position as first among Prescott Sr.'s four sons, and turned Pressie into a frustrated subordinate sibling.

Thereafter, as Poppy flourished in business and politics, Pressie stayed close to the Round Hill Country Club and the world of his parents, serving as a factotum to his father in Connecticut politics and his successor on the Republican Town Committee and at the Greenwich Representative Town Meeting. The reversal of the positions of the two brothers became more glaring when Pressie finally tried for national office himself in 1982, announcing against Senator Lowell Weicker in the Republican primary. Starting at the Senate was a family tradition and the Bushes detested Weicker, but this was a poor choice of moment. Challenging the vulnerable incumbent would only soften Weicker up enough to hand his seat, and possibly control of the Senate, to the Democrats. The awkward work of getting Pressie to withdraw from the race fell to his little brother the vice president, George H. W. Bush.

Pressie's abortive political career pointed to one way in which the Bushes were indeed not like the Kennedys: the imputed line of succession in the Bush family descended vertically rather than horizontally. Of the four Bush brothers, Poppy was the only one who would succeed in following the business-to-politics route established by his father and the only one who would amount to much in either pursuit. Like John F. Kennedy, George H. W. Bush received critical help from his father in establishing his financial base and his political career. Unlike JFK, he needed the illusion that he had done it all on his own.

THE KENNEDY FAMILY'S permanent home is the summer compound Joe bought in Hyannisport, Massachusetts, in 1928. The Bush family summers farther up the Atlantic Coast, in Kennebunkport, Maine. The cedar-shingled house that David Walker and his son Bert built there is the primary scene of the Bush-Walker struggle. Dorothy Walker Bush was born there in 1901 and raised there in summers, competing as fiercely as her brothers, and often beating them at tennis and other contests. She and Prescott were given a bungalow on the property as a wedding present in 1921, and continued to spend summers there with their children through the 1940s. But after Poppy returned from the Pacific, the bungalow became increasingly uncomfortable for Prescott. Bert's ethic of fabulous wealth and brutal competition got on his nerves, in part because of how much it impressed his two oldest sons. Prescott rejected the Walker family ethos that ruled at Kennebunkport, which Elsie Walker Kilbourne once described as "having to be big shots" at everything they did.

Prescott loved golf, tennis, and baseball, liked to win, and was a better athlete than his father-in-law. But he and his wife raised their sons to compete within the boundaries of civility. Poppy learned from his mother to call close tennis shots in and preferred doubles to singles. His sportsmanship is best expressed in his passion for horseshoes—a less than serious game that he takes incredibly seriously. The Walker brothers play without any such irony. Theirs was a family, after all, in which sloppy tennis could get you sent to work in a factory. Visitors have often described a special edge to matches that pitted the Walkers against the Bushes. Both families tease when they play. But the teasing of Poppy and his brothers is funny and mostly benign. The Walker teasing during a tennis match can be personal and nasty.

Bert Walker's grandson Ray Walker told me that his family "treats winning as an end in itself"—a trait he sees in Poppy and George W. Bush as well. One of the things some of the Walkers most wanted to win was Prescott and Dorothy Bush's sons. Bert Walker would let his grandsons tool around on his thirty-eight-foot speedboat, the *Tomboy*, disturbing the peace with blasts of its deafening siren. Pressie and Poppy were fascinated by "Gampy," and, to the irritation of their father, were said to resemble him in appearance and personality.

But Prescott's nemesis in this battle was less his father-in-law than his brother-in-law George Herbert Walker Jr., known as "Uncle Herbie." Herbie was a driven businessman, who began to challenge his father for dominance in the family business after the pattern of his own father in relation to D. D. Walker. After Herbie's death, his widow, Mary Walker, remembered him as "a very aggressive person." His aggression was turned on his own family as well. By the late 1930s, Uncle Herbie was already closer to George and his brothers, Pressie, Johnny, and Bucky, than he was to his own two sons, George Herbert Walker III (known, like his grandfather, as "Bert") and Ray. Uncle Herbie hired Pressie and Johnny to work for G. H. Walker. His own older son and namesake was chosen to run the firm's St. Louis office only after Poppy turned down the job. A baseball lover who co-founded the New York Mets as an expansion team in 1960, Herbie went to every one of George's college games—but often skipped the sports matches of his own sons. "In our younger years, my dad held up George as a model to us," George Herbert Walker III told a reporter in 1988. Ray Walker once described his father's attitude toward his nephew Poppy as "hero worship."

To the irritation of Prescott Bush, Poppy returned the sentiment, displaying tremendous affection and regard for his humorless and arrogant Uncle Herbie. In the White House, Poppy often talked to his aides about Uncle Herbie's ownership of a baseball franchise as the life of Riley—the kind of thing he would have liked to do if he weren't burdened with the responsibility of service and the cares of the world. This became the fantasy of young George W. as well, after his great-uncle Herbie took him to meet Casey Stengel and the legendary St. Louis player Rogers Hornsby in the Mets dugout.

A decade of Poppy's and Uncle Herbie's letters back and forth, preserved on onionskin carbons, reside in the Bush Library. It is an intimate business correspondence that skips seamlessly from drilling rights, offshore rigs, and stock placements to Yale football and family matters. "Dearest Pop," Herbie writes in late 1951 after a visit to Texas with his wife, Mary, to inspect Bush's new company. "I can't tell you how much we all enjoyed our visit with you in Midland and the wonderful hospitality that you and Bar showed us. . . . It was grand to get a good feel of your picture, and I am confident that it is a matter of time until we really start to go places. I am also convinced that you are playing the thing the right way, and I am thoroughly pleased with the whole operation to date." In his letters, Uncle Herbie glories in his role as benefactor to the Bush boys. He asks Poppy what he thinks of his trying to get brother Pressie the job of business manager of the Yale Athletic Association; he recounts brother Johnny's arrival at G. H. Walker & Co.

Poppy's letters back to his uncle are flattering and affectionate. He thanks Herbie and Mary every year for hosting his family at Kennebunkport, for meals and vacations in the Bahamas. The occasional personal letter from Poppy to his father, by comparison, reads like true business correspondence, answering requests for information and registering changes of address. After he and Barbara move to Houston in 1959, Poppy—who would request a $2 refund on a broken toaster—writes to ask whether the senator can get them a discount on beds from the Simmons Company, where he used to serve on the board.

This paternal triangle left wounds on both sides. Prescott envied his son's closeness to Herbie. Herbie's sons wondered why their father was so generous to his nephews and so tough on them. In one of the letters, Herbie confides his frustration with his younger son, Ray, who had quit the JV football squad at Yale, because at 145 pounds he was getting clobbered. "I, of course, feel that he made the decision too early as all the coaches have told me they expected to be able to use him substantially as the season went along," Uncle Herbie writes to Poppy. Ray Walker subsequently took a turn considered bizarre in America's least introspective family when he quit G. H. Walker to train as a Jungian analyst. Today he lives in Vermont, where he nurses bitter feelings about his father and his cousins.

Over the summers, Uncle Herbie tried to lay claim to the affections of Poppy's sons the same way he had with Prescott's. In one of the letters I found in the Bush Library, he describes for Poppy the scene in Kennebunkport, where the six-year-old Little George was visiting with his mother in July 1952, when Poppy was too busy to come. "Dear Pop," Herbie writes:

> I have just returned from Kennebunkport and Georgie, who without any exaggeration has taken the place over and is everybody's favorite. He is a great kid and reminds everyone so much of you. He drove the speedboat alone for about fifteen minutes yesterday and was so sure of himself, demanded the right to bring it into the river and practically docked it. We then had him on the ball field for half an hour and you ought to see me try to knock tennis balls past him. . . . I was particularly touched when he wept buckets at saying goodbye to me. He is such a friendly and wonderfully emotional child and altogether something you should be tremendously proud of. Incidentally, he calls Ray "Uncle Ray" and me just plain Herbie.

The description is fascinating both for the early glimpse of George W. Bush's personality ("so sure of himself"), and as an expression of Uncle Herbie's urge to recapitulate his pattern of avuncular adoption.

When his father died in 1953, Herbie took ownership of both the big house in Kennebunkport and the role of Walker paterfamilias. He had also inherited his father's bullying, egotistical personality, which irritated Prescott much more in Herbie than it had in Bert.

Prescott couched his jealousy about Uncle Herbie's relationships with his sons in moral censure. Like his father, Uncle Herbie was a gambler and a philanderer, who often boasted about his conquests, despite being married. One of the sports he played at Kennebunkport was chasing women—the kind of thing the Kennedys did in Hyannisport. Prescott, who had cut off his own brother James for leaving his wife, found Herbie's boasting about his romantic conquests intolerable. The tensions were exacerbated after Prescott's election to the Senate when Herbie, hoping to capitalize on his brother-in-law's appointment to a congressional committee on nuclear energy, set up a partnership with other investors to get into the business. Prescott eventually refused to visit Kennebunkport while Herbie was there. Instead, he and Dorothy began vacationing on Fishers Island, off the coast of Connecticut. They later bought a house on Hobe Sound, the wealthy enclave on Jupiter Island, Florida.

When Prescott died in 1972, Poppy described him in a note to his friend C. Fred Chambers as an "inspiration" and "the incentive behind everything I did." When Herbie lay on his deathbed five years later, Poppy was far more emotional, calling his uncle "father," "brother," and "best friend." After the funeral, Poppy persuaded Herbie's widow, Mary—with his mother, Dorothy's, help—to sell Walker's Point to him on an installment plan, for the significantly submarket price of $780,000. This infuriated Herbie's sons, who stood to inherit the proceeds from subdivision and development. But the conflict was about more than money. The family jewel was going to their father's surrogate son. Poppy proceeded to remodel and expand the house, turning it into a proper presidential compound. After 1981, the requirements of the Secret Service and the growing brood of Bush grandchildren crowded the Walker cousins out of their family home.

Poppy's hostile takeover of Kennebunkport represented the submersion of the St. Louis clan and the repudiation of its mercantile values. He would turn it into the anti-Hyannisport, a place where nobody drank to excess, everyone went to sleep early (in the right bed), and got up for church on Sunday. Despite his greater affection for Herbie, Poppy was Prescott's son, embodying his morality, good manners, and sense of fair play. The new paterfamilias was, like his father, a man bored with the social whirl, the acquisition of toys, and the accumulation of wealth. He'd rather invite his barber to go fishing for blues. ("He loves all the natives that have worked on the place," his aunt Mary Walker said, some years after selling him the house.) Kennebunkport, with its weathered shingles, was now assumed to be the Bushes' ancestral manse, a Yankee relic rather than a robber baron's playground. In years to come, the public would only have the dimmest sense of the distaff side of Poppy's family beyond his sturdy, spirited mother, Dorothy. Keenly aware of their defeat, the Walkers from time to time flare with resentment. Their occasional sparks are mercilessly extinguished by Barbara Bush, who since the late 1970s has served as "enforcer" not just for her own children, but for her husband's entire tribe.*

George H. W. Bush, who occasionally expresses himself in verse, once wrote a poem about Kennebunkport. It describes a vision in which the departed Bushes and Walkers sit side by side at St. Ann's Church on a Sunday morning—"my Dad and Herby there next to Lou." ("Herby" is Poppy's sentimental spelling from childhood.) In this imagining, family conflict has faded away, with the younger generation carrying on a singular Bush tradition.

I see the brides and the christened face
Soul strength from this sacred place . . .
They're all in bed now in the dorm
The pulse of generations firmly born
The sea's the same—the rocks stay fast
The new ones' strength—generations past.

The Kennebunkport of these verses is no longer Bert and Herbie Walker's hedonistic playground. It is a place to "Just relax and watch

* George Herbert Walker III failed in a run for Congress in 1992, when his father's favorite nephew declined to endorse him in the GOP primary. He was appointed ambassador to Hungary in 2003 by his second cousin, George W. Bush.

the sea / Treasure the strength God's given you." George H. W. Bush's retreat breeds the Yankee values instilled in him by his father—making one's own way in the world and giving something back. In church, "the kids are passing the collection plate." The "firmly born" are all now Bushes, even if their last names are Walker.

There is a double irony here. Prescott Bush, who died in 1972, didn't live to see his ethic triumph in the family struggle. But in the end, the victory wasn't permanent. George W. Bush likes to say he is his mother's son. But many of his most distinctive traits don't seem to come from her or from his father. He is impatient, aggressive, often angry, and sometimes cruel. He's a plunger, not a careful analyst or a patient builder. He loves to compete but can't stand losing. The man's a Walker, through and through.

CHAPTER TWO

Father and Sons

So, when this loose behavior I throw off
And pay the debt I never promised,
By how much better than my word I am,
By so much shall I falsify men's hopes;
And like bright metal on a sullen ground,
My reformation, glitt'ring o'er my fault,
Shall show more goodly and attract more eyes
Than that which hath no foil to set it off.
I'll so offend to make offense a skill,
Redeeming time when men think least I will.

—HENRY IV, PART I

—

IT'S NOT EASY TO BE A BUSH SON. YOU'RE EXPECTED TO CHALLENGE your father, but in a way that indicates respect. Poppy Bush got this exactly right in the spring of 1942 as he was finishing prep school, when his parents tried to talk him out of joining the military. Poppy stood up to Prescott for the first time by saying he was signing up anyway. This was the kind of defiance Prescott had to recognize as a tribute, the reenactment of his own decision to volunteer for the Yale Battalion. It is the only time that the stolid Prescott Bush is recorded as having cried.

Unlike Prescott's fantasy heroics, his son's were entirely real. At eighteen, Poppy Bush became the youngest pilot in the U.S. Navy. He flew 116 bombing runs and was shot down twice over the Pacific. After being hit by enemy fire during a mission in 1944, he stayed aloft to drop his bombs on a Japanese installation on Chichi Jima. Poppy bailed out over the water, the lone survivor of the three men on the plane. Bloodied but not seriously injured, he climbed into his self-inflating raft, and was rescued by a submarine patrolling for survivors of the raid.

He continued to live up to his father's reputation after the war. If not quite the athlete, and nothing of the musician Prescott was, Poppy matched his legend at Yale. Although he was married and faced the challenge of raising a rambunctious baby boy, George Walker Bush, Poppy got through college in three years. As a senior, he was elected captain of the baseball team and to Skull and Bones, where he was "last man tapped"—the top choice of the graduating members. He won the Gordon Brown Prize for "all around student leadership," graduating with a Phi Beta Kappa key and a friendship with nearly everyone else in the class.

After Yale, Poppy was approached to join both family firms. Uncle Herbie offered a job at G. H. Walker that Poppy declined. The partner at Brown Brothers Harriman who approached him understood the family well enough to stress that the idea didn't come from Prescott. While wrestling with the decision, Bush pointedly did not call his father for advice. Having been through the intensity of the war, a comfortable career on Wall Street didn't appeal to him. "I wanted to do something on my own. I did not want to be in the shadow of this very powerful and respected man," Bush later commented. To his friend Gary Bemiss he wrote: "I am not sure I want to capitalize completely on the benefits of my birth—that is on the benefits of my social position." The adverb shows that he recognized making it truly on his own was not really an option.

Bush drove to Texas in a red Studebaker that his father bought him as a graduation present, with Barbara and toddler Georgie to follow. In the family legend, the red Studebaker became the symbol of the ability to strike out on your own and succeed; a replica of it is the first thing visitors see upon entering the Bush Presidential Library in College Station, Texas. To nonfamily members, the idea of the senator's son being a self-made man sounds absurd. Young man Poppy went west, but drawing entirely on his father's business and social connections. The job he took at Dresser Industries was proffered by Neil Mallon, who had been Prescott's confederate in the Skull and Bones "Geronimo" caper. Even more to the point, Prescott was on the oil company's board and hired Mallon as CEO when Harriman controlled it. The job interview would have been a tough one for Poppy to fail.

At the same time, the delusion of independence seems to have been as functional for Poppy as it was for Prescott. Bush was a natural competitor who needed to feel that he was contending on a level playing field. Having seen inherited wealth and position undermine the drive of classmates at Andover and Yale, Poppy saw that having a successful father could also be a drawback. And once he was struggling to succeed in a risky business, Bush realized that family connections wouldn't prevent failure. His own sons amplified these rationalizations, turning them into complaints. Jeb often claimed that being the president's son has been a *disadvantage* for him because it restricted his business opportunities. Neil, the floundering son who embarrassed the family with financial scandal, once said, "I didn't have a red Studebaker," a telling insight into himself and the family's expectations.

Poppy's first job was sweaty, manual labor in the roughneck town of Odessa. But before he had painted too many oil rigs, Mallon, who was keeping close tabs, had him transferred to California to learn the sales side of the business. After a year selling drill bits, Poppy and family moved back to Texas, to the comparatively genteel boomtown of Midland, which was filled with young Ivy Leaguers like himself hoping to make their fortunes. Eager to set up as an "independent," Bush formed a partnership with his Midland neighbor John Overbey to buy and sell drilling rights. Overbey knew the business and the territory. What Bush brought to the table was his gift for making friends and access to seed capital. His Uncle Herbie helped him raise a $350,000 stake in 1951.

Bush's best strike was his choice of partners. In Midland, he and Overbey joined forces with the Liedtke brothers, sons of the chief counsel of Gulf Oil. The venture they formed in 1953, Zapata Petroleum, made a huge, $850,000 investment in a single lease, which eventually yielded 127 performing wells and made Poppy a millionaire on paper before he was thirty. He bought his family a bigger house in Midland, co-founded a bank, built a swimming pool, and pushed for Zapata to move into the emerging business of offshore drilling. The good-natured Poppy's steady rise made the oil business look like an easy field of success to his young sons.

But his work took Poppy further and more frequently away from home, as he hawked multimillion-dollar drilling platforms from Latin America to the Persian Gulf. At the end of the 1950s, the company split, in part over tensions with the Liedtkes about Uncle Herbie's domineering micromanagement. As a result, Bush soon had his own company, the Walker-Bush Corporation, which in 1959 he moved from Midland to Houston, with an eye to his political future as well as the growth of the business.

DIVISION OF LABOR among the Bush generations is unchanging: the women run the family while the men run the world. As Jeb has described it, the structure of his family was "matriarchal." Barbara was by unspoken agreement the custodial parent, doing the principal work of raising six children, figuring out where they would go to school, and managing eleven household moves in her first six years of marriage alone. Big George was the sweeter and less formidable parent. Barbara was the family disciplinarian and protector.

Aspects of Barbara's personality—her acid tongue, her irreverent humor, her long memory for slights—are manifest in her oldest son. Curiously, though, her family figures negligibly in the identities of her children. Though they are related on their mother's side to Franklin Pierce, the fourteenth president, George W. and Jeb seldom acknowledge their maternal ancestry. The disparity in how the family regards the two sides is evident in the forenames of George and Barbara's children and grandchildren, which are mostly culled from the Bush and Walker branches. Only Robin, born in 1949 and named for Barbara's mother, Pauline Robinson, and Marvin, the youngest son, named for her father, refer to the Pierces. To the extent there ever was anything resembling a Pierce ethic, Barbara seems to have wanted neither to embody nor transmit it.

The reason is evident in the unhappy glimpses of her childhood Barbara provides in her autobiography. Growing up in Rye, New York—a suburb slightly south of Greenwich in both location and status—Barbara had an affectionate bond with her indulgent father, who worked as a publishing executive and eventually rose to the chairmanship of *McCall's*. But she had a tormented relationship with her mother, Pauline Robinson Pierce, as well as with her sister, Martha, who was five years older. Her mother's social ambitions were unsatisfied; she didn't make the social register, and neither daughter was picked as a debutante. Insecure Pauline spent beyond the family's means, leading to screaming fights with her husband, who had to borrow to pay her debts. She was also depressive, a trait she passed along to Barbara. Both mother and older sister were beauties—Martha became a model and appeared on the cover of *Vogue*. But Barbara was less lovely and had a weight problem. At twelve, she stood five foot eight and weighed 148 pounds. She internalized her mother's negative image of her, turning a caustic tongue on others and on herself. As a child, she found greater happiness in the household of her friend Lucille Schoolfield, where she recalled there were always fruit or flowers on the dining room table, and where her "second mother" nurtured and cooked.

In 1941, when she met George Bush at the age of sixteen, Barbara was in the market for an alternative family to join permanently. At that stage, she had slimmed down and grown prettier. She plunged headlong into the relationship with Poppy, driven by youthful passion and wartime exigency—but also by the family vindication that came with a socially prominent match. While her fiancé was away at war, Barbara was unofficially adopted by his mother, Dorothy Bush, on whom she came to model herself. There was no question but that

Barbara would drop out of Smith in 1945 after her first year to live with her husband in New Haven. When Pauline Pierce died in a car accident in 1949, with Barbara's father, Marvin, at the wheel, mother and daughter were at odds. Barbara, seven months pregnant with her second child, chose not to travel to New York to attend the funeral.

Barbara Bush is a woman who, as the late journalist Marjorie Williams once noted, was at her most content writing books in the voice of her dog. But in time, her choice to live through her husband and children produced enormous resentment. As Barbara once put it, "In a marriage where one is so willing to take on responsibility and the other is so willing to keep the bathrooms clean, that's the way you get treated." Barbara grumbled about the fascinating life her husband had, while she was stuck home with the brats. She protested that her husband's conflict-aversion forced her to be "the mean one." She complained that for all her efforts, their five children were closer to their father than to her.

In the early years of her marriage, Barbara's tendency to depression was compounded by the bleakness and isolation of Midland. She later described her state of mind during those years as "dormant." Her withdrawal deepened in 1953, when her second child, Robin, died of leukemia. George, who lacks his wife's emotional control, couldn't face the hospital. It was Barbara, alone at Sloan-Kettering Memorial Hospital in New York, who had to make the terrible decision about putting their four-year-old girl through a final operation, which she did not survive. This took a visible toll, turning Barbara's hair completely white before she was thirty.

After Robin died, both Barbara and George seemed equally intent upon not letting the loss affect their lives. One aspect of this was their determination to protect their son, whom they kept in the dark and did not prepare for Robin's death. Thus Little George's formative childhood experience was not only losing his sister when he was seven years old, but losing her by surprise—and then being denied an outlet for his feelings. In acknowledging the mistake she and her husband made in not recognizing that their son needed to grieve just as they did, Barbara points toward the long-term consequence: while their son's sadness was submerged, his anger at his parents never really went away.

LITTLE GEORGE GREW UP idealizing his dashing, good-at-everything dad. In a Rosebud moment he once described, we see him on the floor of the family's ranch house on Ohio Street in Midland (now the George W. Bush Childhood Home, Inc.), sprawled over a family scrapbook. He is fingering a token of his father's valor: a scrap of rubber from the raft that saved Big George's life in the Pacific.

But if he was raised in awe of his father's heroism, Little George also felt the smart of his absence, especially as his mother fell into depression after Robin's death. Unlike Prescott, Poppy wasn't a distant or intimidating father. His sons, George W. (b. 1946), Jeb (b. 1953), Neil (b. 1955), and Marvin (b. 1956), and his daughter, Doro (b. 1959), idolized him, but often from a distance. In the years after Robin's death, Poppy threw himself all the more into building his business, which involved extensive travel. When the family moved to Houston in 1959, he began to spend nearly every evening laying the groundwork for his political career.

Barbara Bush has recounted her oldest son's efforts to cheer her after Robin's death, a role often cited in the formation of his antic personality. The aftermath of the tragedy was a time of closeness that established an unusual bond between mother and son. But it also forged the essential contradiction in the son's feelings toward both his parents. At the age of eight, Little George idolized Big George and resented his absence. He worried about his mother, but later complained that "she kind of smothered me." With his father away while his mother was depressed and burdened with the care of an ever-growing family, Little George absorbed the impossible task of filling Big George's shoes. Barbara's feeling of abandonment pulled him into the role of junior husband. One poignant story has the teenage son driving his mother to the hospital after a miscarriage while his father was away on business. As Barbara later remembered, her son picked her up the next day at the hospital. "He talked to me in the car and he said, 'Don't you think we ought to talk about this before you have more children?' "

The son was also angry, surely, at his father's failure to recognize or help with his difficulties in school, probably resulting from a combination of some form of dyslexia and attention deficit hyperactivity disorder. But George H. W. Bush is a frustrating man to be angry at, because he does so little to reciprocate, leaving the confrontation to Barbara. As an adolescent, Georgie's derelictions mainly provoked expressions of concern and disappointment from his dad, the sting of which his son has often described. In family photos, W. is often off slightly to one side, as if to indicate his reservations about the pretend pose of perfection. On his face there is often a smile-scowl that seems to express his ambivalent attitude toward the superman usually at the center of the picture. Sometimes Little George's adulation and resentment toward his father coexisted; other times they were at war.

Frustrated hero worship was the chief theme of George W.'s life until the age of forty. Little George did everything he could to emulate a father who was treated as champion and paragon within his extended family. But as he grew up, the son discovered that many of the doors his father sailed through only appeared to be open to him. He lacked his father's abilities at sports and academics, as well as Poppy's knack of impressing adults and turning every peer into a pal. If his father was the one for whom everything came easily, George W. was the one for whom it often didn't come at all, even when he tried his hardest. At games and sports, Poppy was a gracious loser. George W. was a sore one.

Nor did the social system in which his dad flourished work in the same way. By the 1960s, having Bush for a last name no longer guaranteed safe passage through the temples of the American aristocracy. To outsiders, Junior's route in life looked like the gilded path of someone born to privilege and taking every advantage of it. But to Little George, the East Coast institutions where his father excelled didn't fit like an old shoe; they chafed like one that doesn't fit. Like his

Walker uncles, he tried to do the same things Poppy did, but couldn't do them as well. Some of the frustration was taken out on his younger brothers. Jeb later recalled Georgie commanding the three of them as an army and staging mock executions. "O.K., you little wieners, line up," Georgie would demand, and shoot them in the back with his air rifle. Jeb, Neil, and Marvin would fall to the ground and play dead.

At Andover, where George W.'s dad was a famous all-arounder, the boy who went by the name of "Junior" was barely a survivor. He spent his first months unable to keep up academically, certain he would be kicked out. His sense of not belonging was bolstered by his friendship with Clay Johnson, a fellow Texan, who subsequently became Bush's roommate at Yale. The smart kids at Andover—along with many of the teachers—scoffed at the two of them. Bush and Johnson jeered back. Junior was not good in class or athletics—a key mark of character at the school and in the family. He had to cope with being treated as dumb, without even being a jock. And while he made friends easily, Bush wasn't universally liked and admired, the way his dad was. It is at prep school that one first sees the joint expression of George W.'s overconfidence and insecurity, qualities often closely twinned. This too is a Walker more than a Bush trait. Prescott and Poppy were neither insecure nor overconfident; they were capable and modest. The Walker men, on the other hand, strut and boast because they're unsure of their abilities.

If at first you don't succeed, pretend you don't really care. At Andover, Junior became known as "the Lip." He bonded with peers by being cutting and subversive, not by being nice to everybody, the way his dad did. Big George thrived as a skillful conformist in a culture of conformity. Naturally respectful of authority, he won rewards by participating fully according to well-established rules. Junior thrived only through calibrated acts of subversion in a period while the unwritten rules were in flux, at a moment when the old principle of class privilege was losing its legitimacy, but the new principle of meritocracy hadn't yet been enshrined. George W. didn't flourish in this ambiguity, but wasn't prepared to challenge the system directly. Instead he would participate ambivalently, leading naughty, ironic cheers from the sidelines, or by creating his own parallel, parody structures. Bush was remembered by his Andover classmates for his mocking "stickball league," for coming up with sardonic nicknames for everyone, and for that smile-scowl, "the smirk" that became his trademark expression.

By the time he graduated in 1964, the automatic standing that came from a family like his was eroding. Asked by the dean of Andover to put down his top three choices for college, since his C average and mediocre test scores might not get him into Yale, Bush listed 1. Yale; 2. Yale; and 3. Yale. On the strength of his family connections, he got in, as did Clay Johnson, despite the dean's feeling that they might be better suited to the University of Texas. But admission to Yale was an ironic reward. The place so conducive to earlier generations of Bushes and Walkers was on the verge of its own social revolution. Bush arrived in 1964 at a university still recognizable as the traditional Yale of the 1950s. In 1968, he graduated from the Yale of the 1960s. The university was undergoing a transformation from a place where Andover boys with family connections could cruise through with Gentleman Cs to a meritocratic institution where WASP scions were more mocked than envied. Under the reforms instituted by President Kingman Brewster and his admissions director, Inky Clark, legacies could no longer expect so powerful a preference. It's unlikely Bush would have been admitted a few years later.

"There were really two Yales back then—one a more or less serious university, the other a cheerful, undemanding party school—and they didn't intersect very much," Bush's classmate Charles McGrath has written. Bush located himself at the center of the latter, avoiding politics and shunning the psychedelic scene. He didn't make the starting lineup of the baseball team, on which his father was captain and his grandfather the star. He was chosen for his father's fraternity, DKE, but by that time its social standing was in decline.

Bush got elected frat house president in his junior year, and faced a campus controversy over the tradition of "branding" new pledges during their initiation ceremonies, a practice that an editorial in the *Yale Daily News* described as "sadistic and obscene." At the last moment, the glowing iron brand was replaced by a hot wire hanger or a lit cigarette. (President Clinton's former spokesman Lanny Davis, who was "branded" on the small of his back by a group that included Bush, attests that the procedure nonetheless leaves a scar.) This conflict was the occasion of George W. Bush's first appearance in *The New York Times*, where he was quoted arguing that the hazing ritual wasn't really torture. It was "only a cigarette burn," he noted, prefiguring later comments.

Bush seems to have been happier in the beer-soaked DKE house than in the dry Skull and Bones temple, which he joined only at his father's urging. Junior adopted the club name "Temporary," expressing his attitude. He ended up making close friends in Skull and Bones, as he does most places. But for him, membership didn't mean what it did to his father, his uncles, and his grandfather. It was a family obligation that turned out to be somewhat better than he expected.

On his Yale classmates, Junior made a curious double impression. Some saw him as a callow bully who made other people feel inferior with slighting nicknames and derisive comments. Others found him genuine and relentlessly likable, with surprising empathy for others and a mostly self-mocking wit. Lanny Davis told me another story about watching with dismay as a bully harassed an effeminate classmate in the dining hall. Bush told the big jock to "shut the fuck up." In a story Bush often told on himself, the star of the Yale football team once spotted him in the back row during shopping period for classes. "Hey! George Bush is in this class!" Calvin Hill shouted to his teammates. "This is the one for us!" Bush replied to Hill's jibe with a "grinning thumbs-up," according to Jim Sleeper, a classmate who witnessed the exchange. Bush's name became a synonym for coasting, not because he was lazier than many others, but because he cultivated the idea that he wouldn't break a sweat. His famous smirk had undergone mitosis into two different expressions. The first was a contemptuous sneer at pretentious people who thought they knew better. The second was an ironic pat administered to his own back. Smirk #1 was at your expense; Smirk #2 was at his own.

The more Yale evolved, the more out of place Bush felt. Those who didn't really know him saw him as the ultimate insider, with a father in Congress and a grandfather, the former "Senator from Yale," serving on the board. But in his own mind, George W. was a double outsider—a Texan among preppies, and a preppie among the hippies. Bush returned the resentment of the new liberal elite, which because it claimed to stand for fairness, felt more entitled than the old WASP elite did. He told his faculty adviser that East Coast snobs and elitists looked down on him for his manners and his father's conservative politics. By graduation, Bush had defined himself as the scourge of intellectual snobs, who were fast replacing the social kind. Contemporaries describe him playing Cool Hand Luke—a brash rebel with a chip on his shoulder, showing up at parties in his leather bomber jacket and smoking unfiltered Lucky Strikes. The existentialist pose was his reaction to feeling awkward in an environment where being a Bush no longer meant automatically fitting in.

Bush later told family members he "didn't learn a damn thing" at Yale. He held a grudge against the place that was strong enough for him to boycott reunions and refuse to contribute to the alumni fund for two decades. His anti-elitist grievance, which became a central part of his presidential story in 1999, was officially laid to rest in 2001, when he returned to claim an honorary degree and give a commencement address. In it, Bush struck his old anti-intellectual pose and reminisced about how little he had studied. But the spot was still sore to the touch. Bush chastised his speechwriters for taking the joke of his failure in college too far. Bush's gripe against Yale won't go away for a simple reason: it was there that he realized he couldn't be his father.

Bush's college years draw to a close with more failed emulation. Like Poppy, who was married while at Yale, George got engaged, to his Houston girlfriend Cathy Lee Wolfman, when he was still a junior. Legend has Barbara intervening against the prospect of a Jewish daughter-in-law, but in fact Wolfman's family had been practicing Episcopalians for some time. The reason they didn't get married was that they had no reason to get married, other than the life map in Bush's head. He postponed the wedding, and Wolfman eventually called it off, with the two parting on amicable terms.

Junior's success at circumventing the five-year waiting list for the Texas Air National Guard has been similarly misunderstood through a generational lens, as oppposed to the more important family one. George surely had no desire to go to Vietnam—another case where, because of the war's unpopularity, the father's heroic opportunities were not available. But if he simply wanted to avoid danger and unpleasantness, there were safer options, like enrolling in graduate school.

WHILE GEORGE W. STRUGGLED to follow his father, his father was also trying to be something he wasn't—a right-wing Texan. Politics was becoming the family business and all the Bush siblings would find roles to play in it. But only George W. was old enough to understand the implications of his father's first defeat in his 1964 Senate race. George H. W. Bush's first campaign for national office reflected the lessons he took from Prescott's political mistakes in 1950 and 1952. In the same way, George W. Bush's maiden effort, his 1978 congressional campaign, reflected what he absorbed from Poppy's failure in 1964.

George H. W. Bush had done some organizing for Republicans in Midland and Odessa, but his political career began in earnest only after the family moved to Houston. There Bush spent more and more time with a group of friends who were focused on making the GOP a viable competitor in Texas. In Lyndon Johnson's heyday, the state—and indeed the entire South—remained dominated by Democrats. But Johnson's elevation to the vice presidency in 1960 created an opening for John Tower, a conservative political science professor. By winning the special election for Johnson's seat, Tower became the first Republican senator elected from the South since Reconstruction.

In 1962, as Prescott Bush was deciding to retire from the Senate, his son was approached to take over the post of Republican Party chairman in Harris County, which includes Houston and its environs. Poppy threw himself into the job with a methodical fervor, visiting all 270 precincts and developing a viable fund-raising operation. The problem he faced was the conflict between his instincts and background on the one hand, and the prevailing local winds on the other. Though hardly ideological, George H. W. Bush came from a distinct political tradition, the patrician, New England Republicanism of his father. The Wall Street internationalism of the Bushes and the Walkers accepted the New Deal welfare state and rejected the isolationism of the party's Taft faction. A supporter of the United Negro College Fund, Poppy joined his father in favoring civil rights legislation. But in Harris County, he had to lead a party organization in which the nativist, paranoid John Birch Society was a rising force.

Poppy's instinctive approach was to genially paper over the differences between moderates and fanatics with good manners. Bush would invite the Birchers to his house, trying to convince them that they shared the same goals, and wrote a memo banning the words "crazies" and "nuts" from intra-party dialogue. He called attacks on the Birchers "reverse McCarthyism." But diplomacy wouldn't win him his first big political opportunity, the Republican nomination to challenge the incumbent Democratic senator Ralph Yarborough. The crotchety, populist Yarborough was vulnerable only because of his status as the sole Southern senator to support the Kennedy-Johnson civil rights legislation.

In declaring against Yarborough, Bush positioned himself much further to the right than he really was, opposing Medicare (which he described as "socialized medicine"), the nuclear test ban treaty, and civil rights, including open housing legislation. Bush contended that the landmark 1964 Civil Rights Act violated constitutional rights, and that the problem could best be handled by moral persuasion at the local level. On each of these issues, Poppy broke with Prescott, who had voted for every civil rights bill, and aligned himself instead with the Republican presidential candidate Barry Goldwater.

While Yarborough's politics were out of step with his state, his political skills were vastly superior to Bush's. Yarborough pummeled Poppy as a spoiled whelp and gave him the back of his hand. He cast the Republican as a Connecticut carpetbagger, and used Zapata's international drilling projects to accuse Bush of undermining Texas producers with cheap foreign imports. He also used Bush's parentage against him. "Big ole Daddy . . . out to buy hisself a seat in the United States Senate," Yarborough drawled at rallies. "Let's show the world that old Senator Bush can't send Little Georgie down here to buy a Senate seat."

For the eighteen-year-old kid who really was called Little George, this created a stew of contradictory emotions. He understood that his father was not close to the forbidding grandfather he once described simply as "scary." The family mythology was all about Poppy making it on his own, with no help from the senator. Junior spent the summer working on the campaign, putting together briefing books on all the Texas counties. Driving a bus around to rallies before leaving for college in September, he saw for the first time a problem he would later grapple with in his own career, right-wing disbelief that anyone named Bush could be an authentic, heartland conservative. At the same time, he must have recognized that his father, talking Texan and touring with a country and western band, was stretching to be something he wasn't.

Little George believed his father would win until he got to the Bush victory party at the Hotel American in Houston. As soon as he walked in, he heard the election being called for Yarborough, who beat his father by more than 300,000 votes out of the 2.6 million cast. This was in part the Johnson tide, but Bush underperformed Goldwater in the state. Georgie turned a chair around to face a wall so people wouldn't see him crying. One glimpses in this moment an essential tension in his relationship with his father: hero worship coping with the hero's flaws.

Decades later, W. described an encounter at Yale with the university's chaplain, William Sloane Coffin, who told him that in losing to Yarborough, his father "was beaten by a better man." Though Coffin denied it, the story is probably true; Barbara Bush has referred to the conversation as a painful one for her son. But by the time he made it public, during his first campaign for governor of Texas in 1994, the anecdote had taken on a great deal of additional freight. The younger Bush had himself assumed Yarborough's populist mantle, making Yale's antiwar minister into an emblem of liberal elitism. Junior surely never thought for a moment that Coffin, who was prosecuted for leading resistance to the draft, was right about his father not being a good man. But politically, he knew that his father had indeed made a mistake. He had suffered from an excess of etiquette, allowing himself to be preppie-baited by a more authentic Texan. This was something his son would do everything to avoid in his own political career.

The elder George Bush drew the opposite lesson from the 1964 campaign: he had tried *too* hard to get elected, betraying his principles in the process. After his loss, he said he was "ashamed" he hadn't spoken out against the Birchers. Bush told John Stevens, his pastor in Houston, "You know, John, I took some of the far right positions to get elected. I hope I never do it again. I regret it." The wording was precise. Poppy didn't say he would not betray his principles again for the sake of winning, merely that he *hoped* not to. Running for Congress in 1966 in a newly created, upscale district, Bush faced no such conflict as he embraced a moderate position on civil rights, and actively sought black support. "I will not attempt to appeal to the white backlash," he declared. "I am in step with the 60s." This time, Poppy won handily. With some help from Prescott, he landed a slot on Ways and Means, the most powerful committee in the U.S. House.

IN 1971, JUNIOR was working for one of his father's Skull and Bones buddies in what he called "a stupid coat and tie job" in the office of an agriculture company. He spent his evenings playing midnight water polo at Chateaux Dijon, the hilariously named apartment complex-cum-singles bar where he lived in Houston. After quitting his job, he spent six months unemployed. He applied to law school at the University of Texas, but didn't get in. His lack of direction was beginning to give his parents cause for concern. The Bushes are not teetotalers, but they seldom lose control—the time George H. W. got sloshed and his oilfield buddies dumped him out on his front lawn is a funny story the family tells. Stories about George W.'s drinking were getting less hilarious. He became obnoxious and insulted people, including friends of his parents. He drove drunk with his younger siblings in the car. He had a tendency to get arrested (twice for pranks and rowdiness in college, once for DUI in Maine). Junior was less and less the charming rascal who could get away with dropping his dirty laundry with his friends' wives, and more and more the guy who needed to get a life. Bush later told a story about the time he quit early on a job his father helped him get. "Son, you agreed to work a certain amount of time and you didn't. I just want you to know that you have disappointed me," Poppy said. As Bush told an interviewer in 1987, "When you love a person and he loves you, those are the harshest words someone can utter."

The mutual frustration of son and parents comes through in the well-worn story from 1973, when the twenty-six-year-old George W. woke his family in the middle of the night by driving drunk into the garbage cans next to their home in Houston. He asked his dad, who had been trying to speak to him, if he wanted "to go mano a mano right here." His father didn't bluster back—he just stared at the spectacle over the top of his reading glasses. The family crisis was averted when Jeb blurted out that George had been admitted to Harvard Business School, where he had applied in secret, to prove he didn't need his father's help. "I don't know if I'm going," Junior said. "I just wanted to show that I could do it." The last admission is the most revealing part of the story. George W. had adopted within his family a technique he would later apply beyond it. He would turn low expectations to his benefit by dramatically surpassing them. To those around him, the prodigal looked like he was squandering his inheritance. But in the back of his mind lurked the idea of a triumphant return.

Junior's Harvard years coincided with a period of growing stress for the family. His father's career had hit a rough patch. In 1970, Nixon encouraged him to give up his safe House seat to take on Yarborough again, and once again he lost. After the defeat, he was given a series of jobs that entailed geographic moves and questionable progress; first to New York to be ambassador to the United Nations in 1971, then back to Washington to run the Republican National Committee in 1973, then to China as American liaison (before the restoration of full diplomatic relations) in 1975, then back to Washington to head the CIA in 1976. If each of these jobs represented a potential step up, each also entailed a level of humiliation. The U.N. position was regarded as a largely ceremonial post, and was far short of the Treasury secretary job Bush wanted. Running the RNC during Watergate meant becoming a Nixon apologist and enabler, and threatened to derail his career. Even Nixon didn't admire Bush for standing by him; he regarded him as spineless, telling John Ehrlichman on the tapes that Bush was the kind of flunky who would "do anything for the cause." Poppy knew this. In 1974, he wrote a pained letter to his sons acknowledging that Nixon considered him to be a privileged and soft Ivy Leaguer. In China, Bush had to bow and scrape to Henry Kissinger, who saw him as weak and treated him accordingly. And if those jobs were fraught with hazard, taking over the CIA in the midst of scandal was a truly poisoned chalice, requiring Bush to publicly disavow any ambitions of taking Nelson Rockefeller's place on the Republican ticket in 1976. Bush believed that Donald Rumsfeld, a rival, had sabotaged his chances by recommending him for the intelligence post.

Barbara's situation was much worse. In China, she had her husband to herself and was happy for one of the only times in her life. But when he moved to the CIA, he was busier with work he couldn't share with her. With their youngest child, Doro, out of the house, Barbara now had time to herself for the first time in her adult life, and nothing much to do with it. Experiencing menopause, she suffered a recurrence of her depression that she acknowledged involved suicidal thoughts. "I was wallowing in self-pity," she later wrote. "I almost wondered why he didn't leave me. Sometimes the pain was so great, I felt the urge to drive into a tree or into an oncoming car." Barbara dealt with these feelings the way she had the black period after Robin's death, without professional help. She viewed depression as a kind of self-indulgence; the cure was to think about others instead of herself.

One form of self-therapy was needlepoint. Barbara spent years stitching a 10 × 14 tapestry depicting frogs, butterflies, and woodland animals amid cattails and lily pads. But the pastoral theme leaves a false impression of quietude. The rug, which was designed by an artist for her to fill in with needlepoint, winks with barbed references: a chipmunk, for instance, refers to her husband's withdrawal from the 1980 presidential race; a rabbit to Jimmy Carter's *Playboy* interview, and the "killer bunny" episode, when Carter was menaced by an alleged "swamp rabbit" while fishing near his home in Plains, Georgia. But the larger message is about her career as self-sacrificing helpmeet. Barbara Bush can tell you which of its dozens of homes the family lived in when she wove each bit of her martyrdom into the fabric.

AFTER GRADUATING BUSINESS school in 1975, George W. reenacted his father's legendary drive to Midland, in a blue 1970 Cutlass, with the intention of getting into the oil business. He taught Sunday school at First Presbyterian Church, just as his father had. And he tried to do what his dad had first done as an oilman, tracking down the ownership of oil leases for $100 a day. The following year, he drew together investments from various family friends to set up his own company, which he called Arbusto, Spanish for "Bush." But he soon discovered that, as at Andover and Yale, his name got him in the door, and could help him raise a pool of capital, but it didn't guarantee success. Even as a loss-making tax shelter, the business barely stayed afloat.

Unlike his father, who at his same age was already worth a million on paper, with a home, a booming business, and a growing family, George W. at thirty was living over a garage surrounded by dirty clothes, out drinking most nights, and getting nowhere in business. In 1976, he was arrested for driving drunk in Maine, this time with his seventeen-year-old sister, Doro, in the car. All around him in Midland was the oil boom of the 1970s, propelled by the OPEC embargo and oil price shocks and bigger than the one in which his father had prospered in the 1950s. But Bush didn't hit more than a trickle. This failure illustrates the inferiority of the Walker approach to the Bush one. His father had approached the oil business systematically, learning it from the ground up and diligently cultivating people who knew where the oil was most likely to be found. His son, who thought success was a matter of rolling the dice with borrowed money, never struck lucky.

Nineteen seventy-seven saw George W.'s first serious attempt to turn his life around. When he heard that George Mahon, the Democrat who had represented Midland in Congress for forty-three years, was retiring, he leapt at a shortcut to the next stage on the Bush trajectory. The conservative district presented a Republican opportunity parallel to his father's in 1964. His parents were stunned when Junior told them he intended to run. This was the Walker plunging instinct at work. The lesson from Prescott and Poppy was to earn a comfortable stake, start a family, and move into politics from a position of strength. But at some level, the boldness of the decision had the desired effect. Whatever his doubts, Big George told friends he was pleased his son was continuing the family tradition and showing that he had the guts to compete.

George W. Bush believed he could escape his father's pitfalls. George H. W. Bush's career up to that point had been defined by his sense of obligation and hierarchy. But waiting his turn and taking orders from Nixon and Gerald Ford hadn't served him well. Rivals had taken advantage of his sense of duty to push him around. After being turned out at the CIA in 1977 following Jimmy Carter's election, Bush Senior was out of work, with his career at a standstill. Junior, by contrast, would not wait in line behind Jim Reese, the Republican who had lost to Mahon in 1976. The younger Bush thought he could avoid the charges of carpetbagging and fakery that had undermined his father because he was a genuine, as opposed to a translated, Texan.

George Senior would avoid visible participation in his son's first campaign, as Prescott had done for him in 1964. Behind the scenes, however, he was similarly active, making calls to Republican officials and asking them not to endorse others. Since Prescott's 1956 reelection victory over Thomas Dodd, the Bushes had become a sort of Republican Partridge Family. This time, Neil, twenty-three and fresh out of Tulane, assumed the role of co-campaign manager, working from Lubbock, the largest and most Democratic city in the district.

The young Karl Rove was detailed from his assignment running George Senior's political action committee to help. Out came Barbara's index file of friends. In poured contributions from the family's fan club. Seventeen-year-old Doro shook the tambourine.

Two weeks after he announced, in July 1977, George's friends Joe and Jan O'Neill fixed him up with Laura Welch, a librarian living in Austin, who had grown up near him in Midland. The story of their first encounter has George W. talking frantically to try to impress her at a cookout. In romance as in politics, his style was the same: he put off doing what was expected of him, then seized at an opportunity to catch up in a hurry.

Like his mother, Laura was perfectly suited to the role of Bush political spouse. Years later, George W. would describe her as "the perfect wife" because she never tried to upstage him. She was bright, literate, and funny, but entirely accepting of a woman's role in the pre-feminist social structure of West Texas. Laura loved her career teaching reading to kids from poor Latino families in Austin's public schools. But she was happy to give up Austin for Midland, teaching for parenthood, and her liberal views to be a Republican politician's wife. Laura saw herself a traditional spouse, raising children, volunteering, and doing a lot of reading. With no East Coast connections, she substantiated George's claim of Texan authenticity. Though the pair lived eight hours away from each other by speeding Oldsmobile, they were engaged in six weeks. After another six weeks, they were married. Their honeymoon was traversing West Texas for his congressional campaign.

On the stump, George W. was a natural. He had a prodigious talent for memorizing names and faces, and flattering ordinary people with his attention. He acknowledged he didn't know anything about agricultural policy beyond thinking that it was unfair that wheat farmers got only a nickel from the price of a fifty-cent loaf of bread. But it didn't really hurt him that his agenda was undercooked. What got him in the end was the issue that doomed his father in 1964: Texanness. Bush's primary opponent, Jim Reese, patronized him as "Junior" and "a personable young man from back East" who was "riding his daddy's coattails." Junior dispatched Reese, but could not do the same with Kent Hance, who cast himself as the local boy fending off a preppie carpetbagger. *While I was at Dimmit High School, Bush was at Andover. While I was at Texas Tech, Bush was at Yale,* Hance would proclaim. In their debate, the Democrat said Washington was messed up "because of all those Yale fellas running the place."

Bush seemed not to take the 1978 loss hard; he had done better than expected on a first try and it was a family tradition to overcome early political defeats. But the election was one he could have won. Nineteen seventy-eight was the year that Bill Clements was elected governor of Texas, becoming the first Republican to hold that position since Reconstruction. Clements took the 19th District by more than thirteen thousand votes; Bush lost it by six thousand.

He might have won if he'd hit as hard as his opponent. Bush lost in part because one of his student supporters (and possibly a Hance agent) ran an ad in the Texas Tech newspaper promising free beer at a rally in Lubbock. Hance's law partner then sent an open letter to four thousand Church of Christ members that began "Dear Fellow Christians," and complained about Bush offering alcohol to get students to vote for him. Hance called this "Yale-Harvard type behavior." Bush refused to retaliate by criticizing Hance for leasing property to a bar near the campus.

The lesson Bush cited in public was one of his father's: the importance of playing fair. He later said he was glad he hadn't defamed a "good man." But the lesson he would apply in practice was a harsher one: that someone named Bush, with his pedigree and connections, was easily caricatured as a Yankee transplant. In future, he needed to play political offense. Bush Senior shook off his first defeat by promising to stay true to himself (if possible). Junior's private vow was "to never be out-Texaned again."

GEORGE AND JEB have always been the family's principal rivals, and by various accounts they are not close. George told Brit Hume in 2003 that they only talk by phone about once a month. ("When he makes a phone call, it's really not to spend a lot of chitchat time," the president said of his brother.) The competition is hard to make out because of the way George and Jeb function as allies when the family's collective interests are at stake, as they were in the 2000 Florida recount. But as a factor in George's drive to succeed, this sibling rivalry is second only to his relationship with his father. And in a way, it is the primary expression of it, since the ultimate stake in the rivalry was inheritance of their father's mantle.

As George is keenly aware, other members of the family have always thought Jeb was smarter. But Jeb has always known that the cousins, aunts, and uncles like George better. Jeb is introverted, relentlessly focused, and serious. Though his political future was always regarded as the brightest by the family, he has never had the glib banter or the gift for friendship of his older and youngest brothers. Asked in 1987 how the brothers were different, Jeb responded: "George is the tightest with his money, that's for sure. He's always been very careful. Marvin is the most personable and he has this great sense of humor. I'm the serious one."

Six and a half years younger than Junior, Jeb grew up as the oldest in a second group of children and in many ways reflects the traits of a firstborn, rather than a later-born, son. Like his father in relation to Pressie, he can be seen as a second son who usurped the place of the first—though in his case, only for a time. Jeb had a different and ostensibly much easier childhood than George; he was born into a more settled family that had moved beyond the crisis of Robin's death. He faced no apparent learning disabilities or struggles with self-control. But somehow Jeb absorbed George's allotted portion of care, while George pranced off with Jeb's share of worldly ease. Where George fooled and funned, Jeb drove as hard as he could in a straight line. He has never played the game of diminished expectations—or many other games, for that matter. His adolescent rebellion was much briefer, and his subsequent embrace of conformity and family obligation more drastic.

From a longer perspective, Jeb's path looks like a more skillful emulation of the paternal pattern. At seventeen, he went to León, in the

Mexican state of Guanajuato, to help build a school for the poor, as part of a course at Andover. There he was smitten with Columba Garnica Gallo, a tiny, middle-class girl from a convent school. His approach to the relationship was patterned on his father's first-love-forever connection with Barbara, but across divides of class, faith, language, and nationality. As with his parents, the relationship was strengthened by an enforced absence. By college, Jeb's rough patch, which involved membership in the Andover Socialist Club as well as the usual pot-smoking, was largely out of the way. To be closer to Columba, he went to the University of Texas instead of Yale, and graduated in just two and a half years. Married at twenty-one, he was a father at twenty-three, inevitably naming his son George Prescott Bush. While his big brother was drilling dry holes back in the town where they grew up, Jeb was getting ahead in the banking business. In choosing Florida over Texas and real estate over oil, he followed the family script more cleverly than his brother. Miami in the early 1980s offered the kind of opportunity Midland had for his father in the 1950s. Soon after his arrival, Jeb tellingly described Miami as "the frontier" in relation to Texas—which had in the intervening decades become a place where social snobbery and established hierarchies made it hard for his immigrant wife and mixed-race family to fit in.

In Jeb's career, we see once again the Bush view of wealth as a means rather than an end. "Making a bunch of money didn't excite me," Jeb said during his first gubernatorial campaign in 1994, echoing his father's feelings in 1964. Once again, we see the Bush self-delusion about independence. Jeb described himself as "a self-made man." Whether he would have thrived with a different last name is impossible to say, but we know Jeb made his nut with help from family connections—all the while complaining about what he couldn't do because of the public spotlight on him. He first accumulated significant wealth with the help of a supporter of his father's, the Cuban developer Armando Codina, who hired him as a leasing agent with a big share of profits, and renamed his company Codina-Bush.

Florida in the 1980s, like Texas in the 1960s, was a Democratic state poised to turn Republican, with a group of feverish conservatives—

the Cuban exiles—leading the charge. Like his dad and unlike his impatient older brother, Jeb was happy to endure a dry policy discussion and a long political slog. Rather than start with Congress, he ran in 1983 for Dade County Republican chairman, a position in which he served as a bridge between the Cuban extremists and the national party establishment—just as his father had for the Birchers in Harris County. Jeb too positioned himself well to the right. "I'm a hang-'em-by-the-neck conservative," he declared.

Jeb worked hard on his father's 1984 vice presidential campaign. W. didn't. After that election, Jeb went back to Florida and diligently built his business and political career. Again copying his father, he hoped to leapfrog from Republican County chairman to the U.S. Senate in 1986, but his father was against it. As the Pressie episode had shown in 1982, it was too awkward to have other family members seeking national office while Bush Senior was trying to make it to the White House. Unlike Junior in 1978, dutiful Jeb took his dad's advice. Instead of running for the Senate, he worked on Bob Martinez's campaign for governor. When Martinez won, Jeb moved to Tallahassee to become Florida's secretary of commerce.

Junior, meanwhile, was floundering in the town he grew up in, a place the rest of the family had been glad to abandon for good in 1959. In Midland, he presided over a string of oil industry washouts. After five years of work, his company, Arbusto, was valued at less than $400,000. A million-dollar investment from another family friend turned the company into Bush Exploration in 1982, but by 1984, it was again on the verge of bankruptcy. In 1985, Bush Exploration merged with Spectrum 7, which lost money on a larger scale with Junior as CEO. The next lifeline was a takeover the following year by Harken Energy, the subsequent losses of which were even more impressive.

Three of Poppy's four sons had set out to follow the father's trajectory. Neil, always regarded as the "nice" brother, attempted to follow the family path of business-to-politics in Colorado, another frontier ripe for self-inventors. Before his involvement with a bankrupt savings and loan led to an investigation and regulatory censure, Poppy and Bar thought Neil might be their best hope to have one of their children elected to high office. But after the Silverado scandal, they realized that Neil was as hopelessly naive as he was sweet growing up. His innocence about the motives of potential partners was bound to get him in trouble again unless others in the family kept close tabs on his business projects. By the mid-1980s, Jeb's career looked the most like a successful recapitulation of his father's, with Neil's attempt as tragedy, and George W.'s as farce. The second son had once again turned the tables on birth order, with Jeb doing in relation to Junior what Poppy had in relation to Pressie. As for the two youngest siblings, Marvin and Doro, neither ever seems to have had any political ambition. In 1986, when he was thirty, Marvin was diagnosed with inflammatory bowel disease, which Barbara blamed on his having to listen to criticism of his father in the press. He was in the hospital for six weeks and lost forty pounds, before having his large intestine removed. After his recovery, he joked to friends that he knew he was dying when his father spent the day by his side, and his brother Jeb called to say, "I love you." Of his four siblings, George W. is closest to Marvin, who along with Doro has been the most regular weekend visitor at Camp David during the second Bush presidency.

DURING GEORGE H.W. BUSH'S first term as vice president, his oldest son continued to struggle with the burden of having a famous father. By his late thirties, George W. had tried repeatedly to duplicate his father's success—in school, sports, the military, business, and politics. Each successive failure heightened his sense of inadequacy. As he later acknowledged to David Maraniss of *The Washington Post*, he was struggling to "reconcile who I was and who my dad was, to establish my own identity in my own way." In another family, it might have been easier for a son to break free of his father's framework. But the Bushes' sense of family cohesion and their mania for secrecy exercised a strong restraining influence.

There's a brilliant vignette from this period in *What It Takes* by George W.'s Yale classmate Richard Ben Cramer, who calls him "the roman candle of the family." The book's opening chapter describes

Vice President Bush's visit to a Houston Astros game in 1986. George W. is furious that only his brother Jeb, Jeb's son George P., and the vice president's chief of staff, Craig Fuller, get to sit in the VIP box with his father, while he and Laura are seated off on their own, several rows back. "Seats ain't worth a shit," the first son growls at his father's political adviser, Lee Atwater, loud enough for Craig Fuller to hear and realize he has made a serious blunder by displacing the first son from the vice presidential box. "I guess the box got a little *crowded*," George W. seethes, as Laura tries to restrain him from making an even bigger scene. "People who think they gotta be here . . ."

Family members saw George W.'s excessive drinking as a response to the pressure he felt to measure up. But alcohol and the belligerence it exacerbated were now creating a potential embarrassment for his father, who was seeking the crown for himself. In *Henry IV, Part 1*, the King complains about the trouble his son Hal's uncontrollable behavior is creating at court:

Thy place in council thou hast rudely lost,
Which by thy younger brother is supplied,
And art almost an alien to the hearts
Of all the court and princes of my blood.

When he struck the Lord Chief Justice, Henry IV's chief of staff, Hal lost his job as counselor to his father. As the King goes on to note, the oldest of Hal's three younger brothers has taken his place as a royal adviser.

Hal's challenger is his cousin Hotspur, who leads the rebellion to seize the crown. In the Bush analogy, Jeb now played that role. He was driven and humorless, but privately preferred by their father and steadily winning the admiration of everyone else. In the first scene of *Henry IV, Part 1*, the King confides that he wishes Hotspur—"amongst a grove the very straightest plant"—were his son instead of Hal, his brow stained with "riot and dishonor." Hal knows that he has "a truant been to chivalry." In Act Three, Hal promises his father, whose reign is imperiled by rebellions, that he will make up for his past mischief by fighting on his behalf.

George W. did the same thing when he turned forty in 1986. He confronted his drinking problem the way his mother had dealt with depression, through willpower alone, though with help from a newfound evangelical faith. He took on his father's enemies, all of them at once, by moving his family to Washington and stepping forward as the "enforcer" for his dad's presidential run. This was George W.'s own term for his role in the campaign, the same one he used to describe his mother's role within the family. The family needed enforcers because the head of household was averse to confrontation. The job Poppy gave Junior was the same role in which Prescott Bush had employed his own oldest son, Pressie. George W. was supposed to apply the old family rules about loyalty. He did so enthusiastically, challenging aides like Lee Atwater in a way his father wouldn't, asking, "How do I know we can trust you?" With reporters, he played gatekeeper and goon. George W., who prided himself on being a shrewd judge of character, would sniff out their motives, mete out access, and bully those who pursued his father's involvement in the Iran-contra scandal or Neil's Silverado troubles. Sobriety and Christianity did not moderate Bush's aggression. Indeed, not drinking seemed to fuel his anger more than drinking did.

Though mistrustful of the press, Poppy liked a few journalists, including Margaret Warner, a *Newsweek* reporter who was close to James Baker. In the fall of 1987, the vice president granted her an interview for a story on whether he could emerge from Reagan's shadow. The resulting *Newsweek* cover story, timed to Bush's presidential announcement, bore the headline "Fighting the Wimp Factor" over a picture of Bush facing into the wind on his motorboat in Maine. The story inside, which questioned whether the patrician Bush could relate to ordinary Americans, remains the single worst piece of press the family ever got. W. responded fiercely, demanding that Warner resign from the magazine (she didn't) and cutting off access to its journalists with squalls of obscenity. His truculent reaction was, like his response to his father's 1964 defeat, a psychologically complicated business. His dad was his hero. To slyly impugn his manhood seemed wildly unfair. But George also knew there was something to Nixon's judgment that his dutiful, cautious, and conflict-averse father might lack sufficient toughness for the presidency. At a deeper level, the opportunity to be the strong son defending a vulnerable father was one that he, like Shakespeare's Prince Hal, had been waiting for his whole life.

If W. stood up for his father in 1988, he also stood up to him. The family's indignation flared again when the press began buzzing about an affair between Bush Senior and an aide named Jennifer Fitzgerald. It fell to George W. to ask his father about the rumors so that he could respond. He quoted to reporters his father's response, which had to be a verbatim quote, because it sounded as much like Dana Carvey's *Saturday Night Live* parody of Poppy as anything Poppy ever said—"the answer to the Big A Question is N-O." What George W. thought of his father's denial is unknown. (Asked in a practice debate if he'd committed adultery, Bush snapped out a different answer: "None of your damn business.") But in asking him the question, George W. was finally confronting his powerful father as an equal. Laura Bush later said, "If there was any sort of leftover competition with being named George Bush and being the eldest, it really at that point was resolved."

George W. thought he'd done the candidate invaluable service in the campaign, and stolen a march on Jeb in the process. His father, he pointed out with pride, now sometimes called him for advice. Lee Atwater's more skillful rerun of Poppy's 1964 campaign, filled with coded appeals to race and insinuations about his opponent's patriotism, left George H. W. Bush with a troubled conscience. Junior bolstered his father's illusion that his path to the White House was the high road. He would tell his father what he knew he wanted to hear: that he should do the right thing regardless of consequence—"the right thing" being whatever it took to win. According to one person who worked with him on the campaign, George W. was intensely concerned with being made to look good in front of his father. In an unguarded moment after his father was sworn in, he described what he had accomplished in his father's eyes to a Dallas reporter. "He had a different view of me, as a person who could perform," George W. said. "He relied on me to do things."

ANOTHER WAY TO CATCH Jeb was through the kind of business success that had eluded him—and toward the end of the 1988 campaign, George W. put one together that fulfilled his father's long-standing fantasy. When he heard from his Yale friend and Spectrum 7 partner Bill DeWitt that the Texas Rangers were for sale, he began working the phones furiously from his campaign office on 14th Street in Washington. Bush enlisted baseball commissioner Peter Ueberroth as an ally and called on friends of his late great-uncle Herbie Walker, who had been an owner of the Mets. Bush swiftly got commitments of $75 million, the largest of them from his DKE buddy Roland Betts and Betts's business partner Tom Bernstein. Bush himself put up only $600,000, but as the rainmaker was given a 10 percent stake by the group. This gave him an immediate paper worth of $7.5 million when the deal went through, well above his brother's. After the city of Arlington committed $135 million to building the team a new stadium, he was worth significantly more. When his partners sold the Rangers in 1998, Bush's interest netted him $15 million.

Right after his father won the 1988 election, George W. moved his family to Dallas so he could take charge of the team. In running the Rangers, he applied a technique that would later serve him poorly as president: he made his personality into his management philosophy. As a manager, Bush prides himself on sizing people up quickly and not getting lost in details. An intuitive decision-maker, he deemphasizes analytic judgment in favor of Walker instinct. Running the Rangers, he thought the team's talent scouts put far too much emphasis on statistics. He insisted that they should pay more attention to "makeup," or essential character. He wanted team players who were good family men, not prima donnas. The man who on first meeting peered into Vladimir Putin's soul and found goodness traded Sammy Sosa to the Chicago White Sox for Harold Baines.

Predictably, the Rangers' win-loss record didn't improve much with this overpersonalized style of decision-making, despite a big increase in player salaries. As Bush himself acknowledged, the team remained "mired in mediocrity" during the five seasons he was in charge, 1989–93.

While the Rangers fulfilled the "Uncle Herbie" fantasy Poppy often talked about, the job was always meant to be transitional, a platform for his entry into politics. George W. distributed baseball cards printed with his picture at home games, and held press conferences. "This job has very high visibility, which cures the political problem I'd have: What has the boy done?" Bush told *The Dallas Morning News* in February 1989. "Well, I'm the businessman who came to town and, at the very minimum, kept the Rangers from moving out."

George W. was already speaking to his father's former aide Karl Rove, who encouraged him to run for governor in 1990. His parents opposed the idea—especially his mother. Doug Wead, who worked closely with him on the 1988 campaign, says Barbara Bush asked him to get her son to give up his foolish notion. "You tell George not to run!" she commanded him. When that failed to settle the matter, Barbara called a group of eight reporters to the White House and offered her discouragement on the record. "I'm rather hoping he won't because everything that happens bad with the administration is [going to be] young George's fault," she said. "I'm hoping, having bought the Rangers, he'll get so involved that he won't do it."

George W. knew what his mother really meant: she was concerned his run would hurt his father's career—and his brother Jeb's. In response, the Roman candle blew up. "Thank you very much," he told his mother through a reporter. "You've been giving me advice forty-two years, most of which I haven't taken." The new president kept his head low as his two enforcers battled it out. When George W. eventually announced that he wasn't going to run in 1990 after all, he said it was because the time wasn't right for him and claimed his decision had nothing to do with pressure from his parents. In fact, it would be the last time he would follow their advice, or heed their warnings, about a major decision.

The conflict between George W. and Barbara, who had become Jeb's champion, continued to simmer. At a state dinner for Queen Elizabeth II, Barbara Bush introduced her eldest son to the British monarch, explaining that she hadn't seated the American Prince of Wales nearby because he was "the black sheep of the family."

"Who's yours?" George W. asked, with his usual cheek.

"None of your business!" the queen responded.

Big George's loss in 1992, coming off his 90 percent approval rating a year and a half earlier, was devastating for the Bushes. Family members worried about the old man, who seemed isolated and depressed. Barbara Bush remained so resentful of the Clintons that she refused their invitation to spend a night at the White House in 1993. Some members of the family felt that the election of a son to a nationally prominent position would be a kind of vindication. The opportunity for revenge on the incumbent Texas governor, Ann Richards, who had humiliated Poppy with her speech at the 1988 Democratic convention ("Poor George. He can't help it. He was born with a silver foot in his mouth.") was irresistible to W. The problem was that despite his affinity for the religious right and the Rangers deal, his parents still saw Jeb as ahead of him in line. Campaigning for Jeb in Florida, the ex-president broke down crying when he tried to describe what the thought of his second son running for governor meant to him. At Thanksgiving in 1993, shortly after George announced that he was going to run against Richards, Barbara yelled that he would soak up contributions Jeb needed in his campaign against Lawton Chiles.

This time George W. was not to be dissuaded. Stealing a quip from his brother and inserting the names of his daughters, he declared: "I'm not running because I'm George Bush's son. I'm running because I'm Barbara and Jenna's dad." The two brothers seeking the governor's office in different states created a contest within the contest. At the outset, Jeb, running against Chiles, was favored to win. George, running against the popular incumbent Richards, was tipped to lose. Both brothers avoided the sibling issue publicly, but George W. did not restrain himself completely. "Jeb will always seem more thoughtful," he complained to one journalist. In another interview, he exposed himself even more. "All I ask," he begged a *Texas Monthly* reporter, "is that for once you guys stop seeing me as the son of George Bush." "I am a Texan in mind and spirit," he told another reporter. "One big difference between me and my dad is that I did go to San Jacinto Junior High School in Midland, Texas, and he went to Greenwich Country Day." This would become one of the son's most familiar lines. It was a version of the contrast Kent Hance had used to out-Texan him in 1978.

Two vignettes from the end of the 1994 campaign illustrate the contradictory essence of George W.'s attitude toward his father—the drive to correct Poppy's mistakes and the demand for his admiration. Don Sipple, who was Bush's media consultant in the 1994 campaign, relates a trenchant story. The Sunday before the election, he visited George W. Bush at his home in Dallas. There he found the candidate, who was running ahead in the polls, brimming with self-confidence, throwing tennis balls into the pool for his dog to catch and smoking a cigar. The adviser remarked on how sure-footed Bush had been in the campaign. "Sip, my man," Bush replied, "don't underestimate what you can learn from a failed presidency."

The second story captures Bush in a more poignant, less cocky mood. On election night, the returns began to come in, indicating that George was winning his race, while Jeb was unexpectedly losing his. Lawton Chiles had staged a last-minute comeback by walking across Florida. In the hotel suite in Houston where George W. was celebrating the good news, his aunt Nancy Ellis heard him speaking to his father over the phone. "Why do you feel bad about Jeb?" he said to his dad. "Why don't you feel good about me?"

The former president's public comment the next day made the same point in a different way. "It's your own son, your own flesh and blood. . . . The joy is in Texas, but our hearts are in Florida."

THE TURNABOUT IN GEORGE'S and Jeb's fortunes continued. After the election, Jeb faced a family crisis, including his daughter's drug problems and the near-breakup of his marriage, which as in his brother's case resulted in a politically helpful religious conversion—to his wife's Catholicism. (He had also converted when he married Columba in 1973, but apparently it hadn't taken the first time.) Jeb emerged from his family crisis more politically moderate, and was elected on his second attempt in 1998. But by that point, his older brother was a successful governor headed for an overwhelming reelection and already planning a campaign for the presidency—again against the advice of his parents, who thought it was the wrong year. George and Barbara eventually became advocates of their oldest son's candidacy. But to her closest friends, Barbara Bush still indicated that she wished it were Jeb, not George, who was running. To her wider circle, she made a joke out of her shock that it was George who was running.

Though disciplined and shielded enough to hide it most of the time, the older son let slip occasionally that the sibling rivalry wasn't quite finished, and probably never would be. There's a moment in Alexandra Pelosi's vérité documentary *Journeys with George*, about his 2000 campaign, where the filmmaker asks Bush a throwaway question about what he's going to do "for the little guy" if he's elected. "I am the little guy," Junior responds. "Jeb is six-four, I am only five-eleven." The answer betrayed not just Bush's tendency to solipsism, but his obsession with fraternal precedence.

As he laid the groundwork for his presidential bid, George W. tapped into the family networks for raising funds and support. But he also focused intently on how to differentiate himself from his father politically. Visitors to the governor's mansion would hear him criticize his father for squandering the political capital he accumulated in the Gulf War, for his violation of his pledge not to raise taxes, and for waiting too long to launch his reelection effort. Covering the 2000 campaign, I found that if you didn't know Bush's opinion on an issue, you could hazard a fairly accurate guess by figuring out what he *wouldn't* think. George W. didn't want to agree with his father, but he didn't want to agree with Bill Clinton either. So he performed what in the Clinton era we learned to call "triangulation." Take affirmative action. His father opposed it when he vetoed the Civil Rights Act of 1990. Clinton was in favor of it. So Bush would need a middle way. And he had one: "affirmative access," which he said could achieve diversity without racial quotas.

The distancing from his father began with George W.'s most fundamental beliefs and tracked through to his policy positions. Where his dad considered religious enthusiasm a form of bad manners, the son was open about his faith and courted the evangelical right with no evident distaste. He would have a vision, not deride "the vision thing." The father had lost in 1992, in the son's view, because of the old loyalty issue. He was too indulgent toward self-interested friends like James Baker, who had resisted giving up the State Department to manage his 1992 campaign. He never should have tolerated the egocentric Richard Darman, who had been an obvious source for the damaging Bob Woodward series that had run in *The Washington Post* before the election. George would only rely on his father's people when they had demonstrated convincing devotion to him—or when he got desperate and had nowhere else to turn.

Where his father was engaged in the details of policy, the son saw himself as a leader who set priorities, tasked people to carry them out, and held them accountable. He wouldn't micromanage the way his father had. His father was methodical, slow to choose a course, and capable of changing his mind. The son was an instantaneous "decider" who didn't revisit his choices or change his mind. His father was mocked for being too "prudent" and nice. The son would be bold and, like his mother, blunt. He told people he wanted to be a "consequential" president, not the manager of an inbox, like his dad.

On social issues including immigration and education, George W. positioned himself as a more effective moderate. His father called himself "the education president," but hadn't taken it much beyond rhetoric. September 11 would not have found Poppy reading to second graders because he didn't visit public schools. His son, "a reformer with results," intended to make the issue of repairing public education his cause, as he had in Texas. He fell in love with a line his speechwriter Michael Gerson had come up with to explain his views on the subject, that as president he would reject "the soft bigotry of low expectations." There was a flash of autobiography here; Bush had suffered the humiliation of being thought mediocre, even if he had at times cultivated the impression. His rejection of the conservative agenda of vouchers and privatization was born of personal experience in public education, and a commitment to it his father lacked.

On fiscal and foreign policy, he positioned himself to his father's right. Conservatives had set up an opposition between Reaganite orthodoxy on economic and foreign policy and his father's squishiness. In cases of conflict, the son sided with Reagan. Where his father had reneged on his "no new taxes" pledge, W. was adamant about his plan for tax cuts. On foreign policy, he would be more hawkish and supportive of Israel, a policy that appealed both to Jews and to Christian evangelicals, in opposition to the proclivities of his father's men, Brent Scowcroft and James Baker. He would be like Reagan, proclaiming, "Mr. Gorbachev, tear down this wall," not like his father, who had refused to make a provocative statement when the Berlin Wall came down.

Scowcroft, even more than Baker, took on a kind of totemic significance for George W. A former lieutenant general in the Air Force, Scowcroft was Bush Senior's national security adviser and epitomized both his realist approach to foreign policy and his careful style of decision-making. Bush Senior thought through the major global issues he faced together with Scowcroft. Where there was strong disagreement among Bush's top advisers, such as over Saddam's invasion of Kuwait or the collapse of the Soviet empire, the president almost always ended up where his national security adviser was. During George H. W. Bush's post-presidency, he and Scowcroft grew even closer. They went fishing together in Kennebunkport, where Scowcroft took an apartment after his wife died, and spent years working together on a meticulous account of Bush's foreign policy called *A World Transformed*. The book made clear that there was no daylight between their views on subjects like the wisdom of not finishing off Saddam in 1991. "Had we gone the invasion route, the United States could conceivably still be an occupying power in a bitterly hostile land," they wrote.

The younger Bush treated Scowcroft as a stepfather—the kind he couldn't stand. Bush Junior let it be known to campaign advisers that he regarded his father's foreign policy right hand as patronizing, meddlesome, and tedious. George W. took a special relish in wooing and winning Scowcroft's star pupil Condoleezza Rice, converting her from the general's balance-of-power realism to a more aggressive and idealist approach inspired by Ronald Reagan.

Seeing the big picture instead of managing the inbox gave George W. permission to know as little as he wanted to, and as little as he did, about every issue other than education. The ignorance for which he was often mocked represented a choice in relation to his father as much as any inherent disability or lack of acumen. It became part of his strategy for being different from his dad.

The outgoing president summed up the matter of George W.'s intelligence acutely after Bush beat Al Gore, "He doesn't know anything," Bill Clinton said of George W. Bush. "He doesn't want to know anything. But he's not dumb."

FOR THOSE TUNED IN TO IT, the son-father dynamic was fully apparent at the 2000 Republican convention in Philadelphia. For the three days, George W. Bush's campaign steadily if subtly diminished his father's one-term presidency, choosing to present the nominee as the true son of Ronald Reagan, rather than of George H. W. Bush. The second night of the convention included a prime-time tribute to Gerald Ford and a speech by the losing nominee from 1996, Bob Dole. Barbara Bush had an evening speaking part, following a Bush "family tribute." But the nominee's father never addressed the hall. In his acceptance speech that last night, George W. Bush praised his father as a "decent man," "a gentle soul," and "the last president of a great generation" that was now passing the country's challenges on to its "sons and daughters." The effect was to cast his dad as a well-meaning failure, as yesterday's man.

I remember staring at George and Barbara Bush as they sat watching all this from a box just off the floor. The expression I caught on George Senior's face was a mixture of parental pride and humiliation. The former president was watching his son accept his party's nomination for the presidency. But he seemed as if he'd rather be anywhere else. He had the pained look of someone being simultaneously honored and dishonored, vindicated and condemned. He appeared almost to be crying and not quite laughing at the same time.

For his son, winning the election, even in disputed circumstances, bolstered the old family delusion about making it on your own. Never mind the thousands of people who had thought they were actually voting for George H. W. Bush when they cast their ballots for George W. in 2000. Never mind that the Bushes had to call in James Baker to lead the Florida recount fight. Never mind his brother Jeb pulling every string on his behalf, or that W. could never have been elected without drawing on what one relative calls "the family brand equity"—a notion of moderation and good sense that countered the risks of his inexperience. George W. Bush thought he had won despite a famous father, not because of him. But the absence of a clean victory meant that many people saw the new president even more as a family subsidiary. In an earlier interview with *Newsweek,* he insisted that people had never voted for him because of his father. "Being George Bush's son," he said, "has its plusses, and it had its minuses."

George W. Bush was sworn in wearing the cuff links Prescott had given Poppy when he went off to war. These have totemic significance in the family; George H. W. Bush called them his most treasured possession, and wore them at his inauguration in 1989. He gave them to George W. as a gift when he was sworn in as Texas governor in 1995. Just two months into his presidency, the younger Bush was trying to flesh out why his education policy would be more significant than his father's, at a school appearance in Milwaukee. He was searching for the word "handcuff" to describe the kind of federal role he didn't want. Instead, he came up with "cuff link." This was more than a Bushism; it was a Freudian slip. For the forty-third president, his father's cuff links were a set of handcuffs. He had yet to break free from them.

ON ALMOST EVERY ISSUE that arose during his first eight months in office, George W. took a stand that in some way drew a line under a limitation or fault of his father's. In foreign policy terms, his opportunity to do this came only after September 11, 2001, when his vice president and secretary of defense united behind the idea of deposing Saddam Hussein. I'll examine this decision in the context of Bush's foreign policy views later. What's relevant in psychological terms is how potent the suggestion of completing his father's biggest piece of unfinished business must have been to him. Bush could defend his father, point up his failure, and vindicate the family name, all in a single stroke. Though his decision was a refutation of his father's realist foreign policy, he expected that his success would win him the appreciation and respect of his parents, and an acknowledgment that he, not Jeb, was the outstanding son.

Bush's self-image as a Churchillian leader, the anti-Poppy, meant he didn't need to delve into endless rounds of diplomacy, or spend time studying the history of Iraq, or worry about what might follow a triumphant American victory. Others could handle those details. Unlike 41, who described his sleepless nights on the eve of the American invasion of Kuwait in 1990, 43 let it be known that he was sleeping soundly as he prepared for war. When Brent Scowcroft, the man closest to George H. W. Bush, argued in a *Wall Street Journal* op-ed that going to war with Iraq risked destabilizing the Middle East, family intimates took the piece for something more—a worried father's only way of communicating with his bellicose son. Bush reacted against Scowcroft the way he usually did, treating him not as a concerned uncle but as an irksome surrogate for his dad. "Scowcroft has become a pain in the ass in his old age," he complained.

A few minutes before going on national television to announce the attack on Iraq, Bush was captured on an internal monitor at the White House revving himself up. "Feels good," he said, pumping his fist. But the battle of Baghdad didn't look like the victory at Agincourt for long. Looting broke out; the weapons of mass destruction, used to justify the war, couldn't be found; casualties mounted as the insurgency emerged; the occupation foundered and failed to end. But as the going got rougher, the son's assertions of independence only intensified. Bush has said on numerous occasions that his father (unlike his mother) doesn't offer unsolicited advice. When Bob Woodward asked the president if he sought counsel from his father about what to do in Iraq, Bush responded that he now briefed his father on foreign policy. Then the president added, "You know, he is the wrong father to appeal to in terms of strength. There is a higher father that I appeal to." He has told several interviewers that without access to all the information a president has at his disposal, his father isn't even qualified to give him advice on the subject. On this basis, no one outside of his national security team is qualified to have an opinion either.

As the euphoria of the initial military victory curdled, the father's position became increasingly awkward. Instead of his son showing up his limitations and failures, which he could have lived with, George W. substantiated 41's wisdom in not going all the way to Baghdad to overthrow Saddam. This was hard vindication, especially since his son was too proud to ask for or accept help. Though Scowcroft had failed to get through to the president, Baker tried again, leading the Iraq Study Group, composed primarily of 41's friends and allies, in a last-ditch effort to persuade the president to reevaluate his course. The report, also known as Baker-Hamilton, represented a reasonable approximation of what 41 might have done if handed the nightmarish entanglement: engage in intensive diplomacy, try to win allies, and slowly begin to disengage.

The elder Bush chokes up so often at sentimental occasions that he stopped trying to give toasts at family weddings years ago. But by late 2006, Bush Senior was crying constantly and in public. He broke down talking about his mother, in an appearance with his daughter Doro, in early October, on *Larry King Live*. He choked up again at the launch of the aircraft carrier USS *George H.W. Bush* two days later, when talking about his pride in his two oldest sons, who were sitting on either side of him. He tried to express that the day in 1998 when Jeb was elected governor of Florida and George W. was reelected in Texas was the happiest day of his life. But he could hardly get the words out.

A more painful episode came on December 4, 2006, when George Senior spoke in the Florida House of Delegates, at a ceremony to mark the end of Jeb's two terms as governor. The former president began to crack when talking about Jeb's 1994 defeat, and how his son didn't whine or complain about the unfair attacks on him in the campaign. "The true measure of a man is . . ." Bush tried to say, now openly sobbing as Jeb approached to comfort him, ". . . is how you handle victory . . . and also defeat."

Peggy Noonan, who wrote speeches for 41, caught the scene. "No one who knows George H. W. Bush thinks that moment was only about Jeb," she wrote in *The Wall Street Journal* a few days later. "It wasn't only about some small defeat a dozen years ago. It would more likely have been about a number of things, and another son, and more than him." Three weeks earlier, 43 had been handed a decisive rebuke in the midterm elections, losing control of the House and the Senate for the Republicans, and signaling the effective end of his presidency. The electoral defeat was a manifestation of the larger one the son was experiencing at the scene of his father's greatest presidential triumph in the Persian Gulf. The Iraq Study Group report would be issued the next day. Baker had warned him that it would criticize his son's strategy, and he knew how his son would react. Challenge would have the usual effect of getting Junior's back up and confirming his resolve.

That was, in fact, George W. Bush's reaction. Instead of agreeing to gradually reduce troop levels, he responded by proposing to increase them—and arguing, perversely, that this followed a recommendation from the report. With his poor decisions and stubborn refusal to adapt, the oldest son had undermined the reputation of careful leadership the family had built over the previous decades. Jeb, the obedient son, the one who was supposed to be president, who even after George Junior's election was regarded as a potential third in the line, now faced an impasse in his career. His older brother had raced ahead and blown up the bridge behind him.

Their father, once dismissed as insignificant and weak, now stood as a perfect contrast to his reckless, swaggering son. But this was no sort of vindication. The former president's public sorrow suggested a recognition that his son had blundered into needless catastrophe because of him. After failing at being the same, George W. had molded himself into his father's opposite. The Oedipal challenge 41 had tried to deny to Don Imus back in 2004 turned truer than he ever imagined. His son had squandered his presidency and damaged the country trying to defend, live up to, and defy him.

According to people close to the family, Barbara Bush spent much of 2007 angry at her son for not listening to his father about Iraq. But her husband didn't blame their son for his mistakes. In private conversations, Bush Senior laid the fault at the feet of Rumsfeld and Cheney. But surely the thought occurred that some of the responsibility was his as well. Trying to respect his son's independence and not interfere, he had watched him disgrace himself. The question must have gnawed at him: had he been a good father after all?

This is the personal side to the Bush Tragedy—the downfall of a dynasty as well as the failure of a president. A son who tried to vindicate his family by repudiating his father's policies ended up doing the opposite of what he intended. He showed the world his father's wisdom and brought shame to his name.

CHAPTER THREE

The Gospel of George

Presume not that I am the thing I was.
For God doth know, so shall the world perceive,
That I have turn'd away my former self.

—HENRY IV, PART 2

—

TWO WELL-KNOWN STORIES ABOUT FAITH FEATURE IN EVERY biography of George W. Bush. He refers to both in the very first paragraph of *A Charge to Keep*, the campaign autobiography he published in 1999. The first of these turning points was a soul-searching conversation with the Reverend Billy Graham that prompted him to reevaluate his life, accept Jesus, and give up drinking. In the summer of 1985, as Bush tells it, his father the vice president invited the famous evangelist to Kennebunkport for a weekend visit. Graham spent an evening taking questions from members of the family about faith. The next day, Graham took a walk along the beach with Bush's eldest son and asked if he was "right with God." Bush said he wasn't, but that he'd like to be.

"Something was missing in my life, and Billy Graham stimulated my heart—I would like to say planted the mustard seed which grew, and started me on a journey, a walk, to recommit myself to Jesus Christ," was how George W. put it in one interview during the 2000 campaign. His wording varies slightly, but the terms "heart," "walk," and "mustard seed" occur in nearly every telling. The mustard seed, like the prodigal son, is a parable from the Gospel of Luke. Jesus tells his disciples that the Kingdom of Heaven is like the tiny mustard seed that grows into a huge plant. According to Bush's story, the conversation with Graham took a year or more to germinate. But it was this meeting that prompted his change of heart, which in an evangelical Christian context means accepting Jesus as one's personal savior. This experience led him to begin "walking," or leading a righteous life. Finding God enabled him to quit drinking, gave his life meaning and direction, and made possible the successful political career that followed.

The other story is about how Bush decided to run for president. He was sitting in a pew in First United Methodist Church in Austin on January 19, 1999, at a private service for friends and family before he was sworn in for a second term as Texas governor. The Reverend Mark Craig, who had been Bush's pastor when he and Laura lived in Dallas, from 1989 through 1994, delivered the sermon. It drew from Exodus, and focused on Moses's reluctance to lead his people. Craig related that Moses pleaded with God that he had family obligations, that he was a flawed man and a poor speaker—a reference that may have been directed at the governor. There is no text or recording of the sermon, but according to accounts in several "faith" biographies of the president, Craig looked at Bush when he said that as in Moses's day, the people were "starved for leadership." Against the backdrop of the Clinton impeachment trial in the House, Craig said the country needed leaders with the courage to "do the right thing for the right reason." After the sermon, Barbara Bush told her son—whom both parents were now encouraging to run for president—that Craig was speaking directly to him.

Bush described the Reverend Craig's sermon as another "defining moment" in the Christian narrative of his life. It was only a few months after the sermon that Bush (with the help of Karen Hughes) wrote in *A Charge to Keep*, "I've heard powerful sermons, inspiring sermons, and a few too many boring sermons, but this sermon reached out and grabbed me and changed my life. . . . As I started my second term as Governor, I was struggling with the decision about whether to seek the Presidency, worried about what that decision would mean for my family and my own life. And Pastor Craig had prodded me out of my comfortable life as Governor of Texas and toward a national campaign."

Neither of these stories is entirely false. There isn't much beach to walk along the rocky shore of Walker's Point even at low tide, but Graham and Bush surely did have conversations in Maine that subsequently took on meaning for George W. The Reverend Craig did preach his sermon in Austin with Bush's presidential campaign in mind. But on closer examination, both of these turning points turn out to be parables of a kind, fables crafted to convey an idea about the protagonist rather than to relate the literal truth of what happened. Almost every detail about his spiritual life that Bush has chosen to reveal shows evidence of being shaped and packaged. The seemingly minor discrepancies reveal a great deal.

A version of the Billy Graham story first appeared in 1988, in a book called *George Bush: Man of Integrity*, which was distributed by his father's presidential campaign of that year. It was compiled by Doug Wead, an Assemblies of God minister whom Vice President Bush began using as an emissary to evangelical leaders in 1985, and who became close to Bush Junior around the time of his religious conversion. In that book, the story goes somewhat differently:

> I remember one night when Dad asked Billy if he would sit around with the family and answer questions and just talk about his life and his view of things, his spirituality. It was one of the most exciting nights I have ever spent in my life. The man is powerful and yet humble. That combination of wisdom and humility was so inspiring to me individually that I took up the Bible in a more serious and meaningful way.
>
> As you know, one's walk in life is full of all kinds of little blind alleys. Sometimes life isn't easy, and so Billy redirected

> my way of thinking in a very positive way. He answered questions of all types.
>
> The next year when he came, he made it a point to call me aside and ask how things were going. He took a real interest in me individually, and for that I am forever grateful.

In this version, there is no walk on the (nonexistent) beach, no pointed question about the son's relationship with God, no admission by Bush that he felt "lost." The private conversation with George W. happens a full year later, which would have been in the summer of 1986—after Bush had already spent nearly a year attending a weekly men's Community Bible Study group in the basement of the First Presbyterian Church in Midland every Monday night.

Other evidence suggests that Bush's religious turn really began fifteen months before his first conversation with Billy Graham. If someone planted a mustard seed, it was likely not Graham in 1985–86 but Arthur Blessitt in April 1984. Blessitt—yes, that is his real name—is an evangelical preacher who has walked throughout the world lugging a twelve-foot-tall, seventy-pound cross. His Web site boasts that he holds the Guinness World Record for the world's longest walk, most recently tallied at 37,352 miles.

Blessitt keeps a careful diary. On April 3, 1984, he noted: "A good and powerful day. Led Vice President Bush's son to Jesus today. George Bush Jr.! This is great! Glory to God." Over the previous week, thousands of people had been coming to hear Blessitt tell stories of dragging his cross through the Amazon at a sports stadium in Midland. Bush heard Blessitt's sermons, which were carried live on local radio, while driving. Though he didn't feel comfortable coming to the Chapparal Center, Bush arranged through an oilman friend named Jim Sale for the two of them to meet with Blessitt and talk about Jesus. In an empty restaurant at the Midland Holiday Inn, Bush looked Blessitt in the eye and said: "I want to talk to you about how to know Jesus Christ and how to follow Him." According to Blessitt's account:

> I slowly leaned forward and lifted the Bible that was in my hand and began to speak.
>
> "What is your relationship with Jesus?" I said.
>
> He replied, "I'm not sure."
>
> "Let me ask you this question. If you died this moment, do you have the assurance you would go to heaven?"
>
> "No," he replied.
>
> "Then let me explain to you how you can have that assurance and know for sure that you are saved."
>
> He replied, "I'd like that."

After telling him how to know Jesus, Blessitt asked:

> "Would you rather live with Jesus in your life or without Him?"
>
> "With Him," Bush replied.
>
> "Would you rather spend eternity with Jesus or without Him?"
>
> "With Jesus."

The three men held hands and prayed together. Blessitt proclaimed "You are saved!" Jim Sale attests that he remembers this event precisely the way Blessitt does.

There are other discrepancies in the "official" version of Bush's conversion. When Bush first told the story in public, a religious reporter contacted Graham, who had no memory of a meaningful encounter with George W. Graham later did his best to get on board with the anecdote that laid the cornerstone of his relationship with yet another American president. Even so, Graham struggled in trying to confirm it. "I don't remember what we talked about," he told *Time* journalists Nancy Gibbs and Michael Duffy in 2006. "There's not much of a beach there. Mostly rocks. Some people have written—or maybe he has said, I don't know—that it had an effect, our walk on the beach. I don't remember. I do remember a walk on the beach."

Something's going on here beyond the tricks of memory. The explanation is that in 1999, when the political purpose was the son's, rather than the father's, George W. reshaped the anecdote to give it greater resonance and political value. Multiple encounters were telescoped into a single one, a process that took place over at least two years was collapsed into a single "defining moment," and the setting was made more dramatic (the beach in Maine rather than a living room) and more personal (a one-on-one conversation, rather than a family question-and-answer session). The exchange that two eyewitnesses remember taking place with Blessitt—"What is your relationship with Jesus?"—"I'm not sure"—was transmuted into a dialogue with Graham—"Are you right with God?"—"No, but I'd like to be."

One can understand why a mainstream politician might wish to do this. Blessitt, seen by some as a kind of madman-messiah, comes out of hippiedom's Christian branch, the Jesus people or "Jesus freaks." In the 1960s, the "psychedelic evangelist" began preaching in a strip club in L.A. and ran His Place, a ministry–coffee house–nightclub, with appearances by bands like the Eternal Rush. Blessitt's book *Life's Greatest Trip* includes some of his poetry: "Get loaded on Jesus,/ 24 hours a day,/ you can be naturally stoned/ on Jesus!" In 1969, Jesus told Blessitt to start walking. He has kept on truckin' ever since. In 1976, he declared he was running for president, though it wasn't clear which party, if any, he belonged to.

Finally, the "mustard seed" reference in the later version is calibrated to resonate with evangelical Christians without sending the wrong signals to the biblically ignorant, who might pause to wonder why it's not a more common herb or vegetable, or just an unspecific "seed." Often, the precision of Bush's religious language cuts in the other direction, making references more generic. He avoids such evangelical terms of art as "born again" and "saved" in his journey-to-faith narrative—and even "Jesus," as opposed to "God." He similarly avoids using the specific terminology "evangelical" or "alcoholic" in reference to himself. This vagueness frees Bush from the assumptions people make when they hear the more conventional terms. According to Doug Wead, Bush's break with the bottle came after he and Laura read an Alcoholics Anonymous pamphlet that emphasized the need for help from a higher power. "The tract brought a lot of things together," Wead told me. Bush has never spoken of reading AA literature; following twelve-step guidance would make him sound like an alcoholic.

Bush has never been able to explain why he doesn't call himself born again. According to one of his Christian biographers, he did use this language before resuming his political career in 1993 after a gap of fifteen years. This makes sense out of another story that caused Bush a lot of trouble in his early days as a presidential candidate—and might have caused him even more if its implications had been understood. In 1993, Bush told Ken Herman, a reporter at the now defunct *Houston Post,* that he believed only those who accepted Jesus could gain entry into heaven. The context was his relating an argument he'd had with his mother some years before. Mother and son phoned family friend Billy Graham to settle the disagreement, in which Barbara contended that heaven was open to people of all faiths. Graham agreed with George W., that heaven was reserved for those who'd been born again, but told them not to worry too much about the issue. When Bush began running for president, he was asked about the comment. In response, he changed the emphasis of the anecdote. The point was now that Billy Graham had cautioned him not to play God; it wasn't up to the governor to decide who got into heaven.

But why was Bush having this argument with his mom about who got into heaven? The story only makes sense when you understand that he, as a recent evangelical convert, believed his Episcopalian mother wasn't going to heaven unless she had a conversion of the type her son had. "Accepting Jesus" is evangelical lingo—it means having a born-again experience as an adult. Though the reporter Bush spoke to happened to be Jewish, and though the Anti-Defamation League complained, the issue had nothing to do with Jews (who mostly don't believe in heaven and hell anyway), or even with Christians and non-Christians. Evangelicals believe that faithful Christians who don't truly accept Jesus into their hearts can't get into heaven. Given George W.'s taunting relationship with his mother, it seems possible that he was defending his born-again transformation and provoking her by saying that she wasn't going to heaven with him.

In the second story, the official narrative better matches the external evidence. Others were in the church and heard the Reverend Craig's sermon. If there's a specific factual distortion in Bush's account, it is a minor one about how personalized the message about moral leadership was intended to be. Other accounts explain that Craig's message was also for Jeb, who had just been sworn in as governor of Florida, and for former President Bush, in retrospective terms, with reference to his ignoble successor. What doesn't add up is Bush's account of the sermon as a turning point in his life. By the time he heard this call from God, his presidential campaign had been under way for more than a year. Paul Burka, a long-standing Texas political journalist, remembers Karl Rove talking about Bush's presidential strategy at a panel discussion nearly a full year earlier. This got Rove into trouble with Bush's chief of staff, Joe Allbaugh, because Bush's advisers had agreed not to discuss the governor's White House aspirations until after he was reelected. Nor does the story of Bush wrestling with his destiny square with the way he handles big decisions. As both he and Laura have noted, he makes up his mind quickly, easily, and definitively. By the time he "heard the call" in January 1999, he had long since decided. In short, the defining moment was a premeditated epiphany.

Casting his decision to run for president as the response to a call from God had the familiar dual effect. For religious voters, it emphasized his sincere faith. For secular voters, it downplayed his personal ambition. Since the days of George Washington, the preferred narrative for presidents is to offer token resistance before accepting a summons to duty. Like the humble farmer Cincinnatus, who was called away from his plow to save Rome, the ideal American statesman is supposed to yield only reluctantly to the civic imperative. Bush gave a religious dimension to that secular myth, turning Cincinnatus into Moses, the reluctant prophet.

The point here is not that Bush didn't feel the emotion he described. It is that he again reshaped the facts to enhance a pious image of himself. What these two faith stories have in common is the way they put George W. Bush's religious experiences to political use. The beliefs themselves may be genuine. But Bush does not appear to surrender to the will of God in the way a conventionally religious person does. If we look closely at his relationship to religion over a period of two decades, we see him repeatedly commandeering God for his exigent needs. His is an instrumentalist, utilitarian faith that puts religion to work for his own purposes. Faith made it possible for Bush to order his life and emerge as a plausible leader. Once he became president, it helped him cope more effectively than his father had with the monumental pressures of the job.

WHAT ARE GEORGE W. BUSH'S religious beliefs? The question, which would seem central to understanding his presidency, comes up again and again, and never receives a satisfactory answer. When religiously inclined writers try to describe Bush's faith, they invariably end up talking about how he uses religion, how he relates to other religious people, and what faith means to him. But they seldom say anything about its content. They describe all the things his faith is not—fiery, judgmental, dogmatic, exclusive—but don't discover positions on even the most basic theological issues that divide and define denominations, such as whether the Bible is literally true, whether Christians should evangelize, or whether salvation comes through faith alone. They overlook the curious detail that he seldom goes to church on Sunday. Often, they end up projecting their own beliefs onto his blank screen.

After reading a certain amount of this godly president literature—*The Faith of George W. Bush* by Stephen Mansfield, *God and George W. Bush* by Paul Kengor, *A Man of Faith* by David Aikman—the recognition begins to dawn that Bush's faith has no theological content. When a Houston reporter asked Bush about the difference between the Episcopal church he was raised in and the Methodist one he began attending after he was married, he replied, "I'm sure there is some kind of heavy doctrinal difference, which I'm not sophisticated enough to explain to you." His religion has often been best described as evangelical, but in various respects it appears not to conform to the definition. Unlike most other evangelicals, Bush blithely uses profanity and as governor would play poker. He doesn't tithe. He didn't try to convert others—one of the central obligations in most evangelical denominations—even before he resumed a political career. He didn't raise his daughters in his faith. On issues that divide evangelical Christians from nonevangelical Christians—and varieties of evangelicals from each other—Bush does not need to feign ecumenical neutrality. He isn't hiding his beliefs; he simply doesn't have many of them.

A better term for Bush's faith is Self-help Methodism. What Bush clearly does believe in is the personal, transforming, and sustaining power of belief in God. "Faith gives us purpose—to right wrongs, preserve our families, and teach our children values," he told congregants at the Second Baptist Church in Houston on the Sunday he announced his presidential exploratory committee in 1999. "Faith gives us a conscience—to keep us honest even when no one is watching. Faith changes lives. I know, because it changed mine." Having a personal relationship with God, praying, and reading the Bible daily were the tools Bush used to get control of his life; they made it possible for him to control his drinking, keep his family together after Laura threatened to leave him, manage his aggressive behavior, cope with the burden of a heroic father, and attain success in business and politics. Finding God made his life "easier to understand and clearer," as he put it.

If Bush proselytizes, it is not for his denomination or even for Christianity, but for the power of "faith" itself. Bush believes that everyone who prays prays to the same God, and that there is "truth" in all religions. He told the Muslim prime minister of Turkey, Recep Tayyip Erdogan, "You believe in the almighty, and I believe in the almighty. That's why we'll be great partners." He had a similar reaction to the Orthodox cross he saw hanging around the neck of

Vladimir Putin on their first meeting. According to staff members, Bush had a problem figuring out how to relate to secular European leaders like Jacques Chirac and Gerhard Schroeder. As Bush's former chief of staff, Andrew Card, told Jeffrey Goldberg of *The New Yorker*: "I can see him struggle with other world leaders who don't appear to be grounded in some faith." He added, "The President doesn't care what faith it is, as long as it's faith."

This instrumental view of religion is inseparable from the way Bush came to it, through a midlife crisis on the verge of forty. The Community Bible Study was an ecumenical movement just catching on in 1984, when a group of men from Midland traveled to California to learn the method. When I visited a session in the fall of 2007, the Midland Bible Study had grown to more than two hundred regular attendees, but still worked the same way: After meeting together for a few songs, the men broke into groups of twelve or fifteen to consider the passage they had read that week. Wealthy oilmen sat side by side with jumpers who worked on their million-dollar rigs for $20 an hour. Each participant had filled out a questionnaire that asked him to relate the week's verses from the Gospel of Mark to his own life and feelings. In some places, Bible study is more like a religious book group. In Midland it is more like a support group, with some business networking thrown in. When I attended, oil had just crossed the $80 mark, and Midland was booming as it hadn't since the early 1980s. But when Bush read the Gospel of Luke with the group in September 1985, the price of oil had just fallen to $9 a barrel. Many of those joining the Bible Study had gone bankrupt, or were on the verge of doing so. Some were suffering from substance abuse problems, and many had been through or were on the verge of family breakups.

This was Bush's story. Laura was losing patience with her husband's drinking and he was deeply worried about losing her and his daughters. According to various accounts, she gave him an ultimatum: me or Jim Beam. He was resistant to the change at first. Several attendees recall his sarcasm at sessions. One version of the history has Bush following his drinking buddy Don Jones, the president of a

Midland bank, into the group. According to another legend, Bush's parents asked Graham to lead an "intervention" after an episode of boorish behavior up in Maine. In any case, the Midland Bible Study supported the behavioral changes Bush adopted in the summer of 1986. In this sense, it functioned as therapy for someone who doesn't believe in therapy, more AA meeting than religious exploration. Prayer—which as a friend of the president's who is still in the Bible Study told me, just means talking to God—gave Bush a sense of serenity and control that enabled him to redirect his stalled career.

The relevant context for Bush's embrace of sobriety was not just Laura's ultimatum and his fortieth birthday, but his father's run for president. At one level, finding God was an act of rebellion against the arid, high church Episcopalianism of his parents. His father once said that when he was marooned in a lifeboat after being shot down over the Pacific, he thought of his family, God, and "the separation of church and state." That principle is perhaps the last one his son would think of in extremity. Fervent, popular faith helped him establish his independent identity. But this was loyal defiance. His new religious identity enabled George W. to become closer to his father, who needed someone to help him navigate the evangelical shoals of a Republican primary. In 1980, when religious leaders asked if he was a born-again Christian, Bush Senior had made the mistake of simply saying "No" (before learning to say that though he hadn't had a single born-again moment, he accepted Jesus as his personal savior). With his behavior under control, the younger Bush now began to win his father's confidence as someone who could help with the problem of the evangelicals. By outdoing his father in religiosity, he could effectively represent the family's political interests, as opposed to being a liability for the family to manage.

Faith produced in Bush a series of positive second-order effects as well. Religion supplied George W. with a richer emotional vocabulary, allowing him to express feelings in a way he hadn't previously been able to do. Over time, his religious outlook tempered his aggression and made him nicer, at least some of the time. It added humility to his repertoire. A religious framework made him more accepting of others, less cutting and judgmental, something he frequently refers to with reference to the parable of the mote and the beam: "Don't try to take a speck out of your neighbor's eye when you've got a log in your own."

In this way, faith and prayer serve to mitigate the Walker personality. But in another sense, they have magnified it. Bush answered his parents' doubts about his capabilities with an exertion of personal will. With religious help, he showed he could accomplish feats they thought him incapable of. And so willpower became his instinctive way of dealing with doubt, criticism, and opposition of all kinds. Rather than prompt him to consider or reflect, skepticism about what he could do provoked him to prove his doubters wrong.

IF BUSH'S THEOLOGY is free of content, his application of it to politics is sophisticated and artful. Evangelical politics is a subject on which he has exercised his intellect, and perhaps the only one on which he qualifies as an expert. Bush began his study in 1985 on behalf of his father's effort to become president. George H. W. Bush regarded televangelists like Pat Robertson as snake-oil vendors. Reflecting his parents' attitude, Neil Bush referred to evangelical Christians in a speech for his father in Iowa as "cockroaches" issuing "from the baseboards of the Bible-belt." For their part, the evangelicals felt no affinity for Bush Senior. They found his patrician background off-putting and suspected the sincerity of his conversion to the pro-life cause.

To help him with this problem, Bush Senior brought in Doug Wead as his evangelical adviser and liaison. Wead had been involved in a group called Mercy Corps International doing missionary relief work in Ethiopia and Cambodia, and gave inspirational speeches at Amway meetings. He was also a prolific memo writer. The most important of his memos is a 161-page document he wrote in the summer of 1985, and a long follow-up to it known jointly as "The Red Memo." Wead argued for "an effective, discreet evangelical strategy" to counter Jack Kemp, who had been courting evangelicals for a decade, and Pat Robertson, who he accurately predicted would run in the 1988 primaries. Wead compiled a long dossier on the evangelical "targets" he saw as most important for Bush. "If [Jerry] Falwell is privately reassured from time to time of the Vice President's personal friendship, he will be less likely to demand the limelight," he wrote. Wead made a chart rating nearly two hundred leaders for factors including their influence within the movement, their influence outside of it, and their potential impact within early caucus and primary states. Billy Graham received the highest total score, 315, followed by Robert Schuller, 237; Jerry Falwell, 236; and Jim Bakker, 232.

Unbeknownst to Wead, Vice President Bush gave the Red Memo to his oldest son. After George Junior pronounced it sound, Senior closely followed its advice. For instance, Wead recommended that the vice president read the first chapter of *Mere Christianity* by C. S. Lewis, a book that had become a popular evangelical tool for winning converts. "Evangelicals believe that this book is so effective that they will automatically assume that if the Vice President has read it, he will agree with it," Wead wrote. Vice President Bush made sure that religious figures saw a well-worn copy on top of a stack of books in his office when they visited the White House and cited Lewis's condemnation of the sin of pride as one of the reasons "we haven't been inclined to go around proclaiming that we are Christians." He also took Wead's advice on how to answer the born-again question; in courting the National Religious Broadcasters with three speeches in three years; in inviting Falwell, James Dobson, and others to the White House; in cooperating with a cover story in the *Christian Herald*, the largest-circulation evangelical magazine at the time; and in producing a volume for the Christian book market.

George W. Bush became the campaign's semiofficial liaison to the evangelical community in March 1987. "Wead, I'm taking you over," he said at their first meeting, over Mexican food in Corpus Christi. He told him to ignore Lee Atwater, whom Wead had been reporting to. Wead recalls how anxious George W. was in political conversations with his dad. "He was a nervous wreck," Wead told me. "He wanted his father to be proud of him." Wead also recalled the son's expressions of his own political interest. The campaign had prepared a state-by-state analysis of the primary electorate in advance of Super Tuesday in 1988. "When he got the one on Texas, his eyes just bugged out," Wead remembered. "This is just great! I can become governor of Texas just with the evangelical vote."

The crucible of the campaign forged a close relationship between the two men. Wead, whom George W. called "Weadie," says the candidate's son was so anxious to avoid any whiff or rumor of infidelity that he asked Wead to stay in his hotel room one night when he thought a young woman working on the campaign might knock on his door. "I tried to read to him from the Bible, because by that time he was sending me these signals," Wead told me. "But he wasn't interested. He just rolled over and went to sleep."

Having Wead put him to bed was a way to advertise his marital fidelity, and to reinforce a distinction with his father, who was facing rumors about the Big A. Wead said Bush also liked having him around as an alternative to the company of drinking buddies from his preconversion period. But Bush resisted religious overtures as firmly as sexual ones. "He has absolutely zero interest in anything theological—nothing," Wead said. "We spent hours talking about sex . . . who on the campaign was doing what to whom—but nothing about God. And I tried many, many times." Wead remembered one exception. When they went through his list of evangelical leaders in 1987, Bush had no interest in any of the names, with one exception: Arthur Blessitt. " 'Wait a minute, tell me about this guy,' Bush says. I told him he was a wonderful innocent person, a Jesus freak, a person of the '60s, a sort of Christian Cheech and Chong guy. And he's nodding like crazy."

The Wead–George W. effort yielded spectacular results: Poppy beat back the primary challenge from Pat Robertson and won 81 percent of the evangelical vote in 1988, exceeding the 78 percent share Ronald Reagan won in 1984. After the election, George W. turned to his evangelical friend for advice about how to handle having a father in the White House. Wead returned with a forty-four-page memo that he later developed into a book called *All the President's Children.* The precedents were not encouraging. Burdened by impossibly high expectations, many sons of presidents struggled unsuccessfully to "complete" the work of their fathers. As a group, they disproportionately fell victim to various forms of failure, alcoholism, divorce, and early death. Bush, who was planning to move back to Texas and run for office, groaned when Wead told him that no presidential child had ever been elected governor of a state.

With the various roles he played in Bush's life—life counselor, political adviser, spiritual companion—Wead became in the late 1980s the first in a series of what might be described as surrogate family members to George W. Like Karl Rove and Dick Cheney, two others who subsequently played this kind of role, Wead originally worked for the old man, before transferring loyalties to his son. Like them, he aided Bush with a crucial transition in relation to his father. What Rove would do in helping Bush launch his political career in Texas, and Cheney in helping him define his presidency, Wead did in helping Bush assert and establish his independent identity as a person of faith. But the experience left Wead troubled about the sincerity of Bush's beliefs. "I'm almost certain that a lot of it was calculated," he says. "If you really believed that there's some accountability to life, wouldn't you have Billy Graham come down and have a magic moment with your daughters? Are you just going to let them go to hell? You have all these religious leaders coming through. If it changed your life, wouldn't you invite them to sit down in the living room and have a talk with your daughters? Or is it all political?"

The success of the 1988 evangelical outreach led to a staff job for Wead in the White House. But once elected, the first President Bush handled the religious right much less effectively than he had during the campaign. He tried to relate to them culturally, rather than emotionally, which yielded the comedy of his claiming to love pork rinds and country music. In August 1990, White House Chief of Staff John Sununu fired Wead for writing a letter to evangelical leaders on White House stationery, in which he criticized a fellow member of the president's staff for inviting gay leaders to the signing of a hate crimes bill. George W. offered to fly to Camp David to take this issue up with his father, but Wead, feeling that his time in the White House was at an end, asked him not to. Nonetheless, the incident created animosity that lingered enough to provoke George W. to do the honors in firing Sununu on behalf of his conflict-averse father in late 1991. With Wead's departure, Bush's relationship with the religious right deteriorated, which prompted him to overcompensate by inviting Pat Robertson to speak at the Houston convention. In 1992, with Ross Perot in the race, Bush's share of the evangelical vote plunged to 59 percent.

GEORGE W. BECAME the keenest student of that defeat. He saw the way his father had been undermined from both sides: failing to bond with evangelicals, while being seen as pandering to them. Contemplating the Texas context, George W. worried less about the hazard of injecting religion into politics. In a state whose political landscape had been reshaped by the rise of the evangelical movement in the 1980s, it was already there. But he still faced the problem of winning the support of Christian leaders. Bush continued to follow Wead's advice about the advantages of associating himself with black evangelicals like the Dallas minister Kirbyjon Caldwell (less likely to draw media criticism) and playing up his faith story. With an eye on his national prospects, Bush thought he could woo the right principally through symbolism and his religious identity. How he tried to do this can be explained in relation to two pictures he hung in the governor's mansion.

In an April 1995 memo, Bush invited his staff to come to his office to look at a painting that his friends the O'Neills had loaned him. The picture is a Western scene of a cowboy riding up a craggy hill, with two other riders following behind him. Bush told visitors—who often noted his resemblance to the rider in front—that it was called *A Charge to Keep* and that it was based on his favorite Methodist hymn of that title, written in the eighteenth century by Charles Wesley. As Bush noted in the memo, which he quoted in his autobiography of the same title: "I thought I would share with you a recent bit of Texas history which epitomizes our mission. When you come into my office, please take a look at the beautiful painting of a horseman determinedly charging up what appears to be a steep and rough trail. This is us. What adds complete life to the painting for me is the message of Charles Wesley that we serve One greater than ourselves." Bush identified with the lead rider, whom he took to be a kind of Christian cowboy, an embodiment of indomitable vigor, courage, and moral clarity. He loved the painting enough that he reproduced it on the back cover of his autobiography and took it with him to Washington to hang in the Oval Office. By then, the president had developed some additional mythology, possibly supplied by visiting ministers. He came to believe that the picture depicted the circuit-riders who spread Methodism across the Alleghenies in the nineteenth century. In other words, the cowboy who looked like Bush was a missionary of his own denomination.

Only that is not the title, message, or meaning of the painting. The artist, W. H. D. Koerner, executed it to illustrate a Western short story entitled "The Slipper Tongue," published in *The Saturday Evening Post* in 1916. The story is about a smooth-talking horse thief who is caught, and then escapes a lynch mob in the Sand Hills of Nebraska. The illustration depicts the thief fleeing his captors. In the magazine, the illustration bears the caption: "Had His Start Been Fifteen Minutes Longer He Would Not Have Been Caught." The illustration has no religious import. The horseman with whom Bush identifies is "wanted dead er a-live," though in a final twist, he turns out to be the hero and his pursuers the real thieves. *The Saturday Evening Post* reused the image the following year to illustrate a nonfiction article about chaos in Mexico entitled "Ways That Are Dark." The caption under the image of Bush's imagined missionaries now reads: "Bandits Move About from Town to Town, Pillaging Whatever They Can Find." The association with the title of the hymn came from the third and final recycling of the illustration for another romantic story published the following year in *The Country Gentleman.* This story is about a son who receives a legacy from his father—a beautiful forest in the Northeast and a plea to protect it from rapacious timber barons.

The other painting he chose for the governor's office underscored his religious conversion. It was a full-length portrait of Sam Houston, the hero of Texas's founding, dressed in a Roman toga and standing amid the ruins of Carthage. Bush's identification with Houston goes fairly deep. Houston was known as "Big Drunk" to the Cherokee Indians he lived with before he sobered up and became a statesman. Houston quit drinking with the help of a late-blooming religious faith. Bush has cited *The Raven*, a classic biography of Houston by John Marquand, as his favorite book. It includes the story of the painting: Houston, who idealized the Roman emperor Caius Marius, had the picture done in Memphis in 1831, sometime before he dried out. To Bush, it looked like something that must have seemed like a good idea in the midst of an epic bender, like the time he came to the party for a three-day golf tournament at the Midland Country Club dressed as Mahatma Gandhi "in a toga that looked like a diaper by the end of the night," as he later put it. "I keep that one up there to remind me that I'm only one bottle away," he once told his Austin minister Dr. Jim Mayfield.

Not until the latter part of his first term did Bush find a way to turn his recovery-movement message into a distinctive political program. During his first gubernatorial campaign, Rove encouraged the candidate to read books by David Horowitz, Myron Magnet, and Marvin Olasky—Bush's trinity of messianic Jews. All three of these writers were on the left before converting to conservatism, though only Olasky had gone all the way to Christianity (stopping along the way at communism). Their collective message was that the 1960s had given sanction to self-destructive behavior and value-neutral social policies of the Great Society. Their neoconservative argument for remoralizing government dovetailed with the anti-elitism Bush had carried as a wound since his Yale days.

At the time of Bush's election in 1994, his view of domestic policy began and ended with this critique. In that campaign and after, he did not emphasize his faith as something that would play a role in his policymaking. But in 1997, Olasky got in touch with him about a state agency's denial of a license to Teen Challenge, a religiously based drug and alcohol rehabilitation center in San Antonio that was in danger of losing its license because of technical violations. Up until that point, most Texans hadn't seen Bush as unusually devout. It took some nudging to get him interested in Teen Challenge, but Bush eventually took up the cause, introducing a bill to free faith-based rehab facilities from state oversight. Olasky's message that religious institutions, not government, were best at helping people change resonated with what Bush had seen and experienced in the Midland Bible Study. He knew faith was a way for people with personal problems to change their lives and behavior. This made him responsive to Olasky's message that church groups, not government, were best at delivering "compassion." Lobbying for the legislation, he became imbued with the idea that religiously based programs could do what the public sector couldn't by changing the human heart. Later that year, Bush embraced Chuck Colson's Prison Fellowship, inviting the organization to run a pilot program in a prison near Houston. Bush visited and sang "Amazing Grace" with his arm around a convicted killer.

As he and Karl Rove mapped out his presidential bid in 1998, Bush faced a problem with conservative evangelicals that was in some ways the opposite of his father's. He knew how to talk the talk well enough to know what the "walk" was. His problem was figuring out how to win and retain the support of the right-wing evangelical leaders he privately called "wackos," without becoming so closely identified with them that the association would damage him in a general election. The answer he and Rove developed was to expand his support for religiously based treatment for drug and alcohol abuse into a larger political philosophy. Thus did "faith-based initiatives" become Bush's signature social policy.

The phrase Bush adopted to encapsulate this philosophy was "compassionate conservatism." Though Olasky has generally been given credit for it, Bush picked the phrase up from Wead, who had been using it since at least 1979, when he gave a speech with that title at a charity meeting. "The Compassionate Conservative" was the title of a chapter of *The Courage of a Conservative*, a book Wead ghostwrote for James Watt in 1985. (Rove was especially concerned that this association not become known, lest Bush's pet idea be connected to the notorious former interior secretary, who had to resign from the Reagan administration after describing his staff as including "a black, a woman, two Jews and a cripple.") Recycling the label like a *Saturday Evening Post* illustration, Wead subsequently lent "compassionate conservative" to Bush 41 aide Ron Kaufman, who used it again as the title of an article about Bush Senior in the *Christian Herald*.

In 1999, both Rove and Karen Hughes glommed on to the term, recognizing the way it could help them cut into areas of traditional Democratic advantage nationally, just as they had in Texas. The word "compassionate" had special overtones to born-again Christians, referring to their duty to be Good Samaritans. But to nonevangelicals, it simply sounded like a way of saying "not all that conservative." It exemplified Bush's ability to speak in code, using language with special meaning for evangelicals that sounded innocuous to everyone else. His other slogan, "Prosperity with a Purpose," also came from Wead and attempted to do the same thing. "Purpose" had religious implications only to the religious. Rove and Bush thought using this kind of loaded language offered a way out of the father's conundrum. Because he knew the religious right, George W. could carry it off. When Bush hailed the "armies of compassion" he envisioned performing social services; evangelicals heard a reference to the church militant. Secular, economic conservatives heard shrinking government, since Washington would be butting out in favor of private charity. Liberals, meanwhile, heard only a curious metaphor for passionate voluntarism.

In his attempt to walk the line between courting evangelicals and sucking up to them, Bush continued to draw upon Wead's advice. The governor encouraged Wead to move from Arizona, where he had failed in a bid for Congress, to Texas to help with Bush's pending presidential bid. In early January, Wead wrote Bush and Rove to accept the job he'd already been performing unofficially, handling evangelicals for the embryonic campaign. One of Wead's first steps was another big memo, an eighty-eight-pager called "Building Relationships: Governor George W. Bush and the Religious Right." It was dated January 15, 1999—four days before the Reverend Craig's "turning point" sermon. The memo made Wead's familiar argument that because courting evangelicals risked a backlash from the liberal media, Bush had to secure his religious base early and quietly. He recommended that Bush do this by emphasizing his personal faith and keeping his cultivation of evangelical leaders invisible to the general public. Wead encouraged George W. to take many of the steps he had urged on his father—go on Robert Schuller's TV program, appear before the National Association of Religious Broadcasters, court the Southern Baptist Convention.

By early 1999, Wead was prodding the governor with almost daily memos faxed to a private number in his residence. He supplied intelligence about where Dan Quayle, Elizabeth Dole, John Ashcroft, Steve Forbes, Gary Bauer, and Alan Keyes stood in their efforts to win over various evangelical leaders, and on the ongoing struggle for precedence among the evangelical leaders themselves. On January 5, Wead warned Bush about Liddy Dole's strong relationship with evangelicals, including Billy Graham, because of her North Carolina roots. "She is very effective at 'Jesus talk,' " he noted. On February 20, Wead proposed that Bush befriend Alan Keyes, who Wead thought was outpacing Bauer as the favorite candidate of the religious right and would be valuable to Bush when he dropped out. "If he continues on his current pace, he could be the candidate on the right and one we would have to have. We could sure use him [at the 2000 Republican convention] in Philadelphia, for example. We could bring in all the right-to-life activists, shut the door and turn Alan loose. He could seal the deal." On February 22, Wead wrote: "the evangelicals are ripe. But it must be harvested and it takes hours of juggling. The key is not just the face to face meetings it is the follow up. That is where the battle is won or lost. . . . It's not just a question of winning the nomination it's a question of doing what you have to in the general without losing your base."

As this last message suggested, Wead was growing frustrated with

Bush's failure to follow his guidance. He wanted to produce a religious book with Bush's cooperation, of the kind he had written about his father. But Wead now lacked the kind of influence on Bush he had a decade earlier. In the years after Wead moved to Arizona to attempt his own political career, the role of intimate counselor had passed to Karl Rove, who had a broader view of politics and who had performed the far more valuable service of getting Bush elected governor. Rove was always wary of other political advisers with a direct line into Bush and wanted to own Bush's key relationships with conservatives himself. Partly for this reason, he didn't like Wead.

Rove also had a different view of how to handle the religious right. Wead thought evangelicals followed their leaders, and wanted Bush to court the most influential figures quietly but assiduously. Rove thought Bush didn't need to stroke the leaders of the religious right because they understood him to be one of their own. But as it became clear that Bush was going to do poorly in the New Hampshire primary, the campaign retrenched. After he lost to John McCain by 18 percentage points, winning the "wackos" became an urgent priority for him. Bush was relying on Ralph Reed and the Christian Coalition to help him stop McCain in the South Carolina primary. Not understanding the dynamics of the Christian right, Rove sent Bush to appear at Bob Jones University, a fundamentalist institution in Greenville known for its anti-Catholicism and its ban on interracial dating. Bush, who takes racial and religious inclusiveness seriously, obviously didn't grasp the implications of this choice of venue. Neither he nor Rove understood that the "young earth" fundamentalists at BJU, who believe in the literal truth of the Bible, represented an extreme subset of evangelicals, and that Billy Graham had broken with them as far back as the 1950s. The visit blew up in their faces. Bush had to apologize repeatedly, and negative reaction from Catholic voters contributed to his defeat in the Michigan primary.

That fiasco reaffirmed Rove, who is an agnostic, in his instincts about the risks of associating with Christian conservatives. Over the next year and a half, Wead's memos grew more plaintive and desperate: "If you are going to touch the religious right you better do it now," he wrote on March 22. "Karl, you mentioned something about not needing to secure the right for purposes of later moving to the middle because the unique doctrine of compassionate conservatism will defy the normal strategic positioning of a traditional campaign. That may be true but there are still some calibrations that will be necessary." But by then, Wead had been shoved aside by Rove. Bush's pretext for not giving Wead a staff job on the campaign was that he needed to avoid people who had worked for his father.

Envy over Rove's closer relationship with the candidate may have pushed Wead toward an act of betrayal he tried to portray as a service to history, his secretly tape-recording nine hours of private phone conversations with Bush in 1999 and 2000. Wead played portions of his tapes for *The New York Times* and a few other journalists at the time his book *All the President's Children* was published in 2003. He later apologized and signed a legal agreement to turn them over to Bush's lawyers and not discuss their contents. These tapes, of which I've obtained a partial copy (not from Wead), provide a glimpse of the man behind the public mask. They capture Bush thinking aloud and rehearsing answers to questions he expected to get on the campaign trail. On one, he acknowledges illegal drug use decades back: "Doug," Bush says, "it doesn't just matter cocaine, it'd be the same with marijuana. I wouldn't answer the marijuana question. You know why? Because I don't want some little kid doing what I tried . . . I don't want any kid doing what I tried to do [pause] thirty years ago."

But the more significant revelation is how politically Bush thinks about religion. Speaking of an upcoming meeting with evangelical leaders, he notes: "As you said, there are some code words. There are some proper ways to say things and some improper ways. I am going to say that I've accepted Christ into my life. And that's a true statement." On another tape, he rehearses his dodges. He goes over with Wead what he plans to tell James Robison, an evangelical minister in Texas, who wanted Bush to promise not to appoint homosexuals to his administration: "Look James, I got to tell you two things right off the bat. One, I'm not going to kick gays, because I'm a sinner. How can I differentiate sin?" For those interested in the details about what kind of sinner he once was, Bush notes that he has another line: "That's part of my schtick, which is, look, we have all made mistakes."

The tapes reveal how calculated George W. Bush's projection of faith is. Wead said that during the countless hours the two spent talking about religion over a dozen years, they discussed endlessly the implications of attending services at different congregations, how Bush could position himself in relation to various tricky questions, and how he should handle various ministers and evangelical leaders. But the substance of Bush's own faith never came up. Wead told me he now struggles with the question of how sincere Bush's expressions of devotion ever were. He often goes over their conversations from 1987 and 1988 in his mind, having grown more skeptical about what Bush was doing. "As these memos started flowing to him, he started feeding back to me what his faith was," Wead said. "Now what is interesting for me, and I'm trying to understand is, was I giving him his story?"

BUSH'S SKILL AT "JESUS TALK" raises an interesting problem. I've edited six books of Bushisms, which collect hundreds of examples of the president's linguistic blunders. The patterns of these slips testify to some sort of relatively minor, undiagnosed language processing impairment akin to dyslexia. But Bushisms are only one aspect of a complex verbal picture. Growing up, Bush developed a glib facility with language that compensates for his disability. In private conversation, he is quick-witted and funny, using practiced tools of memory and physicality to create intimacy. Early on, he seems to have learned to use words to woo or wound, and to calibrate his language to the occasion. In private, Bush can be profane and get in your face, swearing "like a sailor" in a 1999 campaign interview with Tucker Carlson, a conservative reporter he expected to protect him, or telling staff that he would kick Saddam Hussein's "sorry motherfucking ass all over the Mideast." But in scripted and more formal settings, Bush is capable of dignified eloquence.

The greatest surprise is that Bush's verbal clumsiness is matched by an impressive precision. In a political context, he is sensitive to the resonance and nuance of his terminology. As a governor and presidential candidate, he has always avoided the kind of Evangelese that arouses the concern of irreligious citizens. He avoids such terms as "sinner," "heaven," and "hell," as well as "saved" and "Jesus." Instead, during the 2000 campaign, Bush chose more generic words and phrases: "God," "charge," "heart," "love," "faith," "spirit," "service," and "prayer." To secular ears, these sound merely like elevated diction, a reach for gravitas. Christian evangelicals, however, recognize them as references to the born-again experience.

But Bush's familiarity with evangelical culture is limited enough that he sometimes gets his terminology wrong. The irony of his famous debate comment that his favorite philosopher was "Jesus, because he changed my heart" is that it puzzled many evangelical leaders even as it troubled many secular commentators. "Jesus changed my heart" isn't a correct evangelical sentence, because being born again involves an individual choosing to turn to God. According to Wead, the more natural way for an evangelical Christian to express the same sentiment would have been: "Jesus, because he changed my life when I gave my heart to him."

After Michael Gerson began to work with Bush on his speeches, his public language took on an even more elevated vocabulary and precise liturgical reference. He increasingly employed terms like "Providence," "the Almighty," "the Creator," "mission," and echoed phraseology from evangelical hymns ("wonder-working power") and the Bible. He made greater use of Christian metaphors, such as light and darkness. Gerson, a former journalist and evangelical Christian whose first job was working for Chuck Colson's Prison Fellowship, created a formal "voice" for Bush that was both evangelically coded and ecumenically powerful. At an event in Indianapolis in July 1999, Bush laid out his faith-based agenda in a major Gerson-written speech in which he compared asking church-based social programs to do without more public funding to "asking them to make bricks without straw." If you watch the tape of the speech, you can see Smirk #2, the self-satisfied one, flash across Bush's face after he delivers the reference to Exodus. The candidate is pleased with the trick he has just pulled off. In his first inaugural address, Bush offered a corollary New Testament reference to support his faith-based initiative. "I can pledge our nation to a new goal: When we see that wounded traveler on the road to Jericho, we will not pass to the other side."

What happened to Bush's faith-based idea encapsulates a larger problem he encountered as president. What worked in Austin ran aground in Washington because the national political spectrum was more liberal and secular than the one he had grown used to in Texas. In a Texas political debate, calling Christ his favorite philosopher wouldn't have occasioned much comment—Bush declaring a statewide "Jesus Day" didn't. But on a national stage, explicit invocations of religious observance were regarded as exclusionary and possibly outside the boundaries of appropriate public discourse. In Texas, giving state money to Christian programs that were doing a good job rehabilitating drug addicts and prisoners seemed like common sense. In the North, it seemed like a pander to the religious right and a failure to honor the separation of church and state. With his education bill, Bush was able to strike a compromise with Ted Kennedy. But when it came time to pass the enabling legislation for his faith-based programs, no prominent Democrat wanted to be his partner.

Rove's reading of the election results made passing a faith-based bill more urgent. In the 2000 election, Bush won only 68 percent of the evangelical vote, as compared to the 81 percent share for his father in 1988. The discrepancy explained why he lost the popular vote and nearly the electoral one as well. According to Rove's calculations, evangelical turnout had also been poor. Four million Christian voters had chosen to stay home on election day. This outcome might have been taken as vindication for Wead: rank-and-file evangelicals follow leaders that Bush hadn't sufficiently cultivated in 1999 and 2000. Rove had a more self-serving interpretation of the low religious turnout: he blamed the eleventh-hour disclosure of Bush's 1977 drunk driving arrest, a failing that couldn't be laid at the adviser's doorstep. But either way, Bush's poor performance among evangelical voters meant that he had a big job to do in cultivating the religious right in advance of 2004.

Implementing a faith-based policy proved far more difficult than promoting one. In his memoir *Tempting Faith*, David Kuo, who was the deputy director of the Office of Faith-Based and Community Initiatives for nearly three years, quotes Karl Rove at the outset of the administration demanding, "just get me a fucking faith-based thing." Margaret Spellings, Bush's first domestic policy adviser, expressed a similar frustration: "Just get me a damn faith bill. Any bill. I don't care what kind of bill. Just get me a damn faith bill," she said. Kuo had been won over seeing Bush look drug addicts in the eye and put his arm around their shoulders. He thought Bush's sympathy for the afflicted was at the core of his character. Once in Washington, Kuo concluded that most of the White House senior staff couldn't have cared less about what the policy was or how well it worked beyond the level of politics.

Bush's blunt politicization of social policy occasioned the first significant rupture inside the administration, when John DiIulio, the first head of the Office of Faith-Based and Community Initiatives, left in disgust after six months and gave an interview to Ron Suskind for an article in *Esquire*. DiIulio, an academic and serious policy wonk, was aghast that there was no real discussion of domestic policy or apparatus for developing it inside the West Wing. After the interview came out, DiIulio tried to eat his words, but his moment of indiscretion came the closest to producing action. Kuo quotes Bush shouting in a stairwell: "Well, is he right, or isn't he? Have we done compassion or haven't we? I wanna know." Years later, Bush might still be wondering. There is essentially no faith-based program beyond a minuscule $30 million "compassion fund" that channels grants to politically sympathetic Christian groups. The chief work of the White House faith-based office was organizing conferences in swing states at which it touted breaking down largely nonexistent barriers and encouraging church groups to apply for grants that weren't available.

Kuo's view is that Bush got snookered by Rove and other aides. The MBA president didn't notice that the faith-based programs he delegated never got implemented. This is naive, especially given the repetitive pattern. After Hurricane Katrina, Bush stood in Jackson Square in New Orleans and declared another ambitious conservative war on poverty, which fell by the wayside even more quickly. The fundamental explanation of Bush's failure to follow through on his domestic agenda is that public administration was terra incognita to both him and Rove. Bush didn't understand the design and implementation of federal programs because his only prior political job was as governor in a state where the governor has hardly any genuine authority. Rove didn't know how to do it because political consultants don't learn how government works unless they come from government.

What Bush and Rove shared was the machine politician's insight that distributing rewards and aligning incentives can make the public sector work effectively. But when it came to executing a new policy approach in the face of major obstacles, they were essentially at sea. Bush soon discovered that many leaders of the Christian right didn't want government funding because they feared it would prove corrupting. What mattered to them was influence wherever government might intersect with abortion, evolution, and other items on their agenda. And this Bush and Rove gave them. Kay Coles James, a former dean of Pat Robertson's Regent University and a former vice president of Gary Bauer's Family Research Council, was made head of the White House Office of Personnel. She placed evangelicals in sensitive positions at Justice, Interior, State, HHS, the FDA, NASA, and the CDC. Even applicants to the Coalition Provisional Authority in Iraq were vetted for evangelical status—not because it mattered to their work, but on the straightforward principle of patronage. The spoils system placated Bush's constituents on the religious right. What it could not do was put his big idea into practice.

THE FAMILIAR STORY of Bush's response to September 11 is another faith narrative. At first, the president was lost, with no idea what to do. The look on his face in the Sarasota classroom, when his chief of staff, Andrew Card, whispered in his ear that a second plane had struck, was uncomprehending. His first televised appearance, from Barksdale Air Force Base in Louisiana, was shaky and bewildered. The next day, with responsibility for the attacks affixed to Osama bin Laden, Bush again took to the airwaves and quoted from Psalm 23, "Even though I walk through the valley of the shadow of death, I fear no evil, because you are with me." His message was that God would help him, and the nation, make it through this difficult time.

According to this story line, Bush soon found solace and the voice he needed to reassure the country. Many inside the White House later remarked on the sense of equanimity that descended upon him. In his book, *Heroic Conservatism*, Michael Gerson recounts an exchange with Bush after the president delivered a speech Gerson wrote to a joint session of Congress on September 20. After watching the speech on television, Gerson told his boss, "Mr. President, this is why God wants you here." The president replied, "No, this is why God wants us here." Even in Gerson's self-aggrandizing version, this sounds a bit like Bush trying to brush off a pious sycophant. But Gerson took Bush's pastoral role quite seriously. He, more than anyone else, promoted the idea that a providential mantle had descended upon the president.

Bush's private comment to Gerson carries an echo of his first confident public expression. The president was standing on a rubble pile at Ground Zero with his arm around a firefighter, when someone called out, "I can't hear you." Bush responded through his bullhorn with his version of Henry V's St. Crispin's Day Speech—a comparison Gerson makes explicit in his book. "I can hear you. I can hear you. The rest of the world hears you. And the people—and the people who knocked these buildings down will hear all of us soon!"

As he continued to rally the nation, he seemed to frame the conflict through the lens of his religious beliefs. After meeting with his national security team at the White House the day after the attacks, the president stepped outside to declare, "This will be a monumental struggle of good versus evil. But good will prevail." On September 14, at the memorial service at the National Cathedral, he said his responsibility was "to answer these attacks and rid the world of evil." Bush talked about the power of prayer and asserted again that the side of good would prevail because "this world he created is of moral design." Two days after that, answering questions on the South Lawn, Bush used the term "evil" nine times in thirteen minutes. "My administration has a job to do," he said. "We will rid the world of the evildoers." The president invoked and then quickly withdrew the term "crusade" because of the implication that he was defending a Christian civilization against infidel attack. But in the generic sense, it well described his dualistic outlook on the conflict. In the coming months, he employed the term "evil" hundreds of times, culminating in his famous reference to the axis of it, in his 2002 State of the Union address.

Over the coming months, through the war in Afghanistan and the adoption of a plan to invade Iraq, the providential note became more pronounced in Bush's speeches. His suggestions that God was on the American side owed much to Gerson, a graduate of Wheaton College, often described as the Christian Harvard. Gerson was deeply grounded in theology in a way his boss wasn't. In speeches he drafted, Bush now sometimes described his prayers not just as a way of finding strength for the challenges he faced, but as conversations with the ultimate Decider. "We can be confident in the ways of Providence," he told the National Prayer Breakfast in February 2003. "Behind all of life and all of history, there's a dedication and purpose, set by the hand of a just and faithful God."

Such an appearance was a natural occasion for coded "evangelical talk." But the shading of his language in the run-up to the Iraq War suggested something deeper might be happening. As a writer put it in the *National Catholic Reporter*, "We are witnessing a shift in Bush's theology—from talking mostly about a Wesleyan theology of 'personal transformation' to describing a Calvinist 'divine plan' laid out by a sovereign God for the country and himself." Others have imagined glimpses of the end-times eschatology borrowed from the Christian Dominion movement, or the orgiastic Rapture of the *Left Behind* novels of Tim LaHaye. Writers on the left have mined Bush's language for possible explanations of his policies in the Middle East.

It is tempting to seek such theological threads in Bush's comments. All this talk of God and guidance, this biblical imagery, must, we imagine, mean *something*, perhaps tempered to accommodate the strictures of secular leadership. But in theological, as opposed to political and personal, terms, it doesn't—it's mostly resonant speechwriting. Bush's idea of divine providence had no larger significance in terms of his Methodist faith, which rejects the Calvinist concept of predestination. In his book *Heroic Conservatism,* Gerson assures us that Bush did not believe that God was guiding his actions in any explicit way. Eventually, the missionary found a mission and began spreading the good news of democracy with evangelical fervor—a turn I'll examine in Chapter 6. But to look for a theological motivation for this idea is to fall into the fallacy of thinking that Bush's oratory is packed with more meaning than it seems to be, when it usually contains less. To understand Bush's view of the world as driven by religion, as opposed to dressed up in religion, is to commit the same error. The religious aura of Bush's presidency is mostly atmospherics. Faith may give him comfort, but it does not provide him with instructions.

A higher power did not guide Bush's response to September 11 in any way that mattered. The president's biggest decisions followed more closely the advice of a lesser power, his vice president. Religion couldn't guide his response because Bush's faith was a constructed persona, the projection of a chosen identity rather than a framework for looking at the world. The more inadequate he felt to events, the more deeply he delved into the only religious tradition he had access to, the paltry spirituality of the recovery movement. The Christian cowboy reached into his saddlebag and found a painting of himself charging up a hill. There were few resources in his intellectually shallow, self-help faith to guide the immense decisions he had to make.

With no theological grounding or genuine framework of belief, Bush returned from his soul-searching with ecumenical bromides that sounded like they might mean something, but mostly didn't. After September 11, Bush sounded at moments like a religious zealot. But this was entirely misleading. The president did not see the conflict in terms of a clash of civilizations, but rather as one in which all well-meaning believers were on the same side. On occasion after occasion, he praised Islam as a "peaceful religion." And while it was his biblical and bellicose comments that got attention, most of what Bush said in those days was striking in its banality. Love your neighbor. Good will triumph in the end. Have faith—any faith. Pray for whatever. God bless you all. He was zealously proclaiming the message inside a fortune cookie.

If Bush's new language was liturgical in cadence and occasionally in reference, it was mostly political in inspiration. One of his favorite points to make was that he wanted to be a "consequential" leader. Left unstated was the opposition between this and the transitional, inconsequential leader he thought his father was. Sounding religious helped him reframe his presidency in grander, historical terms; he needed faith to be a "war president." The first book Bush read after the attacks was about Lincoln during the Civil War. He seemed to see himself as part Lincoln and part Reagan—the last president he viewed as consequential. His language reflected his notion, and that of his speechwriters, of how Reagan had spoken to the nation as he led the country in a great moral conflict. Reagan's single most famous comment was his calling America's Cold War enemy the "Evil Empire." Applying the analogy to the War on Terror, Bush now spoke a kind of evangelical Reaganese.

In personal terms, religious language expressed how Bush thought he had to appear to the country. Like Henry V, he seemed to think that whatever doubts he might feel in private, he needed to play the part of the fearless leader to family, staff, and nation. He wanted everyone to know that God was guiding him. But this was a hollow certainty and a hollow confidence. As with his conversion by Billy Graham and his decision to run for president, this faith narrative was a conscious autobiographical construction. In this sense, Bush's projection of religious assurance after September 11 is entirely compatible with the premeditation evident in his earlier turn to God.

To say that Bush's religious persona is a calculated projection does not mean it is fraudulent. For practiced politicians, the question of whether any behavior is genuine can seldom be answered. For them, calculation and sincerity are not opposites. The skillful leader harmonizes them, coming to truly believe in what he thinks he needs to do to succeed. Piety, like any other political mask, tends to become a genuine face over time.

THE SECULAR MISUNDERSTANDING of Bush is that his relationship with God has turned him into a harsh man, driven by moral certainty, and attempting to foist his evangelical views onto others. Many of those who know Bush best see the religious influence in his life cutting in precisely the opposite direction. As one of the evangelical staff members in the White House told me over lunch in the summer of 2007, Bush's religion has made him more genuinely humble and less absolutist in the way he defends his views. Believing that he too is a lowly sinner, Bush learned to be more tolerant of the faults of others. Faith has helped him repress Smirk #1, the one that expresses contempt. And it has hardly made him into a zealot. When it comes to spreading his religious views, Bush hasn't bothered trying to persuade his own daughters, or his closest adviser, Karl Rove.

But if his eternal perspective improves Bush's personality, it diminishes any ability he might otherwise have to take in ambiguity and complexity. Early in his presidency, Bush told Senator Joe Biden, "I don't do nuance." That line was probably spoken with self-deprecating irony (Smirk #2), but it captures a truth about the intellectually constricting lens of his faith. Bush rejects nuance not because he's mentally incapable of engaging with it, but because he has chosen to disavow it. Applying a crude religious lens that clarifies all decisions as moral choices rather than complicated trade-offs helps him fend off the deliberation and uncertainty he identifies with his father.

But closing one's mind to complexity isn't mere intellectual laziness; it's a fundamental evasion of freedom, God-given or otherwise. When Henry V shakes off Falstaff, he repudiates immorality, but at the cost of embracing narrowness. A simple faith frees George W.

from the kind of agonizing and struggle his father went through in handling the largest questions of his presidency, and helps him cope with the heavy burden of the job. But it comes at a tragic cost. A too crude religious understanding has limited Bush's ability to comprehend the world. The habit of pious simplification has undermined the Decider's decision-making.

CHAPTER FOUR

The Shadow

I am your shadow, my lord, I'll follow you.

—HENRY IV, PART 2

—

KARL'S FIRST ENCOUNTER WITH GEORGE WAS LOVE AT FIRST sight, in one direction. The year was 1973 and Bush had just started at Harvard Business School. Rove was working for Bush's father at the Republican National Committee office on Capitol Hill. When the chairman's son came home for a holiday weekend, it fell to Karl to give him the keys to his dad's car—a potent metaphor for his subsequent role. Rove recalled his first impression in an interview with Nicholas Lemann of *The New Yorker*:

> "It was the day before Thanksgiving, 1973," Rove said. "Chairman Bush's chief of staff called me and said, 'I've got to be at a meeting on the Hill, the chairman's got to be at a meeting at the White House, the other people in the office have already gone, and the eldest son's going to be coming down from Harvard. He's going to arrive at the train station, early afternoon. He'll call over here when he gets to the train station. Meet him down in the lobby and give him the keys to the family car.' I can literally remember what he was wearing: an Air National Guard flight jacket, cowboy boots, blue jeans, com-

> plete with the—in Texas you see it a lot—one of the back pockets will have a circle worn in the pocket from where you carry your tin of snuff, your tin of tobacco. He was exuding more charisma than any one individual should be allowed to have."

Rove has given off this same *Brokeback Mountain* vibe in other descriptions of the encounter: "Huge amounts of charisma, swagger, cowboy boots, flight jacket, wonderful smile, just charisma—you know, wow," Rove recalled to Frank Bruni of *The New York Times*.

George W.'s good looks and his Cool Hand Luke pose don't fully explain the spell. Nor, impressive though it seemed to a history-and-politics buff like Rove, was it simply his political pedigree. More than any of those things, Rove was awed by the insouciance with which the young man wore his privilege. The kid was Andover, Yale, Harvard, a Bush—and didn't seem impressed with any of it. The smoldering cowboy intensified the effect by taking no notice of the enraptured ranch hand. Indeed, the significance of this first encounter is that Rove immediately begins to idealize Bush, and that Bush doesn't register Rove at all.

Rove carried the torch for years and years, working for Bush's father, and helping with the son's 1978 congressional campaign. Fifteen years after the first encounter, he bumped into the object of his affection again. His worshipful vision intact, he tried to coax Bush into running for governor of Texas. Rove failed, but tried again in the following election, and this time succeeded, launching the most successful combination of politician and professional consultant in American history. This partnership led to their joint victories in 1994, 1998, 2000, and 2004. Through this period, Rove emerged as the sine qua non of Bush's political success—perhaps the only person without whom it simply could not have happened.

Yet the inequality in the relationship never went away. Karl was the perpetual wooer, George the eternally pursued. In ways subtle and direct, Bush tormented his admirer, reminding him that their arrangement was a marriage of his convenience. Bush is ever the put-down artist, but with Rove, there was always a special contempt mixed with his appreciation. During a political meeting in the basement of the Capitol, Rove's cell phone rang. Bush not only evicted him from the room, but locked the door so he couldn't get back in. Bush reacted with genuine cruelty when Rove received public credit for his success, telling him to stop acting like a big shot. On another occasion, he demanded in a meeting that Karl hang up his jacket for him. His attitude to Rove is captured in his brilliantly sarcastic nicknames, which mingle flattery and hurt: "boy genius" and "turd blossom." In Texas, turd blossoms are pale flowers that grow out of cow dung. In the White House, Bush never invited the man most responsible for his becoming president to his birthday parties. He has always made clear that he regards Rove as high-level help, not a close friend. Rove responded to Bush's distance as if it were a form of flirtation, performing greater and greater feats to win his affection.

On the night of his reelection victory in 2004, Bush finally yielded to his suitor, publicly crowning Rove with the title he desired: the Architect. But that designation expresses something different to each of them, a tension that in the second term undermined the success of their partnership and contributed to the failure of Bush's presidency. For Bush, Rove was the architect of his political career. But Rove saw himself as something more: the genius behind a new century's first great political realignment. In the end, it turned out that Rove had an agenda that went beyond George W.'s. His infatuation wasn't with Bush the person. It was with Bush as a vehicle for his own grandiose historical vision.

In the White House, Rove's anger and competitiveness diverted Bush's better instincts. He used his influence to steer Bush away from being the president he originally wanted to be—the kind of center-right consensus-builder he was as governor of Texas—and into a too-close alliance with people both of them found a bit nutty. Rove's dream of long-term Republican dominance positioned Bush as a creature of the party's right wing, and helped to turn him into the most unpopular and polarizing president since Nixon. Rove first made Bush successful, then helped to bring about his downfall by pursuing goals that went beyond Bush's. The problem was that, like a lot of great political theories, Rove's concept of realignment was brilliantly argued, but ultimately wrong.

THE POWERFUL FIRST IMPRESSION George made on Karl was intensified by the contrast between them. Rove, four years younger than Bush, was a skinny kid from Utah, lacking in any sense of style, and obsessed with the mechanics and minutiae of politics. Rove was so uncoordinated, he once noted, that he had trouble shuffling cards. He hadn't graduated from the University of Utah and wasn't sure if he was going back. At twenty-two, he was living from paycheck to paycheck.

Even if he'd been able to afford the ticket home for Thanksgiving in 1973, when he gave the keys to Bush, he didn't have much of a family to spend it with. While Dorothy Bush was smashing lobs at Round Hill Country Club, Karl Rove's grandmother was living in a tar-paper shack in Pueblo, Colorado, with newspaper pasted to the walls for insulation. Her husband, Rove's maternal grandfather, worked on a road crew and sold knives off the back of a pickup truck. Born in Denver, Rove moved at the age of ten to Sparks, Nevada, a railroad junction turned suburb that has since blurred into the sprawl of greater Reno. When he was fifteen, the family moved again to Salt Lake City, where his mother made sales in a gift shop and the man he knew as his father pursued work as a mineral geologist, often away from home. Karl's hobbies in high school were stamp collecting and debate. "I was the complete nerd," he told the *Deseret Morning News*, the Salt Lake City newspaper, in 2002. "I had the briefcase. I had the pocket protector. I wore Hush Puppies when they were not cool. I was the thin, scrawny little guy. I was definitely uncool."

After Rove's first semester at the University of Utah, which he attended on a scholarship, his father announced on Christmas Eve 1969 that he was moving out. It is unclear whether Karl learned at that point that his dad, who later lived openly as a gay man in Palm Springs, was homosexual. But soon thereafter, he found out another family secret from an aunt and uncle. Louis Rove was only a stepfather to him and his older brother. Their biological father had abandoned the family when Karl was an infant. Now his mother, Reba, abandoned them as adults. As Rove told the journalist Thomas Edsall in a revealing 1997 interview that Edsall only wrote about a decade later, his mother "packed up the car, had the house on the market, and moved to Reno and said good luck."

Worse, Reba intercepted the checks Louis sent to help pay his son's tuition at the University of Utah. Karl was living in an improvised bedroom in the attic of a fraternity house, paying his rent by working in a convenience store where he was once robbed at gunpoint. "My mother was one of these people who really thought often of what it was that she wanted in life, and not necessarily what was good or right for her family," Rove said. "And that was just her way. She never grew up. She could never think long term. She was always in the moment." The Edsall piece continues:

> Occasionally, she sent him packages with magazines from his childhood or old, broken toys. "It was like she was trying desperately to sort of keep this connection," he recalled. Finally, in 1981, his mother "drove out to the desert north of Reno and filled the car with carbon monoxide, and then left all of her children a letter saying, don't blame yourselves for this." It was, Rove said, "the classic fuck-you gesture."

Rove has never elsewhere spoken about such things; even his closest associates didn't know this story. Three biographies written while he was in the White House failed to turn up the details of his mother's suicide, or the name of his birth father. Only one of his four siblings has ever been quoted in press accounts.

Rove has not tried to pretend that he is something he's not, only to try to make his family background disappear. The legend of origin he prefers is that of the immaculately conceived political wunderkind. He claims to have written a paper on dialectical materialism in ninth grade, and was reading tracts by Michael Novak, a Catholic theologian influential in Republican politics, while serving as his high school's student president. After working on campaigns in Utah and Illinois, he dropped out of college to become executive director of the College Republican National Committee in 1971.

Rove has many of the classic traits of the autodidact. Having learned by choice rather than compulsion, he is excited about what he knows, and doesn't distinguish between formal and recreational education. When he talks about history, Rove often narrates in the present tense, imparting his feeling for its drama. Having organized his knowledge independently, he is full of idiosyncratic theories. He loves to boast about how much he has read and how much he knows. But there is also an edge of insecurity to the way he lords his knowledge over others. Rove harbors considerable resentment toward middle-class liberals who took better educational opportunities than he had and did less with them. In his first interview after announcing his departure from the White House in 2007, Rove told Rush Limbaugh that Bush's critics were "elite, effete snobs"—while touting Bush's Yale and Harvard degrees as evidence of how smart he is.

The issue of Rove's credentials has never quite gone away. Since dropping out in 1971, he has made several attempts to get a diploma, at the University of Maryland, George Mason, and the University of Texas. Rove loudly broadcasts those academic qualifications he has collected, which include an adjunct teaching position at the University of Texas and some honorary degrees. By rubbing other people's noses in their comparative ignorance, Rove compensates for old wounds of class, which never healed as he climbed the socioeconomic ladder.

In their book *Bush's Brain*, James Moore and Wayne Slater get at Rove's social insecurity with a story from the mid-1980s. Rove, who had moved to a posh suburb of Austin, became embroiled in a bitter dispute with his next-door neighbor Bud Neely, a wealthy doctor. Neely blocked Rove from finishing the construction of a multistory garage that he had begun building in violation of the local zoning regulations. But over the years, Neely couldn't understand the persistence of Rove's anger—he left furious messages on Neely's answering machine, planted survey flags to demarcate their property line, and challenged every conceivable trespass. After Rove demanded a meeting at the border over a gardening dispute, Neely asked Rove why he was still nursing the grudge after five years. "Because you said, 'I came here to get away from people like you,'" Rove told him.

Neely was nonplussed. Not only did he not remember saying it, he felt certain he would never say anything like that to anyone. The point of the story is that even after Rove could live like a rich Republican, he felt that people from the professional class didn't accept him. He might be able to join their country club, but he still wasn't welcome there. Rove has claimed there is more to the story, though his additional charges reflect the same dynamic. He says that Neely accused him of putting a window in the room above the garage so Rove could spy into his bedroom.

In his combination of overconfidence and insecurity, Rove reverses the Bush dynamic. Bush has bottomless social confidence, but is unsteady intellectually. Rove is intellectually cocksure, but lacking in confidence socially. For both of them, the mixture fueled visceral hostility to the establishment. But there are differences. Bush's anti-elitism is anti-intellectual. A son of the aristocracy, he derides a meritocracy chosen on the basis of brains alone. He scoffs at the pretensions of the East Coast. Rove's anti-elitism is intellectual; he resents the class that didn't recognize his brilliance and welcome him in. Where Bush never tires of pointing out that he despises Harvard and Yale despite having attended both, Rove fixates on his exclusion from that gilded world. Over time, their joint insecurity and overconfidence would fuse into a dangerous political aggression. It was politically deadly for those who got in the way of their juggernaut, in Texas and in Washington. And it would eventually prove politically fatal to Rove and Bush themselves, because of the way it encouraged the use of extreme partisanship and prevented necessary compromise.

IN THE SPRING OF 1973, Rove left his paid job at the College Republicans to run for president of the organization, with his friend Lee

Atwater as his campaign manager. In the Watergate era, the group was a school for scandal, and Rove and Atwater were its star pupils. At the group's convention that year in Lake of the Ozarks, they challenged the credentials of every state delegation under an obscure pretext, deferring the decision to an ostensibly neutral referee who was secretly a Rove-Atwater confederate. After the balloting, both sides in the election claimed victory, and the outcome went into electoral purgatory. Rove's opponent leaked a tape from a student training session to *The Washington Post*. On it, Rove could be heard boasting about pranks he'd pulled off. Working for a candidate for state treasurer in Illinois, Rove had impersonated a supporter of his candidate's opponent. He stole some stationery and used it to make an invitation to a bash with "free beer, free food, girls and a good time for nothing." He also recommended such tactics as "dumpster diving" in opponents' trash cans in search of incriminating correspondence. The tape led to Rove being questioned by the FBI. But after Atwater signed an affidavit testifying that Rove was recommending Nixonian dirty tricks only in jest, the investigation ended. Rove was seated as president by the new Republican National Committee chairman, George H. W. Bush.

In the years since, the story of the Lake of the Ozarks convention has become a talisman of Rove's deviousness and need to win at any cost. Those inferences aren't wrong; Rove is a ferocious competitor whose reputation for cunning is well earned. No one has ever accused him of excessive scruples. But the familiar telling overlooks the most interesting point of the story. The prize for which Rove was conniving was social validation. As president of the College Republicans, he would have entreé into Bush's secure, gracious world.

Once installed as president of the College Republicans, it gnawed at Rove how readily his friend Lee developed a relationship with the boss, while he toiled with the mailing lists. Rove often told the story of how Atwater asked to borrow the RNC yacht, so he could impress the woman he later married with a date on the moonlit Potomac. Though not so different from Rove in his lower-middle-class background, Atwater had the roguish charisma to escape it. While he played the bad boy, Rove had no such charm. "I guess I'm more cerebral and lack his great people skills," he said. "And I'm more of a nerd. Lee was a nerd in high school, but then he learned to play the guitar and talk to girls, and I never did." Instead of riding in the chairman's boat, Rove found himself after his term was up doing fund-raising for Gerald Ford's reelection campaign in Richmond, Virginia, a long way from the center of power.

In 1976, Rove married Valerie Wainwright, the daughter of a prominent Houston family with ties to the Bushes. She convinced him to move back to Texas, where she would be closer to her family. The connection helped Rove become the first person hired by James Baker in 1978 to work on the Fund for Limited Government, a vehicle for George H. W. Bush's planned 1980 presidential campaign. Baker was embarked that year on his own, ultimately unsuccessful campaign for Texas attorney general. He managed his friend Poppy's nascent campaign from Houston while Rove traveled the country with Bush Senior and longtime Bush aides Jennifer Fitzgerald and Margaret Tutwiler. Rove left the Bush campaign after less than a year, for reasons that have never been satisfactorily explained. When Bush—prodded by Baker—dropped out of the primaries in 1980 and was subsequently picked as Ronald Reagan's running mate, Rove wasn't asked back to work in the general election. Nor was Rove offered a position in the White House, or work on subsequent Bush campaigns in 1984 or 1988.

Why the elder Bush stiffed Rove in this way remains a central mystery at the heart of his biography. The version Rove gives is that he left the campaign to try to save his faltering marriage, which ended in divorce soon after. But it seems implausible that Rove, whose dream was to work in the White House, would have let his personal life take priority over his political one. He is known for embodying the opposite principle. Nor does it explain why Rove didn't rejoin Bush in any capacity later. In *The Way to Win*, Mark Halperin and John Harris suggest that Rove's problem was a personality conflict with Fitzgerald, a longtime member of the Bush inner circle. It was rumors about Bush Senior's relationship with Fitzgerald that prompted George W. to ask his father the adultery question in 1987.

Rove may have felt the sting of class in this expulsion. Fitzgerald and Tutwiler were both from the party's country club wing. And judging from the hostility Rove later exhibited toward him, James Baker probably had something to do with Rove's exile as well. Rove has long scorned Baker as a washed-up hack. When the journalist Melinda Henneberger asked in 2000 about Rove's lack of experience running a presidential campaign, he sneeringly asked her whether she thought hiring the dinosaur James Baker would be a better idea. "Do you repopulate the campaign with people from 1908? No!"

Left behind by Bush in Texas, Rove signed on to work for the new Republican governor, Bill Clements. After two years, he left the governor's office to found his own direct mail firm, Karl Rove & Company, with Clements as his invaluable first client. Rove's innovation was based on what he'd done for the Republican Party in Virginia, developing a database of contributors and voters. Recognizing earlier than most Republicans and all Democrats the power of targeted lists, Rove invested hundreds of thousands of dollars in mainframe computers and printers that allowed him to tailor the data he collected. He called the subsidiary that handled the database work Praxis Lists, a Marxist reference lost on his clients.

Rove worked for Democrats to round out his client list, but the future of the Republican Party was his focus. By the early 1980s, he grasped the relevance to Texas of the factors that had helped propel Reagan into the White House. The state's population was becoming more suburban, corporations were growing in size and power, and evangelical Christians were on the rise. According to a 2003 story in *Texas Monthly*, Rove was constantly telling people that Republicans were going to one day rule the state. His friends dismissed this as "the Rove bullshit." But by the middle of the decade, Rove & Co. was able to thrive while representing Republicans exclusively. And by the late 1980s, it wasn't bullshit anymore. Texas was turning dramatically to the GOP, with Rove as the strategist in most of the key federal and statewide races. The watershed was reached in 1990. Though Republicans lost the governor's mansion that year to Ann Richards, they won nine out of nine seats on the State Supreme Court (on which they'd had zero a decade earlier) and took control of virtually all the other state offices.

A HALLMARK OF ROVE'S campaigns was their careful planning from start to finish. They seldom departed from the strategy he laid out. They took advantage of Rove's superior technology to segment the electorate, raise money, and drive turnout. Rove candidates tended to emphasize three or four simple and effective issues. The consultant encouraged them to play offense, often by highlighting the Democrats' failures, personal vulnerabilities, or surreptitiously fueling a taint of scandal. None of this was extraordinary, but Rove executed his plans well. What was less usual was the tendency of Rove's political opponents—and his personal enemies—to be victimized by false rumors of homosexuality. In 2004, Joshua Green, a writer for *The Atlantic*, managed to document one of these whisper campaigns in an election for an Alabama Supreme Court seat in 1994. A former employee of Rove & Co. told Green that the firm used University of Alabama Law School students as unwitting conduits for untrue rumors—in this case that the Democratic incumbent Rove's candidate was trying to unseat was a gay pedophile.

By the late 1980s, Rove had arrived. His company was earning a tidy profit. In 1986, he got married again, to Darby Hickson, a graphic designer at his office, and in 1989 they had a son, Andrew Madison Rove. The huge collection of history books in his big new house was perfectly organized. But if Rove had achieved success in business and home life, his ambitions were far from satisfied. He was still little known in political circles outside of Texas. What Rove needed more than anything else, he recognized, was a candidate of national stature to champion.

After his father's victory at the end of 1988, Bush moved his family to Dallas and the two men resumed contact. Rove's worshipful feelings were intact. He still saw in Bush someone with charisma and charm. Bush formed an immediate bond with people, remembered names, and nurtured long-term connections. He had tremendous personal discipline. He also had the Bush name, a business background, and access to capital. Rove latched on to him not just as someone who could win the governor's mansion for the Republicans, but as a vehicle capable of carrying him beyond Texas to Washington. He revealed this conception only in glimpses. "Bush is the kind of candidate and officeholder political hacks like me wait for a lifetime to be associated with," Rove told a Florida reporter in 1998.

The disparity in their social status remained, but Rove and George W. now had something in common. At earlier stages in their lives, both had seen George H. W. Bush as a lodestar. Both felt the sting of having failed him. Now both were building an argument that Bush Senior had been wrong about them. Junior had done this with his work on the 1988 campaign and the Texas Rangers deal. Rove did it by becoming the guru of political realignment in Texas. But in both cases, a rival for Bush Senior's affections was still in the lead. As George was trying to catch up to Jeb, Rove was chasing Lee Atwater, who had elected Bush president in 1988. Atwater and Rove didn't speak often, but Rove still measured himself against the doppelgänger who had broken out ahead of him fifteen years earlier. Atwater's death in 1991, from a brain tumor at the age of forty, created an opportunity for Rove to become the dominant Republican strategist, much as George H. W. Bush's loss in 1992 and Jeb's in 1994 paved the way for George W. to become the dominant Republican politician.

Rove and Bush Junior were soon discussing political possibilities, including a challenge to Senator Lloyd Bentsen, who had beaten his father in 1970 and humiliated his running mate, Dan Quayle, in the 1988 vice presidential debate. Rove wanted Bush to run for governor in 1990, and began floating trial balloons in political circles and the press. In February 1989, before the Rangers deal was even complete,

Rove told *The Dallas Morning News*, "Ownership of the Texas Rangers anchors him clearly as a Texas businessman and entrepreneur and it gives him name identification, exposure and gives him something that will be easily recallable by people." Bush was quoted in the same story saying, "I'm thinking about it, and I might run. But it is too early to make any decisions."

Rove could not persuade Bush to run that year against the wishes of his parents. But the alliance was struck. Rove continued courting Bush, plying him with books to read and laying the groundwork for a future campaign. His role quickly supplanted and soon exceeded that of Doug Wead. Where the former minister had helped Bush with his religious change, the irreligious Rove transformed Bush into a politician. A crucial commonality was that both had worked for the father, but made clear their allegiance to the son. George W. had fully absorbed Prescott Bush's lesson about the importance of loyalty, as underscored by his father's travails after the Gulf War. He saw Atwater, Baker, and other aides who failed to get his father reelected in 1992 as more faithful to their own ambitions than to the man they served. The younger Bush intended to place his trust only in those, like Rove, whose devotion to him seemed absolute. Bush tested the proposition by treating Rove as a kind of surrogate younger brother, who would take his abuse and play dead on command. Karl was what Jeb might have been if he'd remained content in his subordinate status and never turned into his older brother's rival.

Rove's distance from the father and closeness to the son increased in 1992, when he was fired from his meager role on President Bush's Texas reelection team. Rove was suspected of leaking negative information about finance chair Robert Mosbacher Jr.—the son of Bush's commerce secretary—to the syndicated columnist Robert Novak. There was already bad blood between Rove and the younger Mosbacher because Mosbacher had directed three-quarters of a $1 million budget to a consultant named John Weaver, who was Rove's principal rival in Texas's Republican political consulting industry. Weaver and Rove had planned to go into business together a few years previously, but had a bitter falling out after Rove spread a nasty story about Weaver that tracked the familiar theme of his whispering campaigns. He falsely claimed Weaver had made a pass at a young man at a party. After Mosbacher fired Rove, the remaining quarter of Bush's budget pointedly was transferred to Weaver's firm as well.

Following his father's 1992 defeat, George W. and Karl had extensive conversations about what had gone wrong. Bush's view amalgamated Rove's analysis. His father hadn't had a well-developed strategy; he started his reelection campaign too late; he was too reactive; he hadn't spent his political capital wisely; he had been undermined by a primary challenge, then by Ross Perot. Bush felt that rather than define himself, his father had allowed others to define him as someone who didn't care about the economy and ordinary people.

This critique was central to their bond. Rove became Bush's political mentor in 1993 by showing him how he could help him escape his father's fate. Rove recognized the younger Bush as fiercely loyal to his father, yet desperate to escape his shadow. The political plan he presented to George W. was a map of differentiation. He and Bush planned the whole gubernatorial campaign before it began, asserting that others would not dictate its course or timing. Bush would talk potential primary opponents, like the younger Mosbacher and Ross Perot's former campaign manager Tom Luce, out of running. This would clear his path to challenge Ann Richards. Candidate and consultant would choose the issues for the campaign, defining it around Bush's agenda, not his opponent's. Rove would carefully control Bush's image and exposure, avoiding the national media, which only wanted to write about him in relation to his dad, and evading tricky policy questions until they had answers ready.

The trickiest part of this plan was adding substance to Bush's style, turning his appealing instincts into a plausible policy agenda. When Rove asked him in 1993 to write down why he wanted to be governor, George W. listed "cultural change from the 1960s," "personal responsibility," and "liberal guilt." This list reflected not just Bush's abiding hostility to the elite he abhorred from his years at Yale, but also his understanding that his father had lost to Clinton by being a weak domestic leader, with no distinctive policy approach of his own. His father had been known for the vague noblesse oblige embodied in pabulum phrases like "a kinder, gentler nation" and "1,000 points of light." This mushiness, and the elder Bush's passion for foreign policy, had allowed Clinton to turn "personal responsibility"—as embodied by his two-years-then-out welfare policy—into the signature of his winning campaign.

Rove's status as a self-educated man made him the ideal policy tutor. He could guide Bush into serious subjects without triggering his gag reflex. In 1992, Karl began bringing policy experts and conservative writers to Dallas to home-school Bush according to a curriculum of his own design. The most influential of the books he gave Bush was Myron Magnet's recently published *The Dream and the Nightmare: The Sixties' Legacy to the Underclass.* Vance McMahon, who became Bush's policy director in Austin, remembers seeing a row of twenty-five copies on the shelf in Rove's office. In the book, Magnet argues that the libertinism of the 1960s was most destructive not to middle-class students, whose social structures helped them cope with drugs, single parenthood, and divorce, but to the lower class, who lacked safety nets. In a way, this was the story of Rove's own disintegrated family. The book resonated differently with Bush. Magnet condemns liberal academics who helped to undermine traditional moral values. These were the people Bush couldn't stand at Yale, the William Sloane Coffins and Strobe Talbotts, who thought they knew better than people like the Bushes and the Walkers. George Junior now had a better counter to their elitist arrogance. He could answer their intellectual pretensions with a firm, clear concept of right and wrong. With cultural resentment increasingly at the center of the GOP's story, Bush saw the populist persona he had forged in opposition to his father gaining real political traction.

Together, Rove and Bush worked out four issues he could use to challenge the popular incumbent: education (on which with Laura's help he knew what he was talking about), juvenile crime (a trendy spin on law and order, based on John DiIulio's since-discredited idea of a demographic bulge of "super-predators"), fixing welfare (the hot social issue of the day), and tort law reform (which Rove had used to great effect in reshaping the Texas Supreme Court). Bush followed this script with a martial discipline, refusing to be drawn into discussions of topics he didn't know as well. He stayed fanatically on message, even when Richards tried to provoke his famous temper by taunting him as "the Shrub" and "Prince George." To the surprise of some of his closest friends and relatives, Bush never took the bait.

The campaign did also have some of Rove's less salubrious trademarks, such as an untraceable rumor campaign that the divorced Richards was a lesbian. But after an impressive debate, in which Bush not for the last time vastly exceeded low expectations, Rove didn't really need to reach very far into his bag of tricks. His candidate won by a comfortable, seven-point margin. Bush had overcome not just the doubts of his parents, but those of the press and public as well. As with his turn to sobriety, he had done it through the exercise of personal will. Rove knew better than to claim credit for a triumph so crucial to his hero's identity.

DESPITE HIS CRITIQUE of his father's mistakes, George W. honored the family belief that politics should be kept separate from governing—and that the people who worked in the latter ranked above the people who helped with the former. As governor, he would talk to Rove throughout the day on a dedicated phone line, but didn't want the relationship more visible than it had to be. His political adviser wasn't given a title or an office in the Texas capitol. Instead, he ran Bush's political operation from his own office, and joined meetings held in a kind of boiler room in the capitol basement. Rove's role included vetting appointments, cultivating constituencies, developing policy, and maintaining relationships for the governor. As Bush's "prime minister," he had influence over everything that mattered, even if he was explicitly in charge of very little.

At the same time, Rove's power was balanced by Bush's communications director, Karen Hughes, and his chief of staff, Joe Allbaugh. This is a point that admirers of Bush from his Austin days often emphasize. Among the Washington press corps, Hughes is thought of as Bush's propaganda minister, a slavish apologist who during the 2000 campaign would answer questions by reciting from Bush's speeches. But in Austin, Hughes was considered a person of substance and a moderating counterweight to Rove, who was seen as an ally of conservative interest groups. Hughes had relationships with people who were not part of the Republican base. In *The Right Man,* David Frum describes her as a "mother substitute." Selflessly devoted to Bush, she would tell him things he wasn't eager to hear, which no one else did. Allbaugh, a Republican campaign hand from Oklahoma brought in to establish order, had direct authority over Rove and helped to keep his megalomania in check.

After the 1994 victory, Rove came to view Bush the way a jockey does the greatest horse he will ever ride. He idealized and feared him, knowing the skittish beast could end his dreams of fame and fortune if he wasn't properly stroked and tended. Bush, on the other hand, viewed Rove as a skilled servant who needed to be reminded who the boss was. The new governor bridled at suggestions that he was being directed by Rove. He made a point of harshly reprimanding his political guru in front of others, the way his mother sometimes slapped down aides of her husband's she thought were getting too big for their britches. Part of Rove's role was to provide an outlet for the governor's storms of anger. Their relationship was co-dependent. Rove couldn't make himself important without Bush; Bush couldn't prove himself without Karl. If Bush was nastier to Rove than to anyone else in his circle, it may have been because he knew he needed Rove's help, and hated needing help from anyone.

Bush's churlish treatment of Rove revealed not only his touchiness about his independence and his dislike of being managed, but the family's view of political consultants as seasonal help. The worst thing Rove could do was assume privileges reserved for relatives. Once, when Rove recited his familiar criticisms of George Senior's mistakes on the record, the governor reamed him out, telling him never to criticize his family again. Rove apologized. He learned that while Bush might choose to disparage his father, outsiders were never to insert themselves into their relationship. Rove dealt with Bush's abuse by passing it down the chain of command. He instilled enough fear to keep his subordinates from complaining, and developed the reputation of being awful to work for.

Where Bush succeeded in Texas, it often had little to do with his political guru. In his first year in office, he focused on building his relationships with the key figures in the state. His most important decision was to lavish his charm on the two Democrats who had the most sway over his fate, Speaker of the House Pete Laney and the late lieutenant governor, Bob Bullock. With Bullock, a big personality who held the post that in Texas is in many respects more powerful than the governorship, Bush acted as if he was back at DKE House. At a breakfast meeting in 1997, Bullock told Bush he planned to support a bill the governor opposed. "I'm sorry, but I'm going to have to fuck you on this one," Bullock said. Bush got up, seized the lieutenant governor by the shoulders, and gave him a moist smooch on the lips.

"What the hell did you do that for?" Bullock spat out, ostentatiously wiping his mouth.

"If you're going to fuck me, you'll have to kiss me first," Bush replied.

This is a good illustration of the cultural gap that would make life in Washington more difficult than Bush expected. In Texas, people think that Bush giving a big wet smacker to a homophobic old bubba is about the funniest thing that ever happened. Bush loved telling the story, and even made the mistake of repeating it to Tucker Carlson in 1999. To Washington ears, it's obnoxious, immature behavior—an illustration of Bush Junior's failure to completely grow up. Bush knows how to calibrate his antics, and didn't try this trick with Tom Daschle or Nancy Pelosi. But once in the White House, he was missing his favorite tool. He couldn't use his outrageous personality to bond with people in informal settings and overcome partisan differences.

When it came to the substance of policy, the governor rejected Rove's advice on the signature initiative of his first term, an education proposal that would have shifted the burden of paying for public schools from the property tax to a new value-added type of tax. Rove objected to Bush allowing a tax increase, the very issue that had doomed his father with conservatives. But his political argument didn't carry much sway with Bush, who with Laura's encouragement had become possessed of the notion that he was doing the right thing for underprivileged children. When the bill went down to defeat in the legislature, both of them had learned something. Thereafter, Rove understood that the way to sell a position to Bush was the same way you sold one to his father, by arguing that it was the right thing to do, and framing any political advantages around the ethical choice. Bush learned that Rove had a sound feel not just for campaigns, but for the irreducibly political aspects of governing.

Even though Bush lost the school funding fight, taking a relatively liberal position had longer-term political benefits that Rove did not anticipate. The new governor came across to Texas Democrats as moderate, caring, and pragmatic. Mark McKinnon, an Austin-based media adviser who had worked exclusively for Democrats, changed sides to work for him. So did Matthew Dowd, the state's leading Democrat pollster. McKinnon and Dowd became Rove's most important collaborators.

Many in the local media became admirers as well. Political reporters saw Bush as moderate and reasonable, and became friendlier in response to his flattery. Bush worked the Texas press corps brilliantly. His most obvious form of cultivation was remembering a journalist's name and pulling out unlikely personal details. Bush might ask a reporter about a sick parent or make sure to call on one who brought his daughter to a press conference—and then invite them up to his office afterward. But most politicians learn those tricks. Bush's signature is knocking reporters off balance before they can do the same to him. In an interview, he puts you on the defensive with a hostile-sounding comment that suggests he has you pegged—as the representative of a liberal outfit, a policy wonk, someone trying to put him on the couch or play "gotcha." This produces a wave of relief when he offers a bit of jocular camaraderie that suggests access will continue. On reporters he sees frequently, he bestows nicknames: "Stretch" (David Gregory of NBC), "Super-Stretch" (Bill Sammon of *The Washington Times*), "Pancho" (Frank Bruni of *The New York Times*), "Dulce" (Candy Crowley of CNN). This prep-school technique is both a form of flattery and an expression of dominance. The recipient of a nickname is made to feel important, but on the basis of an identity defined by Bush.

AS FAR AS ROVE was concerned, Bush's reelection as governor was merely a warm-up drill for the presidential campaign that would begin immediately afterward. Victory was a foregone conclusion, so 1998 became a test of how far Bush could reach into the other side's pocket. Bush won with 69 percent of the vote, and hit Rove's benchmarks by winning 27 percent of the black vote and 49 percent of the Hispanic vote. Nearly winning a Latino majority represented a real achievement for a Republican. In a year when Clinton's impeachment caused Republicans to lose congressional seats nationally, Republicans swept all of Texas's eighteen statewide offices. Eliminating Democrats meant that Rove's work in Texas was finished. The state's political realignment was complete.

Once, when he was asked if the Republican takeover in Texas would have been possible without George W. Bush, Rove told the journalist Wayne Slater, "If George W. Bush didn't exist we'd have to find a way to create somebody like him." It's a revealing admission, both about Rove's view of Bush as a vehicle and in its suggestion of an agenda that went beyond the candidate. Rove's new goal wasn't just to elect George W. Bush president. It was to do nationally what he had done in Texas: develop the kind of political machine that would ensure Republican dominance for decades to come. Having directed one blockbuster, Rove naturally wanted to cast his leading man in the even bigger sequel.

As someone who sees politics in historical terms, Rove was constantly looking to other campaigns that might provide him with a transformational paradigm. The two most obvious examples to consider were FDR's 1932 victory and Ronald Reagan's in 1980. But neither of these was quite right. Roosevelt arrived at a moment of crisis, and reordered American politics by fundamentally changing the role of the federal government, circumstances that hardly pertained to a Republican in 1998, at the height of an economic boom. Nineteen eighty provided a better model, but that conception was too limited. Rove wanted Bush to lead a political transformation of his own, not just complete the work of a predecessor. He thought the pattern to follow might be the rise of the conservative hero Theodore Roosevelt, who shared his candidate's youthful vigor and ability to appeal across the political spectrum.

Testing his Bush–as–Teddy Roosevelt hypothesis might also satisfy Rove's perpetual quest for academic credentials, Rove had applied and been accepted to the Ph.D. program at the University of Texas government department. But in 1998, he still lacked sufficient credits for a BA, the requirements of which included a research essay. Rove had already written a paper about Wendell Willkie, the 1940 Republican presidential nominee, but for bureaucratic reasons, he couldn't count it toward his degree. So in the spring of 1998, while running one Bush campaign and conceptualizing another, he enrolled for the second time in a U of T writing seminar with the intention of examining Teddy Roosevelt's role in the 1896 presidential election.

The adviser Rove found for his paper was Lewis L. Gould, a leading scholar of the Gilded Age then in his last semester of teaching. Gould was the author of several books about William McKinley, who had picked Roosevelt as his running mate in 1900, bringing about TR's accidental presidency when McKinley was assassinated in the first year of his second term. Gould suggested Rove refocus his research on the underappreciated McKinley. In his tutor's view, McKinley was the first modern American politician because of the way he used the media and technology. This notion appealed to Rove, who loves nothing better than an argument that everyone's assumptions are wrong.

In the process of writing his thirty-page paper, Rove became fixated on the parallels between 1896 and 2000. McKinley, the last president of the Civil War generation, was not exactly a stand-in for Bush, but both were smarter and more their own men than contemporary opponents gave them credit for. Mark Hanna, the strategist behind McKinley's career and presidential victory, was an even more relevant figure for Rove. The outstanding political practitioner of his era, Hanna was strategically minded, ferociously organized, and brilliant in his application of new technologies to politics. For a man described as Bush's brain, the relationship between an underrated president and his reviled guru was highly suggestive. It was Hanna, as much as McKinley, who put together the coalition of big business and Northern industrial workers that would end the era of Southern dominance and drive American politics in the period ahead. Republicans kept the White House in six of the eight subsequent presidential elections, and dominated Congress until the New Deal, when the next major party realignment took place.

After journalists started making more of a meal out of the Hanna comparison than he found helpful, Rove revised his analogy, dismissing Hanna as the "Don Evans of the McKinley campaign" (Evans, a Bush friend and fund-raiser who became secretary of commerce, had little substantive role in the White House). Rove now indicated that the historical figure he really identified with was Charles Dawes, who later served as Calvin Coolidge's vice president. At a speech at the University of Utah in 2002, Rove noted that McKinley relied on Dawes, a young lawyer who ran his operation in Illinois, for political intelligence.

This is misdirection, a standard Rove technique. Dawes was vastly less important to him, and to McKinley, than Hanna. But more than he personally identified with any individual antecedent, Rove analogized 2000 to the 1896 campaign itself. He drew many of his parallels from *The Presidential Election of 1896* by Stanley L. Jones. Rove cast the

GOP as once again the optimistic, modernizing party and the Democrats as backward-looking romantics. McKinley "saw that the issues that had dominated American politics since the 1860s had sort of worn themselves out," Rove explained to a reporter in 1999. He said that McKinley's GOP figured out how to "take its fundamental principles and style them in such a way that they seemed to have relevance to the new economy, the new nature of the country and the new electorate."

Rove's version of 1896 became a template for 2000. He hoped to raise a new Republican coalition by chipping away at the old Democratic one. The fattest target was the growing demographic of Latino voters, for whom the Spanish-speaking Bush had already demonstrated an affinity. Rove thought Bush could make headway with Hispanics nationally by championing immigration reform and economic mobility, and by elevating the status of Mexican-American relations. Bush invited the governors of five Mexican states to sit behind him at his inauguration, something it's hard to imagine any border-state Republican doing today. This was at a moment when Pete Wilson, the governor of California, was supporting Proposition 187, a ballot initiative that would have denied public education and other government benefits to illegal residents. In Texas, by contrast, George W. pointedly decried immigrant bashing.

Rove thought Bush could also win over Hispanic and non-Hispanic Catholics by pronouncing his commitment to a "culture of life," and traveling to Rome to meet John Paul II (whom Bush pronounced "a great Pope"). Bush could also cut into the Democratic Jewish vote by supporting Israel in a way his father hadn't, and into the African-American vote by disavowing attacks on affirmative action and handing out faith-based grants to black churches. The elderly would appreciate his support of a Medicare prescription drug benefit. His broadest attempt to pillage an area of Democratic strength was in education. Before running for president, Bush pulled his daughters out of St. Andrew's Episcopal School and enrolled them in the public Austin High School.

Eighteen ninety-six was a financial model as well. Hanna raised an unprecedented $3.75 million for McKinley by tapping into the country's industrial base, with contributions as large as $250,000 from Standard Oil—the equivalent of $6 million today. His campaign spent the money it raised with notable efficiency, applying what Hanna called "business principles" to politics for the first time. With his family network and a fund-raising operation run by Don Evans, Bush could do the same. A system of incentives for big fund-raisers called "pioneers" helped Bush collect more than $100 million, more than any other presidential candidate in history. In 2004, Bush's kitty would reach $257 million.

Rove drew an analogy to McKinley's "front porch campaign." Rather than crisscross the country by railroad, McKinley invited delegations to visit him at his home in Canton, Ohio. In 1998 and early 1999, a procession of governors, donors, advisers, and influential figures in the party came to see Bush at the governor's mansion—the joke in Austin was that only Iowa legislators could now get time with him. Rove's strategy had the advantage of limiting Bush's exposure to the national media until he was more conversant in a variety of domestic and international topics. "He's ready to talk about national issues," Rove said. "But once you start, you can't stop. He doesn't want to do it on the [media's] time frame."

Another point Rove took away from his McKinley study was about the need for a unifying theme. By 1998, he, Bush, and Hughes had fastened on the flexible message of "compassionate conservatism" drawing on Bush's faith-based programs. If Bush was calculating in his use of religion, Rove, the unbeliever, was directly cynical in his attempt to frame the governor's faith in a way that could appeal to the GOP's evangelical base without alarming the moderate center. The 1896 election was also notable, Rove pointed out, for its innovative use of technology to target variations on its message to ethnic constituencies. "There were 14 pieces of mail and publications to every voter who voted in the 1896 election—a Croatian American list, the first mass-produced political publication in Yiddish. It was a pretty amazing campaign underneath the surface," he mused. In

2000, Rove intended to use technology to parse the electorate much more finely.

In framing the campaign around this comparison, Rove was off on a frolic of his own. To be sure, the candidate had no objection to transforming American politics. But Bush wasn't one to sit around reading about bimetallism and the Wilson-Gorman tariff. With his keen nose for ulterior motives, Bush sniffed out that his guru had another agenda, but mistakenly assumed it must be a financial one. He told Rove that if he was going to run his presidential campaign, he'd have to sell his business. This was a kind of symbolic penance, proof that Rove served no other master, including himself. After selling his company at considerable financial sacrifice, Rove declared his fealty with almost creepy hyperbole: "I have no persona other than Bush's guy." He was his shadow, and he would follow.

IN ONE WAY, Rove's strategy clearly succeeded. He got his man to the White House, in a year when historical models suggested that Al Gore should have been the victor. But in another way, it just as obviously failed; Bush did not earn a plurality of the vote. As Rove put it, they had won "by a chad." His stubbornness about sticking to the master plan was partly at fault. Part of the Rove playbook is always playing offense, which meant that Bush had to make forays into enemy territory. In the last few weeks of the campaign, Rove pumped resources into New Jersey and California, states Bush was never going to win. In a show of confidence, he sent Bush to Sacramento days before the election. In the end, Bush lost California by 13 points. Had that time and money been spent in Florida, Pennsylvania, Wisconsin, or New Mexico, Bush might have won without the taint of quasi-legitimacy that hung over his first term—and without having to call on James Baker and his little brother to bail him out. This arrogant miscalculation came close to making Rove the goat instead of the genius of American politics.

Even before the post-election fight ended, Bush's chief pollster,

Matthew Dowd, was working on a study of what went wrong. The memo Dowd distributed in December suggested that Bush's centrist strategy had been flawed from the outset. Over the previous twenty years, the share of the electorate available to candidates on either side had dwindled from 24 percent to 6 percent. In other words, the American political center was disappearing. Rove liked to say that elections were a balance between persuasion—winning the undecided—and motivation—turning out the base. Dowd's statistics suggested that Bush had tilted too heavily toward persuasion. Four million evangelical voters had stayed home. What's more, there weren't that many undecided votes available in the first place. Rove began carrying a laminated card in his wallet documenting the historical decline of the swing vote. Rove's so-called 72-Hour Project, a massive effort to identify and turn out the Republican base on the final three days before the 2002 midterm elections, verified Dowd's data, and showed how effective a base-in as opposed to a center-out strategy could be.

Some liberal analysts have argued that Rove took one look at Dowd's data from 2000 and decided that Bush needed to govern as a divider after all. In fact, Rove never gave up on his idea of chipping away at Democratic constituencies, an effort most transparent in Bush's 2002 decision to protect the steel industry, with an eye to winning West Virginia and Pennsylvania in 2004. But Rove's emphasis shifted strongly toward motivating the base, which pushed Bush to the right on a range of social, economic, and environmental issues.

There were other reasons why Bush turned right in 2001 and 2002. The polarizing post-election fight and the shadow of illegitimacy that hung over his first term made comity with the Democrats harder to achieve where Bush was inclined to try. Washington Democrats turned out to be unlike Texas Democrats, whom he could compromise with and still mostly get his way. And unlike in Texas, where Democrats controlled the legislature, Bush's own party ran Congress, which meant he might not have to negotiate.

But another reason he governed as he did is that Rove was not just thinking about reelecting Bush but also beyond Bush. If his goal was merely to win 51 percent of the vote in 2004, Rove didn't need to change strategies. In 2004, Bush would have the advantages of incumbency and a record of accomplishment. His own example in Texas showed how to increase a majority by governing from the center. All Bush needed to do to get reelected was cut more deeply into the Democratic share of the Hispanic vote, the Jewish vote, the black vote, the Catholic vote—all areas where he had room to do better.

If, however, the problem wasn't just reelecting Bush in 2004, but assembling a majority that could last thirty years, if he wanted to be Hanna and not just Atwater, Rove had to do something more than shave points from the other side. He had to build a durable coalition of rising groups, the way Hanna had. He would need the financial resources of big business, the shoe leather of the evangelicals, the cultural resentments of lower-class men, and the anxieties of the suburban middle class. Teaching people to despise the Democrats was in tension with his 2000 approach to enlarging Bush's share of the swing vote. But Rove didn't think this shift in emphasis would harm Bush. He thought it would ensure his reelection while putting in place the building blocks of a lasting Republican majority.

Bush gave Rove enough authority to chase this dream. One way George W. thought himself an improvement on his father was his greater taste for politics. Instead of compartmentalizing it, he would integrate it into policy. He wouldn't send his political guru to the RNC, as his dad had done with Atwater after 1988, or resist thinking about his reelection campaign until it was upon him. Rove would work from the West Wing and help design the president's domestic agenda. On the other hand, Bush drew the line at Rove's involvement in foreign policy, where his role was limited to selling policies he had no hand in formulating. Bush's contempt for his immediate predecessor was grounded in the belief that Bill Clinton had made decisions on the basis of polls and focus groups. Bush didn't want to see polling data outside the context of a political meeting. Even as the 2004 campaign drew near, he admonished Rove not to show him polls more than once a week.

The irony here was considerable. In 1993, there was a mini-furor over Clinton's political adviser James Carville even having a White House pass. From his habitat in Hillary Clinton's old office, Rove acted not just as White House political chief, but as Republican CEO, presiding over the most thoroughgoing politicization of the executive branch since Nixon's day. Clinton might have had Dick Morris poll about the best place for him to go on vacation, but Rove's Office of Strategic Initiatives had effective oversight over Bush's entire domestic policy shop, such as it was. As John DiIulio revealed in his *Esquire* interview, the new White House was completely dominated by the political arm. In the second term, Rove's policy role was made explicit when he was named deputy chief of staff. But he recognized the need to keep up the illusion that Bush's presidency was far less political than Clinton's. Describing the president's attitude, he quoted Sam Houston from *The Raven*: "Do right and damn the consequences."

Rove's Machiavellianism meant that unlike in Texas, there was little check on his authority. He persuaded Bush to send Allbaugh into exile at the Federal Emergency Management Agency, which he left in 2002, to be replaced by a political hack named Michael Brown. Rove maneuvered to reduce the clout of both Karen Hughes and Dan Bartlett, a close aide to Bush who worked under her. Andrew Card, the White House chief of staff, spent much of his time arbitrating the poisonous bickering between Rove and Hughes. The constant friction helped drive her back to Texas in 2002. The other two people in a position to check Rove's power, Laura Bush and the president's father, were unwilling to get involved. With domestic policy politicized to an unprecedented degree, cabinet secretaries like Paul O'Neill, Christie Todd Whitman, and Tommy Thompson found there was no percentage in opposing Rove—especially when he saw eye-to-eye with the vice president, as he did on energy and environmental issues. Thanks to Rove, being a cabinet secretary in the Bush White House meant serving as a figurehead, an ambassador with social status but no policymaking authority. O'Neill was open about his humiliation. Whitman was discreet about hers. Thompson kept his mouth shut entirely.

To be a moderate Republican in the Bush years meant becoming increasingly frustrated as Rove steered outcomes to woo constituencies on issues ranging from global warming (the coal industry) to tax cuts (the wealthy) to fetal stem cell research (Catholics). In delivering the spoils, Rove—and Bush—quickly lost touch with any impulse they might once have had about limiting the growth of government. After the thrill of Bush's initial tax cuts wore off, his explosion in federal spending disenchanted some economic and libertarian-minded conservatives. But unlike evangelical and business leaders, small-government conservatives were a weak lobby.

The writer Thomas Beer wrote an early biography of Hanna in which he described him as "the human machine." Hanna ran his machine from his home in Cleveland, sending telegrams and dispatching messengers by railroad. Rove ran his machine from his BlackBerry, on a separate account billed to the RNC. His thumbs moving so fast they blurred, he maintained constant contact with party and campaign organizations in fifty states, figures on the evangelical right, and influential members of the conservative movement. The level of detail and precision with which Rove planned and monitored was extraordinary. If Bush was the delegating CEO president, Rove was the hands-on COO who ran everything and everyone. He involved himself in candidate selection for congressional races, and even for state offices. He exercised rigid control over appointments, making sure they rewarded supporters and contributors. Of course, even the most prodigious of multitaskers couldn't run the entire Republican empire on his own. Rove wired his machine through an unofficial network in which intermediaries helped to keep invisible his role in punishing traitors and servicing allies.

September 11 has colored everything that came before it, but there is an interesting, if academic, debate to be had about how far Rove had succeeded in moving Bush to the right before the attacks. At the outset of his presidency, the president was still inclined to follow his

Texas script. He reached out to Representative George Miller and Senator Ted Kennedy, the Democratic leaders on education, to forge a compromise around his No Child Left Behind bill, which served the conservative goal of raising standards while promising a liberal increase in funds. Bush similarly joined Democrats in expanding Medicare to cover prescription drugs and argued for a sweeping immigration reform bill, though he did not yet seek to introduce one. With his appointments, Bush demonstrated a principled commitment to racial inclusion that he never abandoned. His was the first Republican administration in which blacks, Latinos, and women had a genuinely equal role. This moved the GOP beyond tokenism and put the specter of his father's racially divisive 1988 campaign to rest. On September 10, 2001, the Bush presidency still could have gone either way, just as Clinton could have in the fall of 1993—and remained capable of tacking back to the center, just as Clinton did after the 1994 midterm elections.

Rove not only prevented the needed navigational correction; he stood on the accelerator. It was not Bush's reaction to the attacks, but Rove's that put an indelible political stamp on the War on Terror. In the fall of 2001, Bush's consistent message was that he would not politicize the conflict. But Rove, who saw an opportunity to build his coalition, was under no such orders. In January of 2002, he sent precisely the opposite message to the party. At the Republican National Committee's winter meeting in Austin, Rove argued that the GOP should use terrorism as an issue in the upcoming midterms. "We can also go to the country on this issue because they trust the Republican Party to do a better job of protecting and strengthening America's military might and thereby protecting America," he declared.

Rove's Austin speech counts as one of the turning points in the Bush presidency. Until then, Bush had presided, however imperfectly, over a moment of national and international solidarity. Had he moved in a more bipartisan direction, as Roosevelt did after Pearl Harbor, Bush might have become the kind of unifying leader he wanted to be. But here the shadow pulled the body. Driven by his need to win and his bias toward conflict, Rove persuaded the president to turn the national moment into a partisan one. He got Bush to pick a fight over the Department of Homeland Security, and to use it as a cudgel against vulnerable Democrats in the 2002 midterm elections. This involved an impressive about-face. Bush moved from opposing the creation of a separate cabinet department, which Democrats wanted, to supporting one and bashing Democrats for not wanting it badly enough. Reinforcing Bush's own worst instinct to politicize the war against terrorism was Rove's greatest disservice, and a major contribution to the failure of the Bush presidency. For the rest of his time in office, Bush would remain a polarizing figure, with none of the ability he showed in the first months after September 11 to bring the country together.

The catastrophic blunder of politicizing the War on Terror was obscured for a time by how well Rove's new emphasis on base motivation, as demonstrated by the 72-Hour Project, appeared to be working. In midterm elections, the party that controls the White House typically loses congressional seats. But in 2002, Republicans won back the Senate, which they had lost when Jim Jeffords switched parties, and gained four seats in the House. This was Rove's triumph. The positive electoral feedback raised his stature even higher within the administration and the Republican Party, which now regarded him as a hero and a genius. But it also prevented Bush from recognizing that his vision of governing as a consensus leader was slipping away. For Clinton, the defeat of 1994 was the most powerful warning possible about how far his presidency had drifted from his original intentions. It gave him an opening to reshuffle staff and adjust course. In 2002, Bush received no such signal about the way his presidency was getting away from him, and made no such correction.

ROVE'S SUCCESS IN 2002 pointed in the direction of a base-driven strategy for 2004, which he laid out in stunning specificity for the rest of Bush's political team in February 2003. This plan, and the conservative machine Rove built to implement it, worked at every level. His McKinleyite micro-targeting was now delightfully precise. The campaign didn't just buy the mailing lists of *Field & Stream* and *Golf Digest*. It devoted a share of its TV budget to buying time on *Will and Grace,* a show whose pro-gay message was at odds with Bush's advocacy of a constitutional amendment to ban gay marriage, but that turned out to be popular with security moms. The Democratic apparatus, including labor unions, registered a vast number of new voters in the battleground states. But if Rove's effort registered fewer voters in places, it did a better job of identifying likely supporters and turning them out to vote.

Yet for all Rove's acumen, his 2004 victory has to be regarded as the result of a flawed strategy brilliantly executed. There are few controlled experiments in politics, and as in business, success tends to be treated as conclusive evidence. But a more moderate set of policies and a less political approach to the War on Terror might have resulted in a bigger margin for Bush, and left him in a position to govern effectively in his second term.

Whether or not a more moderate strategy would have worked, Rove's crowning achievement turned out to be a Pyrrhic victory. Second-term blues have afflicted every postwar president, but Bush's were distinctive in how quickly and thoroughly they set in. The president's crude notion of "political capital," which Rove encouraged, meant that after an undisputed victory, Bush was sure to lead off with something large and controversial. As he often repeated, you had to use political capital or lose it, citing his father's ebb in popularity after the first Gulf War as the quintessential illustration. But Bush's version of this theory never made much sense other than as a knock on his dad. "Political capital" is shorthand for the political scientist Richard Neustadt's idea that presidential power is really the power to persuade. Bush never saw it that way. His version took the financial metaphor quite literally. After an election, or when his poll numbers were good, he was flush and therefore free to buy whatever he wanted. Having political capital didn't mean trying to persuade anyone. It was a license to run roughshod over Congress and ignore criticism. Of course, Bush behaved essentially the same way when he wasn't riding high in the polls.

What Bush proposed at the outset of his second term reflected not only his own towering self-confidence and exaggerated sense of a mandate, but also Rove's historically minded ambition. In Rove's view, remaking Social Security around a system of private accounts was the cornerstone of turning the antiquated liberal welfare state into a conservative and individualistic one. It was a big idea that he could count on Bush responding to in much the way he had to the faith-based agenda and the notion of remaking the Middle East. The phrase Bush used to frame his proposal—"the ownership society"—suggested the grandeur of Rove's aspiration. Molding a new relationship between the people and their government on the order of FDR's New Deal or LBJ's Great Society would create a new political model. Workers would come to think of themselves as shareholders and investors, and thus part of the Republican Party's natural base.

What undermined the Bush-Rove Social Security proposal was not the idea of private accounts per se, which could have attracted the support of many Democrats in a less toxic political environment, especially if framed as an add-on to the existing system. What doomed the plan, and with it Bush's entire second-term agenda, was the way he and Rove had bullied both allies and opponents in Congress over the previous four years, and the way they won in 2002 and 2004. Their political style so poisoned the atmosphere as to make negotiation and agreement on major social change impossible. Democrats, who felt burned by Rove's use of terrorism and gay marriage as wedge issues, were in no mood to make a deal with their tormentors. With Bush increasingly unpopular because of Iraq, Democrats sensed political advantage in refusing to work with him, and they hammered it home. By this time, dislike of Bush had collapsed distinctions on the left to an extent that willingness to negotiate with him on Social Security was treated as a form of treason. The Democratic success in blocking privatization of Social Security dashed Bush's hopes of winning other transformational changes on immigration and tax reform, and made plain that he would be essentially a lame duck in domestic and economic policy for his entire second term.

In a similar way, internationalist-minded supporters of both parties who might otherwise have welcomed the president's idealist turn in foreign policy were in no mood to take it seriously. Bush had lost the credibility needed to lead not just because of misrepresentations in the argument for invading Iraq and his mishandling of the occupation, but because of now almost continual revelations about politicization and mismanagement in every corner of Republican-run government. The Social Security defeat was followed by a series of scandals, which usually posited Rove near the center: exposure of Valerie Plame as an undercover CIA agent; FEMA's incompetent response to Hurricane Katrina; Republican fixer Jack Abramoff's shakedown of Indian casino owners; the contracting scandals in Iraq; and the Justice Department's political replacement of federal prosecutors.

Each of these episodes pointed to the inept public administration first glimpsed in the fizzling of Bush's faith-based initiatives. Rove had put hacks everywhere in the name of rewarding constituencies and perpetuating long-term conservative dominance. In one way or another, these fiascoes all pointed to his arrogant political machine. But neither simple incompetence nor excessive politicization quite explains the failures of government in the Bush-Rove era. The breakdown owed something as well to the anti-elitism that was their shared bond and the overarching Republican story of their political era.

Though they did not attack the federal bureaucracy in the frontal way Newt Gingrich did, Bush and Rove had even less affection for bureaucrats, experts, and critics. They regarded federal officialdom and the Washington establishment as snobbish, blinkered, and liberally biased. For Rove, those who ran the government a level down were intellectual inferiors who acted like social superiors. For Bush, they were the internalized parental voice, the people who thought they knew better than he did and had to be proven wrong. It would be hard to find an agency that pressed these buttons more than the CIA, or a person who embodied the type they abhorred more perfectly than Valerie Plame's husband, Joseph Wilson, the vain former ambassador whose criticism of Bush in a *New York Times* op-ed piece touched off the scandal that led to Rove's near-indictment. Bush and Rove didn't hate the *idea* of government. They merely despised the people who do the government's work.

THERE WERE SIGNS that by early 2006 Bush was beginning to recognize the harm that Rove's long-term, "strategic" approach had done to his presidency. As Rove testified again and again to Patrick Fitzgerald's grand jury about his role in the leak of Plame's name—and as Bush came to realize that Rove had misled him about his involvement—the Architect's authority over policy diminished. After Bush replaced Andrew Card in 2006, the new White House chief of staff, Josh Bolten, brought Rove to heel. As the 2006 midterm elections approached, Bush resisted Rove's time-tested base-motivating strategy. On *Fox News Sunday* in May, Chris Wallace asked the first lady about the Marriage Protection Amendment that Rove and congressional Republicans were planning to reintroduce. "I didn't know Karl was an elected official," Laura Bush responded. This marked the first time that she had slapped down Rove—or anyone working for her husband—in public.

Even as the edifice Rove built was crumbling, he continued to argue that realignment was just around the corner. "I believe we are entering a new political system—a new structure in which one party tends to dominate politics, as Democrats did in the New Deal system," he e-mailed a reporter just before the 2006 midterm elections. At a postmortem session in the Oval Office, Rove told Bush that the loss had been a fluke, a matter of bad luck. Had three thousand votes gone the other way in the Montana Senate race, and seventy thousand switched in a dozen congressional districts, the result would have been a Republican victory. The verdict didn't indicate any flaw in his master plan, a case he continued to make after resigning his White House post in August 2007.

It is remotely possible that Rove's realignment theory will be vindicated, that we will one day look back on 2000 as the beginning of a new era of conservative domination. In such a context, the Republican debacle of 2006 might look like the one in the 1974 midterm—an interruption in a longer upsurge resulting from specific causes (Iraq, as opposed to Watergate). That might hold true in a longer perspective even if Democrats recapture the White House in 2008, as they did in 1976. Rove could one day be seen as the visionary behind a grand political transformation, even if Bush is brushed aside as a failed president. Rove played little or no role in the two big policy decisions that caused Bush the greatest harm—the post–September 11 executive power grab and the invasion of Iraq. The argument might be made that the president's bad choices undermined his adviser's brilliant plan, rather than the other way around.

If so, Rove's historical dream would be fulfilled. Mark Hanna died in 1904 but remained a figure of fascination, even as McKinley was dismissed as a mediocrity. Many of his Progressive Era contemporaries recognized Hanna as a brilliant modernizer whose methods had something to teach, notwithstanding his goals. It is not hard to detect a similar undercurrent of envy in the liberal vilification of Rove. More than they ever wanted him frog-marched off to prison, Democrats want their own evil genius. Even Rove's bitterest enemies recognize him as the outstanding political practitioner of his era. Both parties will study his victories and copy his techniques for years to come.

But even if Rove's reputation somehow flourishes, he will have served Bush badly. Rove was devoted enough to gain Bush's trust. He was ruthless and capable enough to win three elections in which Democrats had enormous advantages. But in the end, Rove loved his own scheme even more than the preppie with the tobacco-can imprint on the ass pocket of his jeans. His grandiose historical ambition came at the expense of Bush's best interests. Rove got Bush to the White House, but led him off course and prevented him from recognizing it until his presidency was too broken to fix. His contribution to the Bush Tragedy is substantial. Indeed, there was only one other person—other than the president himself—who was capable of contributing more.

CHAPTER FIVE

The Foremost Hand

You shall be as a father to my youth,
My voice shall sound as you do prompt mine ear,
And I will stoop and humble my intents
To your well-practiced, wise directions.

—HENRY IV, PART 2

—

TOWARD THE END OF *HENRY IV, PART 2,* THE LORD CHIEF JUSTICE receives word of the King's death and ponders what will happen to him when Harry is crowned in his place. As Henry IV's attorney general, the Lord Chief Justice once threw the Prince in prison. He has just tried to arrest Harry's friend Falstaff. Harry's three younger brothers try to console the Lord Chief Justice about his situation, but they're feeling a bit queasy themselves.

Harry enters the rooms. He tells his brothers he isn't going to act like some Turkish sultan and secure the throne by killing them. He intends to be like a father to them as well as an older brother. Hal then casts a cold eye on the Lord Chief Justice and asks whether he should forgive the older man's past treatment of him. In response, the Lord Chief Justice flatters Hal's reformed self-image. If Harry had been his father the King, afflicted by a wayward son who disrespected his authority, wouldn't he have wanted the Lord Chief Justice to perform the difficult task of bringing the boy to heel? And now that he's going to be King himself, won't Harry need precisely this kind of selfless loyalty? In the first signal of Hal's sudden-onset adulthood, he embraces the Lord Chief Justice's argument and says he's putting him in charge of everything. Twice he declares the older man to be his new "father." As he prepares to call Parliament and appoint ministers for his new government, Harry says that under his reign, the Lord Chief Justice "shall have foremost hand" in war and peace. Everyone breathes an enormous sigh of relief; the voice of experience will now guide the callow regent.

Six hundred years later, a similar exhalation was heard in Republican circles when the presumptive nominee named former Defense Secretary Dick Cheney as his running mate. Though George W. Bush had shown unexpected mettle as governor of Texas, he faced doubts about whether he had the knowledge or experience to run America's foreign policy. In a pop quiz posed by a reporter, Bush failed to name the president of Pakistan or recognize the term "Taliban." In the midst of a war in Kosovo, he referred to the locals as "Kosovarians." Alumni of previous administrations traded even more alarming anecdotes. Paul Wolfowitz was stunned to hear Bush ask, in one of his foreign policy tutorials in 1999, whether Germany was in NATO. Cheney embodied the experience and equanimity that characterized 41's handling of the Gulf War and the disintegration of the Soviet empire. He also knew how to run a White House and deal with Congress.

To Bush, Cheney had the advantage of being part of his family circle without the baggage of being too close to his father, personally or politically. If George W. identified Brent Scowcroft with the cautious, realist approach to foreign policy that ended the first Gulf War prematurely, he took Cheney to embody his father's stronger qualities, as manifested in the original decision to attack Saddam. The relationship grew through 1998 and 1999 as the former defense secretary assisted Condi Rice in schooling the governor in foreign policy. Bush found in Cheney the tough-minded approach he was looking for. Like him, Cheney believed in the confident assertion of American power. At a personal level, however, Cheney was anything but assertive; he was seemingly egoless. Feted along with Colin Powell and Norman Schwarzkopf in a ticker-tape parade up Broadway, Cheney was the only hero of the Gulf War not to write a self-glorifying memoir. And Cheney was trustworthy. The soul of discretion, he made clear his loyalties now belonged only to the son. After clinching the nomination in March 2000, Bush asked Cheney if he wanted to be on his list of possible running mates. Cheney said no. Whether this was a heartfelt response or playing hard to get one can only speculate, but Cheney couldn't have flirted more devastatingly. Not wanting the job made him the perfect eunuch to guard the seraglio—a position parallel to that of Warren Christopher, who was playing the vice presidential search role for Al Gore.

Cheney gained more of Bush's confidence in daily conversations about possible running mates through June and into July. Bush told friends that his first choice was Colin Powell. But Powell wouldn't accept. As the other top contenders for the job disgorged their flaws, Cheney himself became more and more alluring. Unlike former Missouri senator Jack Danforth, he didn't patronize Bush as a novice in need of guidance. Unlike Pennsylvania governor Tom Ridge, he didn't raise the hackles of the party's pro-life faction. Unlike Oklahoma governor Frank Keating, who had let a supporter put his children through college, he had no skeletons in his closet. What's more, most of the official contenders were young and vigorous men of ambition. They would have agendas of their own in the White House. Given his cardiac history—three heart attacks, beginning when he was thirty-seven—the fifty-nine-year-old Cheney wouldn't be aiming to succeed him. Like Laura, he would be a contented #2, who wouldn't upstage his #1.

After the selection, George H. W. Bush revealed that while he was delighted with his son's choice, it had not been made on his recommendation. This comment reflects the extent to which Cheney already understood how to game the father-son dynamic to his own advantage. He recognized that the son's quest for paternal approval was in constant conflict with his need to assert independence. To be favored by Dad was crucial, and Cheney worked his friends Baker and Scowcroft to make sure that happened. But to be proposed by his dad would be fatal, and Cheney made sure that didn't happen. The ideal scenario was for the son to come upon the good idea of choosing Cheney on his own, and win his dad's admiration for it. As Robert Draper reports in *Dead Certain*, Karl Rove opposed the choice, arguing that the former defense secretary was seen as his father's man. But here Rove's intrigue against a potential rival for Bush's confidence was too transparent—and his comprehension of the Bush dynamics a bit too crude. Cheney wasn't personally close to his father, or aligned with Bush Senior philosophically in the way Scowcroft and Baker were. His allegiance was transferable.

In asserting influence over Bush, Cheney faced a challenge bigger than Karl Rove's envy. He would have to figure out how to harmonize his presence with that of Condi Rice, who had grown extraordinarily close to the candidate. Rice had become Bush's foreign policy translator. She could explain world affairs to the governor without making him feel bad about what he didn't know. Rice could also vouch for Bush's seriousness with the *Foreign Affairs* crowd. A disciple of Brent Scowcroft who had served as a midlevel official in his father's White House, she knew Bush Senior's world intimately. But unlike her former mentor, she wasn't one of its core components. The consummate protégée, Rice was able to do what she had done so silkily with other powerful mentors. She merged so closely with Bush Junior's views that, as the two evolved together in subsequent years, there was no saying where his ended and hers began.

This mind-meld turned into a foreign policy friendship as close as Scowcroft's with Bush Senior. In the White House, 43 would speak to his national security adviser around eight times a day, more than he did to any other aide. Bush would complain about having to meet with boring foreign leaders; Rice would patiently explain why he had to. After Bush was reelected, Rice was reluctant to abandon her physical proximity to him to become secretary of state. Perhaps because she had no family life, her relationship with the president became her strongest emotional bond. In one of the great Freudian slips ever to occur at a Washington dinner party, Rice referred to George W. as "my husb—." From Foggy Bottom she would write Bush letters, describing what she had done that day. It might seem excessive to say that in Bush's surrogate family, Rice played the role of his lost sister, Robin—if Bush himself didn't use the term "sister" to describe their relationship to other world leaders. Cheney knew better than to challenge this intimate connection and also that he didn't need to. Unlike Rove, Cheney didn't crave personal closeness to Bush. He merely wanted influence, and he understood that where Bush went, Rice would follow.

Another pitfall Cheney had to avoid was conveying any sense that he thought of himself as tutor to the dauphin. Others might depict the relationship that way, but Cheney treated Bush with the respect he had shown the previous presidents he had served. This meant keeping a certain distance. The running mate did not presume to be Bush's buddy. Deference also meant downplaying his role publicly. Cheney, who is congenitally secretive, is more secretive about his conversations with the president than about anything else. But there is every reason to think that even by the time he led the search committee, Cheney's self-abnegation reflected calculation as well as instinct. Seeing how George W. reacted against what he took to be the meddling and condescension of Brent Scowcroft, he made sure to convey the opposite impression. He would hang back, letting Bush come to him. Cheney had figured out how to play on the son's sense of his reborn self, flattering the maturity of his judgment just as the Lord Chief Justice does Prince Hal's. There was no need to spell out the implicit proposition: *You have the self-confidence and inner security to rely on me.*

Bush fell for this elder statesman pitch completely. At the press conference announcing his choice, he pulled one of his father's "Message: I care" moments, explaining his political motivation too well: "It speaks volumes that I'm willing to pick somebody who is as strong a man as he is, that I'm comfortable with having excellence by my side." Bush and Cheney would be collaborators and peers, but with no doubt about who was in charge.

DURING THE POST-ELECTION BATTLE, Cheney had a fourth heart attack at his home in McLean, Virginia. He was rushed to George Washington Hospital, where doctors implanted a state-of-the-art pacemaker and a wire-mesh stent to let blood flow through an occluded coronary artery. Friends and allies looking for an explanation of the extreme positions Cheney has taken in the years since have posited that his health problems might have affected his personality and thinking, as heart bypass surgery sometimes does. Some who worked with him in the Ford and Reagan administrations said that after September 11, they didn't recognize Dick Cheney as the same person. He had become harsher, darker, and more suspicious. Alan Greenspan suggests this sort of mysterious transformation in his memoir, *The Age of Turbulence*. Brent Scowcroft took a similar view. "Dick Cheney I don't know anymore," he told a *New Yorker* reporter in the fall of 2005. You might call this theory the Stent That Invaded Iraq.

But the notion of a changed Cheney is demonstrably wrong. It wasn't Cheney's heart that encouraged Bush in the worst decisions of his presidency: to invade Iraq, to do it with Rumsfeld's inadequate war plan, to suspend habeas corpus for detainees in terrorist cases, push aside the Geneva Conventions, allow intelligence officers and military personnel to engage in torture, or authorize the wiretapping of American citizens without warrants. It was Cheney's head. Those policies, and their negative consequences for American security and stature, all flowed from Cheney's long-standing beliefs about executive power and foreign policy, areas where Bush came to office with little or no understanding of his own. Cheney's mild manner and his association with mainstream Republican politicians and institutions—Gerald Ford, Donald Rumsfeld (in an earlier incarnation), George H. W. Bush, the Republican Study Group in the House, and the American Enterprise Institute (also in an earlier incarnation)—misled some people about his politics. When he was in Congress, a *Washington Post* story described Cheney as a "moderate." The congressman asked an aide to correct the paper's error.

Cheney's views have not moved in more than thirty years. He developed his political philosophy while working in the Ford administration, where he found himself defending presidential prerogatives in the wake of Watergate, and opposing Kissinger's policy of détente. In his mind, the two ideas were closely related; Cheney advocated a view of executive and military power robust enough to defend the nation from communism and, later, terrorism. This bred a view of the world that is anti-elitist, but in a way different from Bush's or Rove's anti-elitism. Where Bush reacts against intellectual pretension and Rove against class snobbery, Cheney believes in *la trahison des clercs*, the notion that intellectuals are irresponsible and do not take fundamental threats to freedom seriously.

To understand Cheney's philosophy, it helps to know a bit of his biography. The descendant of homesteaders on both sides, he was the oldest of three children born into a Democratic, middle-class family in Lincoln, Nebraska. His father, a man said to have been even more monosyllabic than his son, worked a desk job in the Soil Conservation Service, a branch of the Agriculture Department. When Dick was a teenager in the 1950s, he and his family moved to Casper, Wyoming—like Midland, Texas, an oil boom town amid a desolate expanse. At Natrona High School, he was captain of the football team and senior class president. By the time he graduated, he was dating the homecoming queen, Lynne Vincent, who came from a middle-class, public service background similar to his own.

Lynne was capable, shrewd, and seemingly more ambitious than Dick. She got her boyfriend into Yale by introducing him to Thomas Stroock, a local lawyer in whose office she had a part-time job. Back in 1959, Stroock had only to call the admissions office to get Cheney and another promising football player from Natrona High School in with full scholarships.

By the time he got to Yale, Cheney's personality was already well formed. He was taciturn and unflappable—a Western type who loved fishing, hunting, and wide-open spaces. "He never talked much," his wife, Lynne, told a reporter, describing his demeanor around the time of the first Gulf War. "But he is even quieter now." Ken Adelman, a former Reagan administration arms control official who was one of Cheney's closest friends until Adelman began criticizing the Bush administration's management of the Iraq War, said that for years he begged Cheney to take him on a fly-fishing trip in Wyoming. Cheney refused on the grounds that Adelman talks too much. In this sense, Cheney's obsession with secrecy reflects not just his beliefs, but his nature. He needs no excuse not to gab.

At Yale, Cheney was unhappy from the first. He didn't know what he was doing there, didn't fit in easily, and missed his girlfriend, who was at the University of Colorado. After his first year, his grades weren't good enough for him to maintain his financial aid and he had to resort to loans. At the end of his sophomore year, Yale told him not to come back at all. It's not entirely clear what went wrong. Cheney has alluded to being disorganized and having too good a time. Though his idea of a good time lacked the exuberance of Bush's at Yale a few years later, the notion that he had a beverage problem is substantiated by two drunk driving arrests in his early twenties. Two comments—"I didn't relate to Yale at all" and "I didn't like the East"—are about as far as he's gone in explaining the underlying issue.

Cheney returned to Wyoming, where he enrolled in Casper Community College and worked as part of a construction crew laying power transmission lines. With a prod from Lynne, whom he married in 1964, he transferred to the University of Wyoming, where he got his BA in political science. He stayed on for a master's degree while working as an intern for Republicans in the state legislature. Cheney got out of Wyoming with the help of a prize-winning essay he wrote about his experience in the statehouse. This led to a grander internship with Warren Knowles, the governor of Wisconsin.

Dick and Lynne both enrolled in the University of Wisconsin, where he studied for a Ph.D. in political science and she worked on her English dissertation about Kant's influence on Matthew Arnold. Lynne's pregnancy with their first daughter, Elizabeth (b. 1966), qualified him for a family hardship deferment until he was too old to be drafted. Like Bush, Cheney objected to serving personally in Vietnam, but did not oppose the war itself. He reacted strongly, however, to the antiwar protests in Madison, which sometimes blocked the young father, who had become quite serious about his studies, from getting to his classes.

Given the subject of Cheney's thesis—using computer models to find patterns in congressional roll call voting—one can understand why he found the live observation of politics more appealing. Thanks to a fellowship from the American Political Science Association, he won an internship in Washington, working in the office of Representative William Steiger, a rising Republican star from Oshkosh then completing his first term. Elected in 1966 at the age of twenty-eight, the congressman was only a couple of years older than Cheney—and only forty when his promising career was cut short by a fatal heart attack.

Steiger was friends with the biggest friend-maker in his big class of Republican freshmen, Poppy Bush. An issue Bush and Steiger were already discussing when Cheney arrived on Capitol Hill in 1969 was the antiwar movement on campus. Bush Senior was especially incensed about protests at Yale, where his oldest son was graduating that same year. The issue fell under the jurisdiction of the House Health, Education and Welfare Committee on which Steiger served. Bush and Steiger planned to co-sponsor a bill that would cut off funds to universities that tolerated violent protests. Cheney organized a tour for the two congressmen to observe the worst of the campus unrest. At Madison, where Cheney was on hiatus, the three found themselves the only men in suits at an SDS rally. They were also allowed to audit a faculty meeting. The episode seems to have played a part in the development of Cheney's anti-elitism. The young aide, who had been planning to return to Wisconsin to finish his thesis, was disgusted by the apathy of liberal academics in the face of the crisis.

Cheney's hiatus from academia became permanent after he went to work for another young GOP hotshot by the name of Don Rumsfeld. As a member of Congress, the former fighter pilot had backed Gerald Ford's effort to depose the ineffectual "Two Cadillac Charlie" Halleck as House minority leader. The coup succeeded, but the enemies Rumsfeld made in the House Republican Caucus blocked his ambitions to become Republican whip. So in early 1971, Rumsfeld approached President Nixon about an executive branch job. Nixon, who admired Rumsfeld's ambition and cunning, offered him the position of special assistant to the president and chairman of the Office of Economic Opportunity. When Rumsfeld asked Steiger for advice about whom to hire, Cheney volunteered and wrote an unsolicited twelve-page memo about the OEO based on his experience with the Health, Education and Welfare Committee. Steiger passed the memo to Rumsfeld. Rumsfeld, who had been totally unimpressed by Cheney in an earlier interview, now offered him the quintessential behind-the-scenes Washington job of special assistant.

Rumsfeld's and Cheney's careers would remain so intertwined that it is impossible to understand one without the other. To succeed as Rumsfeld's co-pilot, the young aide had to develop a valuable skill: the ability to subordinate his own ego and image to those of his aggressive, self-promoting boss. The tongue-tied young Cheney was perfectly suited to this role—and for the student of politics, there was no better perch. Though they would cease speaking for several years after Cheney declined to endorse Rumsfeld's abortive 1988 presidential bid, and though Rumsfeld would eventually go from Cheney protector to Cheney protectorate, the alliance between the two men was still in force thirty-five years later.

The Office of Economic Opportunity was the lead agency in LBJ's War on Poverty, disobligingly inherited by Nixon. For the ambitious Rumsfeld and his omnipresent sidekick, it presented the challenge of how to succeed by failing. Both did their best to prevent the agency from serving Democratic interests or satisfying liberal critics. But running a liberal agency made Rumsfeld temporarily liberal. In his non-

OEO capacity, Rumsfeld let it be known that he was encouraging Nixon to end the Vietnam War more quickly. Managing a lefty bureaucracy pointed Cheney further away from the spirit of the times. The experience deepened his aversion to the elitists he had encountered at Yale and Wisconsin. But Cheney's primary perspective was pragmatic, not ideological. Working under Rumsfeld, he learned how to get things done in Washington and avoid having them done to you.

After two years, Nixon moved Rumsfeld to a similar hardship post implementing his wage and price controls. Rumsfeld took the job stipulating that he was a free-marketer who didn't believe in the policy. That was fine—no one else did either. Cheney now managed the hopelessly ineffective Cost of Living Council. When Nixon talked Rumsfeld into becoming ambassador to NATO in 1973, Cheney left to advise corporations about the ways of Washington. Both men were lucky to get out of the White House just as the Watergate investigation was gathering steam. As soon as Nixon resigned, Gerald Ford asked his friend Rumsfeld to head his instant transition, which meant Cheney resuming his old role. Cheney's Secret Service code name in the Ford White House was "backseat," which caught the essence of his powerful but deferential role.

His loyal service was soon rewarded. One of Rumsfeld's Rules—a self-aggrandizing anthology of bureaucratic wisdom, half Machiavelli, half *Poor Richard's Almanac*—was always to have a successor ready to take over your job. When Rumsfeld finally persuaded Ford to move him to the Defense Department, Cheney became, at thirty-four, the youngest chief of staff in the history of the presidency. He had risen from intern to the most powerful staff job in Washington in six years.

WHILE AMERICA SLEPT through the Ford years, Cheney was developing his reputation for administrative skill and the views on executive power and national security that have guided him ever since. Their original context was the Republican reaction to the Democratic reaction to Watergate. In 1974, Democrats swept the election three months after Nixon's resignation. In the House, they gained 49 seats, obtaining a 291–144 majority. In the Senate, their new majority was a filibuster-proof 61–38. With the Vietnam War winding down, the largest issue confronting the Watergate babies in the new Congress was how to roll back what Arthur Schlesinger termed "the Imperial Presidency." This movement—which began while Nixon was still in office—produced a raft of hearings and reform legislation intended to restrain the executive and redress the imbalance of power between the branches. The moment led to the War Powers Act, which attempted to give meaning to Congress's constitutional authority to declare war, the Church and Pike committee hearings on abuses by the CIA, the Foreign Intelligence Surveillance Act of 1978, the Freedom of Information Act, and the Presidential Records Act.

Working first with Rumsfeld, then on his own, Cheney resisted this movement as an unwarranted power grab and an assault on the proper separation and balance of powers. With Ford further weakened by his two unpopular pardons—of the ex-president and the Vietnam draft-resisters—the fight between Congress and the White House turned bitter. Cheney and Rumsfeld encouraged Ford to treat the War Powers Act as an unconstitutional usurpation of power by simply ignoring it. Ford did so in the *Mayaguez* incident, when he launched a rescue of passengers and crew aboard a military vessel seized by Cambodia without notifying Congress. Cheney and Rumsfeld engineered the resignation of CIA director William Colby, whom they thought too accommodating toward the Church Committee. They sealed the CIA's "family jewels," the fruits of an internal investigation into activities violating the agency's charter, in a vault. And they continued to assert Nixon's dubious doctrine of executive privilege, carving out a Freedom of Information Act exemption for the White House.

Historically, the argument for a powerful chief executive is no more conservative than it is liberal. In practice, every American president has asserted his constitutional authority relative to Congress, regardless of party. Through most of the twentieth century, Republicans resisted expansions of domestic and military authority by Democratic presidents. But when a Republican was in the White House, conservatives became friendlier to the idea of executive power. In championing the executive branch in the 1970s, Cheney was at the leading edge of a movement that would blossom under Reagan. Republicans wanted to bring more power to the presidency and the states, where they ruled, and take it away from Congress and the courts, where they didn't, and didn't expect to. Ensconced in the West Wing, Cheney forgot about his computer models and began developing an argument about how the federal government should work. "Restoring Executive Power" became his great unpublished thesis.

It would be unlike Dick Cheney to lay out directly the philosophy of government he was developing. In Wyoming, it's the women who are the talkers. The clearest expression of what Dick learned during the Ford years comes through the curious vehicle of his wife, Lynne's, literary career, which she pursued while staying home with their two young daughters. The novel of Lynne Cheney's that has attracted the most attention is the one with a wagon-train lesbian theme, *Sisters* (1981), published only in Canada, which she has not allowed to be reprinted. ("She took off her dress, her petticoat, her corset, her stockings. Even her lacy undershift and drawers were wet, clinging to her body before she stripped them off . . .") The only novel of hers that sold at all was the comedy *Body Politic* (1988), which she co-wrote with Spiro Agnew's former press secretary Vic Gold, whose previous project was ghostwriting George H. W. Bush's campaign autography, *Looking Forward*. In it, a malignant vice president closely modeled on Nelson Rockefeller dies in flagrante, and the White House chief of staff contrives to keep his death secret for reasons too absurd to explain.

But it is in the first and least cringe-inducing of his wife's three attempts at fiction, *Executive Privilege* (1978), that Cheney's political theory comes through. This may be the only potboiler ever written to promulgate the doctrine of separated powers. Along the way it captures other ideas her husband had developed by that point—the need for executive branch secrecy, the incompetence of the CIA, the media's ruthlessness, and the acceptability of official lying in a good cause. The clunky exposition of these ideas is relieved by a shapely minx from the weekly *Newstime* who aspires to bed her boss.

The plot turns on a leak of the Oval Office visitor logs. Someone (who turns out to be the evil vice president—this is Lynne's literary crutch) has revealed to *The Washington Post* how the president spends his time over the course of a week. This leads to a Watergate-style scandal when President Jenner, a sort of Ford-Cheney mash-up, entangles himself in deception to save the life of a Catholic priest in the Philippines who hopes to overthrow Ferdinand Marcos. Jenner's Oval Office soliloquies sound rather like the after-work musings of the author's husband:

> I have a right to confidentiality from the press just as much as from Congress and the Courts. . . . How can I expect the discussions in this office to be open and free if everyone has to sit around and worry about how his words will look on the front page of the *Post*? . . . As I think back on the other men who've worked in this room, it seems to me that the history of the presidency in the twentieth century is the history of a gradually weakening institution. . . . What happens in the next crisis like this, or the next after that, if we let this office grow weaker until it doesn't have any kind of moral force?

Dick Cheney's ideas about the need for executive power emerged in tandem with strong views on how that power should be used in relation to the Soviet Union. On Ford's orders, Rumsfeld and Cheney at first left foreign policy to Henry Kissinger, who had unprecedented authority as both secretary of state and national security adviser. But over the course of their first year, the duo took on Kissinger and his moderate ally, Vice President Nelson Rockefeller. For Rumsfeld this was partly a matter of personal ambition; he was courting the Republican right wing and angling to replace Rockefeller on the ticket in 1976. For Cheney, it was a question of conviction; he opposed détente with the Soviets and was a skeptic of the arms control agreements Kissinger was trying to negotiate. Though they were loyal to Ford, Cheney and Rumsfeld were by the end of his administration closer to the views of Ronald Reagan, who was challenging Ford in the primaries. As deputy chief of staff, Cheney didn't succeed in getting Ford to invite Aleksandr Solzhenitsyn to the White House. But as chief of staff, he persuaded Ford to drop his challenge to the "morality in foreign policy" platform plank proposed by Reagan's supporters. At the time, the notion of injecting a moral dimension into foreign policy stood in opposition to Kissinger's realism. The adoption of the plank spelled the demise of Kissinger's influence in the GOP and the end of détente.

Cheney's hawkish critique of Kissinger's policy blossomed into a wider obsession with threats to American security and the growing conviction that hardly anyone took them seriously enough. He and Rumsfeld encouraged Ford to lean on his new CIA chief, George H. W. Bush, to authorize the Team B exercise of 1975, a reexamination by outside experts of the CIA's conclusions about Soviet nuclear capability and intentions. This was the first big moment of the neoconservatives. Team B was headed by Richard Pipes, a hawkish Soviet expert at Harvard. On the recommendation of Richard Perle, Pipes hired the young Paul Wolfowitz as a member of the staff. Both the personnel and the approach of the Team B group prefigured what happened in 2002 with intelligence about the Iraqi threat. In its classified report, Team B reached darker conclusions about Soviet power and intentions than the CIA had: The Soviets were much stronger militarily than the United States believed, and their leaders meant what they said about spreading socialism. In the event of war with the West, they intended to use nuclear weapons. Team B was more wrong than right in its analysis of the Warsaw Pact's military capabilities. From the point of view of its participants, however, the results were vindicated when the Berlin Wall came down. Taking the communist threat more seriously had helped unmake the Soviet empire.

After Jimmy Carter was elected, Cheney returned home. He

didn't want to challenge Alan Simpson for the Senate in 1978, so he looked instead to the House, where Wyoming has only a single seat. In justifying his interest in the race, he faced the opposite problem from George W. Bush, running against Kent Hance in Texas's 19th District the same year: instead of too green, he looked overqualified. After serving as White House chief of staff, seeking a return to Washington as a freshman member of the minority party seemed like requesting a demotion.

Running for the House made more sense in the context of Cheney's emulation of his mentor. Rumsfeld treated his having been elected to Congress as a distinguishing qualification in the Nixon and Ford cabinets. It was what made him qualified for any job on the planet. Cheney thought winning an election would help him shake the stigma of "staff guy" and establish him as an independent political actor. What's more, there was no better offer on the table. Despite having his first heart attack in the middle of the campaign, he won the race by a comfortable margin.

In Congress, Cheney remained a political scientist. He spent most evenings at home with Lynne working on *Kings of the Hill*, a study of eight speakers of the house from Henry Clay to Sam Rayburn. The book might have been called *Legislative Power*. Though less spicy than Lynne's novels, it too embodied a curious, ideologically tinted view of the branch he now served in. Cheney saw Congress's role as blocking the growth of domestic government—something it has seldom been good at. When the legislative branch functioned properly, he argued, it served the public good by impeding rash and wasteful action, and by preventing special interests from getting their way. But without strong leadership from the speaker's chair—the situation Cheney observed in the 1980s under Tip O'Neill—what James Madison called the "mischief of faction" would be left to run amok.

This research had applied value as well. Cheney used what he learned about the intricacies of precedent and procedure to move up the House hierarchy. At the beginning of his second term in 1985, he was elected chairman of the Republican Policy Committee, the number four spot in the leadership. In 1988, he rose to minority whip, the number two post, and the one Rumsfeld had aimed for and not gotten. This was a symbolically important moment in their relationship. Rumsfeld was stuck in Chicago, where he had returned to take a job running Searle Pharmaceutical. He had lost out in 1980 when Reagan chose his rival George H. W. Bush as his running mate. He lost out again when another nemesis, Al Haig, blocked his path to any top-level administration job. Now his protégé, Cheney—who had declined to endorse his presidential campaign—was rising ahead of him. It would take Rumsfeld a while to get over this.

Cheney cut an unusual figure in Congress. He was in a way a figure from a different era, someone who cared more about his influence than public attention. And while he sought personal power within Congress, he wanted to take constitutional authority away from it. From the other side of the fence, Cheney continued to press his Ford administration arguments that the legislative branch shouldn't interfere with presidential prerogatives or covert action. When it came to the Reagan Doctrine of rolling back communist expansion in places like Angola and Nicaragua, Cheney didn't stop at supporting the president's foreign policy. He opposed Congress's authority to challenge it through measures like the Boland Amendment, which forbade funding to the anticommunist contra rebels.

It was during his congressional period that Cheney began his long association with David Addington, the secretive aide who has been called "Cheney's Cheney." Addington, who had grown up in Montana, worked as a lawyer at the CIA under William Casey from 1981 until 1984. He joined the minority staff of the Intelligence Committee while Cheney was chairman. Over the years, he would become Cheney's most trusted and influential staff member, relating to him in much the way Cheney had related to Rumsfeld. Addington was disciplined, diligent, and ferociously conservative. He became ubiquitous while staying invisible, all the more powerful because he didn't want any credit.

Addington helped to shape a document Cheney has cited as the major expression of his views on presidential power, the Republican dissent from the Iran-contra investigating committee. The 1987 Minority Report is a broadside in favor of unfettered presidential authority in foreign policy and an attack on congressional interference. At its core is a long essay arguing for an executive as the constitutional "sole organ" in foreign affairs, a phrase from the 1936 Supreme Court decision in the *Curtiss-Wright* case. It quotes extensively from a historical document central to Cheney's framework: *The Federalist* No. 70 by Alexander Hamilton. In it, Hamilton uses the famous phrase "energy in the executive." A powerful executive, Hamilton argues, is "essential to the protection of the community against foreign attacks." Dick Cheney updated Hamilton in language that might have been borrowed from Lynne's novel *Executive Privilege*. "The country needs a President who can exercise the powers the Framers intended," the report declares. "As long as any President has those powers, there will be mistakes. It would be disastrous to respond to the possibility of error by further restraining and limiting the powers of office. Then, instead of seeing occasional actions turn out to be wrong, we would be increasing the probability that future Presidents would be unable to act decisively, thus guaranteeing ourselves a perpetually paralyzed, reactive, and unclear foreign policy in which mistake by inaction would be the order of the day."

Cheney's critics, who have a tendency to make his views into a caricature, would later fasten on one phrase in the report: "the Chief Executive will on occasion feel duty bound to assert monarchical notions of prerogative that will permit him to exceed the law." But this is ripped from its context in a way that reverses its intended meaning. In that passage, the Minority Report is rejecting, not defending, an argument Thomas Jefferson made in support of his decision to negotiate the Louisiana Purchase without consulting the Senate. Jefferson argued that the president sometimes has to ignore the written law to protect the country. The authors of the Minority Report counter that only Hamilton's idea of a strong executive can prevent the president from sometimes ignoring the Constitution and behaving like a king in foreign affairs. The full sentence reads: "To the extent that the Constitution and laws are read narrowly, as Jefferson wished, the Chief Executive will on occasion feel duty bound to assert monarchical notions of prerogative that will permit him to exceed the law." In other words, Cheney and Addington wanted to give the president enough power that he wouldn't feel obliged to steal any.

The rest of the Iran-contra Committee Minority Report is a diatribe against involvement in foreign affairs by the legislative branch, which it describes as meddlesome, vacillating, and untrustworthy. The report contends that the fundamental problem in the scandal was not the Reagan administration's clandestine support for the contras, but the Boland Amendment, which prohibited such aid. In the view of Cheney and his colleagues, Reagan was legitimately frustrated with a Democratic Congress that didn't take seriously Soviet expansion in Central America and was constantly infringing on his constitutional powers and undermining covert ops by leaking details to the press. The report becomes most energetic in denouncing Congress for failing to protect classified information. It ends with recommendations about dealing with the *real* problem, namely congressional leaking. New rules should curtail congressional access to national security secrets, and more severely punish those who reveal them, including members of the press. Cheney also wanted to give presidents a line-item veto to block Boland-like attempts to limit their foreign policymaking power.

Cheney developed these themes further in a speech entitled "Congressional Overreaching in Foreign Policy," which he presented at an American Enterprise Institute conference in March 1989. He argued that Congress's vacillation and indecision left it "ill equipped to handle many of the foreign policy tasks it has been taking upon itself lately." These tasks included diplomacy, where congressional Democrats had tried to force Reagan to abide by the unratified SALT II arms control treaty; covert operations, where they had leaked information from classified briefings; and military action, where they tried to override the president's constitutional authority with the War Powers Act.

In Cheney's view, the legislative branch was built for comfort, the executive for speed. "At its best Congress is a deliberative body whose internal checks and balances favor delay as a method of stimulating compromise," he noted. "At its worst, it is a collection of 535 individual, separately elected politicians, each of whom seeks to claim credit and avoid blame." The presidency, by contrast, "was designed as a one-person office to ensure that it would be ready for action." Cheney's AEI speech is notable for its repeated reference to the "inherent" as opposed to the "express" powers of the presidency. Congress, Cheney said, could not use legislation to limit "the scope of the inviolable powers inherent in the presidential office." In the George W. Bush years, this wee term "inherent" would assume gigantic proportions.

In articulating his idea of the presidency, Cheney again cited his favorite *Federalist* letter, No. 70, and its argument that the characteristics of the executive branch were "decision, activity, secrecy and dispatch." Hamilton's string of nouns encapsulates the executive vision Cheney brought to the Bush White House. Cheney's notion of a strong president and a weak Congress was in some sense an artifact of a historical period in which Democrats seemed to be the permanent rulers of Congress and Republicans dominated the White House. Cheney and his allies didn't want the legislative branch Lilliputians (who happened to be Democrats) to tie down Gulliver (who happened to be a Republican). But Cheney showed that his view was a principled one when circumstances changed. He didn't modify his constitutional theory to take the side of the Gingrich Congress in its foreign policy tussles with Bill Clinton.

The need for executive power to protect the nation's security was not bloodless theory to Cheney. Through the Reagan years, he participated alongside Rumsfeld in secret "continuity of government" exercises that gave vivid dimension to the potential need for extra-constitutional action in defense of the country. As described by James Mann in *The Rise of the Vulcans*, these elaborate scenarios modeled the way the government might function in case of a Soviet nuclear attack that took out the president and vice president. Participants on three teams would be dispatched in the middle of the night from Andrews

Air Force Base to military bunkers—secure, undisclosed locations—where they would practice running the remains of the country. What's significant about Cheney's participation in these war games is the way they immersed someone whose outlook revolved around security threats in fantasies about the destruction of the country. When Cheney said in his appearance on *Meet the Press*, five days after September 11, that American intelligence would have to cross over to "the dark side," he was referring to a place he had visited before.

AFTER FORD LEFT OFFICE, Cheney maintained his relationships with Brent Scowcroft, who had been Ford's national security adviser, and James Baker, whom he had hired to help run Ford's unsuccessful reelection campaign. Cheney and Baker became hunting and fishing buddies during the Carter years. When George H. W. Bush's nomination of John Tower to be secretary of defense ran into trouble in 1989 because of revelations about Tower's boozing and lechery, Scowcroft and Baker, now working for Bush, called Cheney to the White House for advice about a substitute. In a pattern that would be repeated, Cheney counseled them without expressing overt interest in the job himself. Naturally, he left the meeting as their preferred choice.

Cheney's Capitol Hill colleagues liked him enough that his Senate confirmation was a formality. The only objection to his nomination barely rated a mention in *The New York Times*. Robert Byrd, the long-winded West Virginia senator, rose to challenge Cheney's view that the president didn't have to notify Congress about covert action. ("On the scale of risks," Cheney had said in his AEI speech, "I am more concerned about depriving the President of his ability to act than I am about Congress's alleged inability to respond.") The press has been blamed for many failings in covering the Bush administration. But perhaps the most egregious was neglecting to explain during the 2000 campaign something that hundreds of conservative intellectuals understood: Cheney's radical ideas about presidential power. At times, Presidents Ford, George H. W. Bush, and Clinton all invoked executive privilege in the inevitable scuffles with Congress. Abraham Lincoln, Woodrow Wilson, and Franklin Roosevelt asserted extraordinary powers in wartime. But not until the second Bush did the argument for an inherent and all-encompassing commander-in-chief authority become an explicit theory of presidential action.

In the first Bush administration, Cheney's extreme views on executive power were obscured by his position at the Defense Department. He felt strongly that 41 should not go to Congress to request a resolution to push Saddam Hussein out of Kuwait, because it would imply he needed permission to act. But Bush disagreed and the congressional vote to authorize the war closed the question. At Defense, the more urgent issues were budgetary and managerial. Cheney proved a skillful manager despite his lack of military background. He installed Addington as his gatekeeper and asserted his authority over the brass. Most notably, he accepted the inevitable post–Cold War spending cuts without too much fuss.

Cheney collected the peace dividend without accepting the premise that the Soviets were washed up. The defense secretary's refusal to accept victory in the Cold War became a running joke in the first Bush's administration. Colin Powell, whom Cheney named to head the Joint Chiefs of Staff, performed a comic riff about his boss carrying on about "the bear" rising from slumber. In the spring of 1990, CIA chairman William Webster called Soviet reforms "irreversible." After Cheney responded by predicting that Mikhail Gorbachev would fail and be replaced by a traditional, anti-Western leader, Bush had to make plain that he disagreed with his defense chief. "Dick Cheney was negative," Brent Scowcroft and George H. W. Bush write in *A World Transformed*. "He believed that it was premature to relax Cold-War style pressure." As the Soviet Union's collapse became undeniable, the internal debate turned to one in which Cheney and his policy planning chief, Paul Wolfowitz, argued for accelerating it by embracing Boris Yeltsin while James Baker (who carried the day) argued for promoting stability by sticking with Gorbachev.

When Saddam invaded Kuwait, all the Bush players assumed their regular battle stations. Baker advocated diplomacy, Powell his famous doctrine of going big or staying home, Scowcroft drawing a line in the sand, and Cheney a blunt assertion of American power. But Cheney never fit the personality stereotype associated with hawks. He was comfortable having his subordinate, Powell, become the big media celebrity in the run-up to the war. It's hard to imagine a Donald Rumsfeld ever standing for this. Where Cheney rebuked Powell was for exceeding his authority in raising the question of whether liberating Kuwait was worth the cost and making his case for a continued strategy of "containment" directly to the president. This was both a procedural issue about civilian control of the military and a substantive one about how to respond. The defense of the Arabian oilfields was historically a high defense priority for the United States. Cheney, again bolstered by Wolfowitz, thought that if Saddam wasn't forced out of Kuwait, he would soon be beyond the reach of sanctions. Oil would make him so powerful that the rest of the world would appease him. Bush sided with Cheney (and Scowcroft) when he ordered the deployment of 425,000 troops to the Persian Gulf.

As part of the buildup, Cheney—assisted by Paul Wolfowitz's deputy and fellow neoconservative I. Lewis "Scooter" Libby—became immersed in a study of Saddam's biological and chemical weapons programs. Saddam at that time really did have stores of anthrax, botulinum toxin, and VX nerve agent. He had used sarin and mustard gas in the Iran-Iraq War and against Kurdish civilians in his own country just two years earlier, in 1988. Supporters and opponents of the war alike feared that Saddam would deploy these horrifying weapons against U.S. troops. As secretary of defense, Cheney now confronted the issue of how to protect American forces and deal with the contingency of a chemical or biological attack against Israel. In the event, Saddam did not use weapons of mass destruction, but Cheney was left with vivid imaginings about what might have happened if he had.

With the Gulf War concluded, discussion inside the administration turned to the question of what the world might look like after the Cold War. Much of the debate took place around the development of a policy document known as Defense Planning Guidance. The 1992 version was drafted by Scooter Libby and Libby's aide Zalmay Khalilzad. It made a bold case for the post–Cold War world as one in which the United States dominated as sole superpower. The classified, study, which was leaked in draft form to *The New York Times*, proposed extending American security commitments to the new democracies of Eastern Europe. Its most controversial suggestion was that the United States should project enough military might to discourage any possible rivals to its global hegemony. Cheney had not driven this conclusion, but he agreed with it. In private discussions, he embraced the notion of a Pax Americana established through unchallenged military supremacy in a unipolar world.

After Bush left office, Cheney briefly indulged the fantasy of turning his Gulf War celebrity into a presidential run. He put Addington in charge of his political action committee and began raising money. But he soon recognized that his lack of charisma and distaste for public performance were insurmountable obstacles. Cheney was more comfortable padding the corridors at the American Enterprise Institute, where he took up scholarly residence alongside his wife.

Though AEI had its roots in the mild, corporate Republicanism of the Ford administration, it had by 1993 tilted in a neoconservative direction. Cheney himself wasn't a neocon. He had not started out on the left, he wasn't Jewish, and he approached foreign policy as a nationalist hawk, not a freedom-sowing idealist. But his infrequent public comments increasingly reflected the company he kept with AEI fellows like Richard Perle and his friend Ken Adelman. As he had with Wolfowitz and Libby at the Pentagon, Cheney found himself agreeing with the neoconservatives about most things. His exposure to their ideas continued after he became CEO of Halliburton at venues like AEI's annual World Leaders Forum in Beaver Creek, Colorado, where former President Ford had a ski chalet. The signatures of Cheney and Rumsfeld appeared alongside familiar neoconservative names like Wolfowitz, Libby, Elliott Abrams, Norman Podhoretz, and Midge Decter on the statement of principles promulgated by the newly formed Project for the New American Century in 1997, which called for "a Reaganite policy of military strength and moral clarity."

But on one subject, Cheney and the neocons did not agree. The neoconservatives constantly argued that stopping the Gulf War after just one hundred hours with Saddam still in power—a decision they blamed on Colin Powell—had been a strategic and moral blunder. They contended that the United States had betrayed Kurdish and Shi'ite rebels, who had been massacred after Norman Schwarzkopf allowed Saddam's helicopter gunships freedom of the skies. Cheney didn't accept this critique. Rumsfeld's name, but not his, appeared on a subsequent Project for the New American Century letter to Clinton calling for the removal of Saddam. Nonetheless, the judgment must have weighed on Cheney's conscience.

HOW DID DICK CHENEY get George W. Bush to make him the most powerful vice president in the history of the office? Despite considerable effort by our finest journalists, we know nothing about how he sold the policies that embodied his views on executive power and foreign policy to the president. The crucial transactions have taken place behind closed doors, in meetings with no other participants. Given Cheney's mania for confidentiality, Bush's poor memory for facts and dates (as opposed to names and faces), and the administration's aversion to documentation and public information, we may never know what happened. The dining room adjacent to the Oval Office where Cheney and Bush hold their private lunch meetings is our political era's Chamber of Secrets. We know who went into the room and we know what came out. We can only hypothesize, however, about what happened inside.

Any theory seeking to explain how Cheney persuaded Bush will have to include a political psychology of their relationship. Here's mine: In the course of the 2000 campaign, Cheney came to understand himself and Bush clearly. He saw his own strengths and limitations plainly. He was someone who could weather a campaign, but the life of a politician was not for him. Cheney hated performing in front of an audience, and had no facility for it. He was uncomfortable with the pressure to reveal his feelings and talk about his family. And he didn't think voters would elect a cardiac cripple. But there was something Cheney could do better than anyone: run the show from behind the scenes. He knew where the invisible levers were and how to pull them. So he would have to fulfill his ambitions indirectly, something he was disposed to by nature and habit anyway. Cheney really was that rare creature, often spoken of but seldom seen in Washington, who could get things done because he didn't care about getting credit.

By inauguration day, Cheney had mastered, perhaps with some help from his wife the novelist, the subject most critical to his success: the mind of George W. Bush. An understanding of Bush's narcissism was the tool he used to "manage up" so brilliantly. Cheney stoked Bush's anti-elitism and hostility to the press. (Bush: "There's Adam Clymer—major league asshole—from *The New York Times.*" Cheney: "Yeah, big time.") He pricked Bush's obsession with disloyalty and showboating by aides and cabinet officers, drawing an ongoing contrast with his eternally confidential, mumbly wisdom. He soothed his sensitivities. Cheney saw that Bush, like his father, wanted to believe his choices were pure, "the right thing to do." But most important, Cheney appreciated, in a way more subtle than Rove did, the way in which Bush needed to make himself his father's antithesis.

When it came to domestic and economic policy, George W. had already figured out how to distinguish himself from his dad. But in foreign policy, the area where his father excelled, the son was still struggling. Cheney figured out how to frame choices for Bush around contrasts to his father's views, without couching them as explicit criticisms of the old man. Cheney knew better than to say that abrogating the ABM treaty was a reversal of his father's policy. He'd say it was the decision Reagan would have made. Cheney learned to get at this with 43's own shorthand. Describe something as what Bush denigrated as "small ball"—cautious, incremental, or involving complicated trade-offs—and it was as good as dead, because it sounded like 41. But present an idea as bold, game-changing, and the right thing to do, Cheney told Rumsfeld (who passed the wisdom on to Colin Powell), and the sale was half made. By flattering the younger Bush's Oedipal complex in this way, Cheney became the latest in Bush's series of surrogate family members—the hawk as substitute father.

Cheney knew that Bush Senior had wanted to hear all opposing sides of an argument, to gather as much information as possible. He was comfortable withholding his own views in order to encourage a fuller debate. The elder Bush would agonize over difficult decisions for weeks or months, sometimes change his mind, and occasionally even acknowledge error. On foreign policy, 41 filtered advice through Scowcroft, a trusted, honest broker. Cheney recognized the way in which Bush 43 saw this decision-making model as emblematic of his father's reactive style, his lack of vision, and his aversion to conflict and risk. George W. even had a name for the judgments reached too methodically. He called them "process decisions." In retaliation, the son made himself into the most decisive executive of all time—the Decider, in the brilliant nickname he bestowed upon himself when defending his decision not to fire Rumsfeld in 2006.

This Bush did not want to host debates in his office or hear a range of opinions. He would begin a foreign policy discussion by stating his own views—and would bristle if someone had the temerity to challenge them. He did not intend to use his national security adviser as a filter for differing opinions. He definitely didn't want to read long, boring memos. Bush was the first president to have graduated from business school, but his management model was like a parody of a bigwig executive's attitude. He believed in making big decisions quickly and firmly, delegating all details and implementation. He rejected rethinking, micromanaging, or getting too absorbed in details. He also took the term "management style" a bit too literally, treating businesslike comportment (his answer to his father's good manners as well as to Clinton's undiscipline) as centrally important. Bush was fanatically punctual, always wore a coat and tie in the Oval Office, and pointedly called out the rudeness of others, like letting a cell phone ring in a meeting or being, God forbid, late.

Cheney, who had never been to Harvard Business School but had actually been a big-shot CEO at Halliburton and run the Defense Department, recognized the opportunity created by Bush's aloofness. The president's management from 40,000 feet gave the vice president, in alliance with the secretary of defense (and unchallenged by the national security adviser), tremendous capacity to shape the internal battlefield. Opposing viewpoints wouldn't even have to be heard inside the Oval Office. So long as they agreed on the correct course, Cheney and Rumsfeld could frame decisions for Bush, interpret those decisions for the rest of the executive branch, and control what Bush learned about the results.

The once "disorganized" Cheney also knew how to create the crisp, businesslike atmosphere Bush craved as a prop of his sobriety. Out of habit and respect, the vice president maintained a reserve and formal distance that kept the relationship from becoming too personal. Even at a private lunch, Bush was always "Mr. President." Like Rove, Cheney grasped that Bush's overconfidence concealed an abiding intellectual insecurity. The worst thing an adviser could do was try to steer Bush too openly, either by talking to the press about his own views or trying to persuade him in an open meeting. But so long as the president felt and appeared to be in command, the vice president could take the lead on virtually anything he cared about. On crucial decisions, he would work on Bush in private. When Cheney wanted the president to strip terrorist suspects captured in the United States of access to any existing civilian or military court, he circumvented the National Security Council process, as well as the interagency working group that had been created to address the problem. According to a *Washington Post* series on Cheney, he simply presented Bush with an executive order at a private lunch meeting in November 2001. Condi Rice and Colin Powell learned about Bush's decision from CNN.

If Bush didn't need to be in the room, steering outcomes was that much easier. Cheney requested, and Bush approved, an all-access pass to "every table and every meeting," according to White House Chief of Staff Josh Bolten. As a matter of precedence, the vice president, or the voice representing him, outweighs everyone else at the table. To be included in the meeting is to have the power of the last word. What authority Rove didn't soak up from the cabinet, Cheney did. In areas related to energy, the environment, and economic policy, EPA Administrator Christie Todd Whitman and Treasury Secretary Paul O'Neill learned, to their immense frustration, the VP's office reigned supreme. Before long, Rove had come up with his own nickname for Cheney. He called him "the management."

None of this would have worked if Cheney was fighting Bush's instincts. But the arguments Cheney made played to the biases that even liberal presidents with a better grasp of the Constitution and more foreign policy experience are susceptible to: power belongs to the commander in chief; Congress is irrelevant; the press goes too far. Unlike Brent Scowcroft, whose messages to 41 were most often about how his foreign policy choices were constrained—by the balance of power, international law, and practicality—Cheney was all about telling Bush what he was free to do. The vice president built his power over Bush by finding ways to give power to Bush.

The issue of executive authority first arose in the Bush administration around Cheney's Energy Task Force. After the vice president's office declined to provide information to Congress or cooperate with a General Accounting Office investigation, the GAO went to court to extract records of the deliberations. Many people assumed that in resisting even the disclosure of participants so fiercely, Cheney must be hiding something—embarrassing details about Enron's participation, perhaps, or a conflict of interest with his old job at Halliburton. But tilting the discussion toward oil and gas industry interests and away from environmental concerns didn't embarrass Cheney in the least. As a series of letters to Congress from David Addington and Cheney himself made clear, nondisclosure was itself the point. How

Cheney feels about this issue comes through in *Executive Privilege*, where the fictional President Jenner states his credo: "I have a right to confidential meetings with the people who work for me, and I'm not going to undermine it by going over the log with the White House press corps and telling them what's going on when." Over the next several years, Cheney and Addington would put similar words in the mouth of a real president, who would take principled stand after stand against media inquisitiveness and congressional meddling.

Cheney had a sound argument about the need for privacy in presidential policymaking. But the Energy Task Force case, which Cheney won in 2002, had much further-reaching implications. It established the vice president's office as a kind of advocacy institute for presidential power, located inside the White House. The goal, as Cheney framed it, was "to leave the Presidency stronger than we found it."

THE THEORY OF EXECUTIVE power that the president advanced after September 11, 2001, was not George W. Bush's. It was Dick Cheney's, developed in response to Watergate, deepened during to Iran-contra, and given vivid dimension by his years of playing first-strike paintball. The terrorist attacks triggered a trained reflex; Cheney headed immediately for a "secure, undisclosed location" and tried unsuccessfully to keep Bush secreted away at another.

One of the first debates to arise after the terrorist attacks was whether they posed an "existential" threat—a challenge to the survival of the constitutional order. For Cheney, there was never any question but that they did, and that they must be treated as such, even if the odds of an attack that could disable the government were one in one hundred. In trying to understand their reaction to September 11, it is important to remember that Cheney and Bush both fervently believed that the country would face additional attacks—this was conventional wisdom at the time. And even before the anthrax letters,

Cheney assumed that another wave would likely involve weapons of mass destruction—a view that played an essential role in the argument for invading Iraq. To the vice president, a threat that serious justified almost anything to prevent it. Cheney expressed this viewpoint immediately in the days after the attacks. "It's going to be vital for us to use any means at our disposal," he said on *Meet the Press*, in his first public appearance after September 11. But because of the way warfare had been regulated during the 1990s, which the U.N. General Assembly declared to be the Decade of International Law, Cheney and his legal team were worried that those means would be far too limited.

That Cheney was able to translate his instincts about the need for extraordinary presidential power so effectively into policy was not just a reflection of his bureaucratic shrewdness. It was a function of his having clear, well-developed ideas ready to fill the intellectual vacuum around the president. Bush's personal reaction to the attacks was to reach for religious guidance and define issues new to him as simple moral choices. That left a lot of details for the vice president and his crew to fill in. But Cheney did more than fill a void with flawed ideas. Inside the Chamber of Secrets, he persuaded Bush to go for broke while persuading him he was choosing a reasonable, moderate course. Bush saw his sweeping arrogation of authority not as the strongest plausible reaction, but as the minimum required under the new situation. He wasn't arresting political opponents as traitors the way John Adams did under the Alien and Sedition Acts. He wasn't suspending habeas corpus outright or rejecting the authority of the courts, the way Lincoln had during the Civil War. He wasn't rounding up Arab-Americans and putting them in camps, the way Roosevelt did with Japanese-Americans. Even though the courts had upheld all of those measures, the president was merely claiming the modest additional powers his people told him they needed to catch the evildoers and defend the country from another, potentially more devastating attack.

Neither Bush nor Cheney is a lawyer, but Bush relies on lawyers the way a businessman does, asking them to find a way to do what he wants, without engaging deeply in their reasoning or argumentation. When called upon to defend legal interpretations made on his behalf, he has done so in the vaguest of terms, often in ways that suggest he doesn't fully understand the constitutional issues at stake. Bush's unfamiliarity with constitutional doctrine left the field to Cheney, who engages the law the way a legislator does, as a core aspect of his work. After September 11, Cheney expanded his executive power institute into a legal "war council," as the group called itself. This network included John Yoo in the Justice Department's Office of Legal Counsel, David Addington in the vice president's office, and Alberto Gonzales, White House counsel and later attorney general. Yoo, a specialist in international law, was the principal theorist. Addington, though he modeled himself on Cheney in keeping the lowest possible public profile, refusing even to have his picture taken, was the whip, getting recalcitrant lawyers at the Justice, State, and Defense departments to go along. Gonzales lent presidential authority to the operation.

In the briefs, memos, and advisory opinions drafted by these lawyers, claims of presidential power went far beyond restraining congressional involvement in foreign policy and withholding information for security reasons. The Cheney council asserted that an undeclared war formed the basis for executive power unprecedented in American history. Its claims covered four overlapping areas: 1) the ability to detain anyone, citizen or not, at any time, indefinitely, in secret and without recourse to the courts; 2) the insistence that military personnel and intelligence officers were not fettered by the Geneva Conventions, or other national and international laws governing human rights; 3) the power to use extreme interrogation methods, amounting to torture, to extract information; and 4) the right to monitor communications of all sorts without judicial warrant.

From the outset, the Cheney lawyers took the position that these were *inherent* powers of the presidency in wartime, which belonged to the commander in chief of the armed forces, whether Congress chose to authorize them or not. Where the Constitution did not expressly grant such authority—or seemed to give it to Congress—they asserted that it belonged to the president, because not giving it to him wouldn't make any sense. At the heart of this case was Cheney's old friend, *The Federalist* No. 70. He and Addington often quoted Hamilton's dictum that "national security decisions require the unity in purpose and energy in action that characterize the presidency rather than Congress." The war council also argued that the president's war powers were not subject to judicial oversight.

In defense of this stance, Cheney and Bush have fended off challenges from Congress, from the judiciary, from internal dissenters in the administration, from human rights organizations, from international institutions, and from allied governments. They have insisted that the courts could not review detentions they ordered; where judges have ruled otherwise, Bush has asked Congress to strip the courts of jurisdiction. The war council has gone to the Supreme Court to argue that the president doesn't require congressional authorization for military tribunals and warrantless wiretapping. Where the high court has ruled that they need more specific authorization, Bush and Cheney have asked for it grudgingly. In the rare cases where Congress has imposed limitations on him, Bush has added signing statements to bills reserving the right to ignore what he doesn't agree with.

A QUESTION THAT MUST be asked is why Cheney set Bush on the hard road for all of these battles, which did so much to damage international respect for the American rule of law. Why not simply ask for legislation to adapt the existing system of military justice to try terrorist detainees—something the Supreme Court all but recommended in its *Hamdan* decision? Why resist the FISA court, which functioned as a virtual rubber stamp for Justice Department prosecutors anyway? When Bush finally did what the Supreme Court required in 2006 and asked Congress to authorize the Guantánamo system of justice, Congress was quick to oblige with a sweeping Military Commissions Act that legalized virtually everything he and Cheney wanted. Eventually, the administration had no recourse but to seek legislative approval for its surveillance activities. This too Congress granted in August 2007. When surrounded by yes-men, why stand on the privilege of not needing to ask?

The explanation is that for Cheney, the means—unilateral executive authority—were more important than the specific ends they served. Cheney and the war council thought military tribunals, extraordinary rendition, secret CIA prisons, waterboarding, and the rest were necessary to prevent another terrorist attack. But they didn't just want those policies to be allowed. They demanded the power to do whatever they thought necessary to preserve the constitutional order in a crisis. The vice president's fight for executive authority was the culmination of a lifelong crusade to restore what he saw as the proper balance and separation of powers. He stated this case clearly over several decades. But before September 11, Cheney's views were largely ignored by the press for one simple reason: he expressed his arguments in broad daylight.

Indeed, executive authority was the one subject on which Cheney bordered on expansive. On a December 2005 trip to Oman, he spoke to a group of reporters on board Air Force Two. One journalist asked the vice president the shrewd question of how serving in the Ford administration, when presidential power was diminished, shaped his view of executive authority. Cheney's response is worth quoting at length:

> Yes, I do have the view that over the years there had been an erosion of presidential power and authority, that it's reflected in a number of developments—the War Powers Act, which many people believe is unconstitutional. . . . I am one of those who believe that was an infringement upon the authority of the president . . . a lot of the things around Watergate and Vietnam, both, in the '70s served to erode the authority, I think, the president needs to be effective especially in a na-

> tional security area. . . . I've got enormous regard for the other body, Title I of the Constitution, but I do believe that, especially in the day and age we live in, the nature of the threats we face, it was true during the Cold War, as well as I think what is true now, the president of the United States needs to have his constitutional powers unimpaired, if you will, in terms of the conduct of national security policy. That's my personal view. . . . So when you're asking about my view of the presidency, yes, I believe in a strong, robust executive authority. . . . I think you're right, probably [at] the end of the next administration, you had the nadir of the modern presidency in terms of authority and legitimacy, then a number of limitations that were imposed in the aftermath of Vietnam and Watergate. But I do think that to some extent now, we've been able to restore the legitimate authority of the presidency.

This was Cheney's lifelong goal, his personal battle. And at the end of 2005, despite his own unpopularity, the mess in Iraq, and the fact that the Bush administration was widely judged incompetent and ineffective, Cheney thought he'd largely succeeded in making the presidency stronger.

Since those comments on the flight to Oman, the most powerful vice president in American history has also become the most reviled. Cheney was already deeply unpopular when he flaunted his contempt for public information about an issue far easier for most people to understand. He might have been forgiven his carelessness in shooting his friend Harry Whittington in the face at a quail-hunting party in Texas in February 2006. But it was harder to excuse his attempt to cover up what had happened. Cheney didn't tell the president's office about the accident for twelve hours. Then he had a friend leak an understated version of events to a friendly local paper near the Armstrong Ranch, where the accident occurred. And when word got out, Cheney didn't tell the truth. The vice president claimed he'd been thirty yards away when he fired, a distance not consistent with Whittington's injuries.

But as with Bush, unpopularity and bad press have little obvious effect on the vice president. With his approval rating in the teens, he pressed the case for preemptive action against Iran. Faced with the possibility that visitor logs to his official residence might be subject to the Freedom of Information and Presidential Records Acts, he demanded that the Secret Service destroy them. Addington now argued that the office of the vice president was exempt as part of the legislative branch from these laws, because of the vice president's constitutional role in presiding over the Senate. This was the logic of Alice in Wonderland in the service of Orwell. If such a loophole were upheld, it would make organizing policymaking through the vice president's office a legal way to ensure secrecy—forever. We would have not only an imperial presidency, but also an invisible one.

Cheney's indifference to popular opinion once seemed like his most appealing characteristic. But not caring what other people thought of him turned out to be an enormous liability when lashed to flawed principles. The vice president saw no need to persuade the public, compromise with Congress, or even defend the White House's major decisions. With a less isolated president, this might not have mattered. But Bush had no working feedback mechanism either.

It is possible that Cheney thinks even now that his effort to restore "robust executive authority" has been a success. Despite some eloquent words about presidential authority not being a blank check in the *Hamdi* decision, the Supreme Court has actually constrained Bush very little. Even with the Democrats in control of the legislative branch, there has been nothing like the post-Watergate movement to restrain executive excess. In the final phase of the Bush presidency, it is probably accurate to say that Cheney's view of executive power has been widely discredited without being significantly constrained.

But even if some of his most controversial policies are still standing, Cheney has failed on his own terms. His vaunting of executive power over all other considerations in the name of protecting the country may have temporarily strengthened the hand of the administration in relation to Congress. But in the end, his assertion made his president, the presidency, and the nation less rather than more powerful. Cheney's open-ended claims of executive authority and privilege have had a devastating effect not just on Bush's political standing, but on America's moral credibility. The president failed in part because Cheney, his foremost hand, refused to accept that a liberal society has some intrinsic disadvantages in fighting terrorism. An American president cannot embrace the dark side, especially while framing his policies in absolutist terms. Cheney did what he thought he had to do to protect the country. But the choices he led Bush to make called into question America's integrity, consistency, and its rule of law.

The alternative approach to Cheney's has been eloquently articulated by the leading jurist of a nation for which terrorism has long been an undisputed existential threat. In a 1999 case, the Israeli Supreme Court reviewed the question of whether torture was allowable in a "ticking time bomb" scenario. Israel at the time was suffering from a wave of suicide bombings and there was enormous pressure on the courts to give the security services a free hand. In this environment, the Court was presented with a case brought by a human rights organization challenging the Shin Bet, the Israeli internal security service. The human rights advocates argued that interrogation methods used on Palestinian prisoners amounted to torture.

Writing for the majority was the court's president, Aharon Barak. Barak's family was killed in the Holocaust. When he was a small child, a Lithuanian family saved his life by smuggling him out of the Kovno Ghetto in a suitcase. His opinion in the case, *The Public Committee Against Torture in Israel v. The State of Israel,* argues that preserving the rule of law and recognizing individual liberties are at the heart of a democratic state's security needs. Barak states the anti-Cheney position eloquently: "We are aware that this judgment of ours does not make confronting that reality any easier. That is the fate of democracy, in whose eyes not all means are permitted, and to whom not all the methods used by her enemies are open." But, the judge wrote, democratic legitimacy and adherence to standards of human rights confer a security advantage as well, one that terrorists can never have.

"At times democracy fights with one hand tied behind her back," Barak concluded. "Despite that, democracy has the upper hand."

CHAPTER SIX

An Amiable Monster

Be it thy course to busy giddy minds
With foreign quarrels; that action, hence borne out
May waste the memory of the former days.

—HENRY IV, PART 2

—

THERE'S SOME SUPPORT FOR THE DYNASTIC READING THAT GEORGE W. Bush intended to invade Iraq from the outset of his presidency to avenge his father. "After all, this is a guy that tried to kill my dad at one time," Bush declared at a political fund-raiser in Houston in September 2002. Considerable doubt has since arisen around the incident Bush was referring to, a supposed plot by Saddam to blow up the former president with a car bomb on a visit to Kuwait in 1993. The Kuwaiti government quickly convicted, but subsequently commuted the death sentences of all six co-conspirators. No evidence tying them to Iraq was found after the Coalition Provisional Authority took possession of the files of the Mukhabarat, Saddam's notorious secret police. But there's little doubt that Bush himself believed what intelligence officials told the family after that incident: that Saddam planned to murder not just George W.'s father, but the other family members visiting Kuwait with him: his mother, Barbara, his wife, Laura, and his two youngest brothers, Neil and Marvin. The incident cast a long shadow in the family. According to family intimates, the Bushes felt they were at risk so long as Saddam remained in power.

Dribbles from the administration confirm the notion that Bush had a personal focus on Iraq well before September 11. His first treasury secretary, Paul O'Neill, claimed that getting rid of Saddam was on Bush's agenda from the earliest days of the administration. "It was all about finding a way to do it," he told the journalist Ron Suskind, whose book *The Price of Loyalty* cast O'Neill as a heroic dissenter. Less than a month into his term, Bush told his speechwriter David Frum that he was determined to dig Saddam out of power. According to former terrorism czar Richard Clarke, Bush pulled him aside in the White House Situation Room on September 12 and asked him to look for evidence that Saddam was behind the attacks. When Clarke said that Al Qaeda was responsible, Bush replied, "I know, I know, but . . . see if Saddam was involved. Just look." According to Bob Woodward's *Bush at War*, Bush told aides immediately after 9/11: "I believe that Iraq was involved, but I'm not going to strike them now."

As suggestive as these shards may be, they point to a desire to oust Saddam rather than a decision to do so from the outset. Of the top-level players in the administration, only Paul Wolfowitz directly advocated military action against Iraq before September 11. From the collective perspective of Bush's foreign policy team, Iraq fell into the category of big problems that weren't urgent. His people were instinctually critical of Clinton's proportionate responses to Saddam's provocations and felt they might have to act more decisively at some point in the future. But the same category of problem also included North Korea and Pakistan's nuclear programs, Russia's growing authoritarianism, and China's belligerence toward Taiwan. Iraq policy in the early months of the administration focused on reforming the existing policy of sanctions and was left to Colin Powell. In the immediate aftermath of September 11, Bush rejected Wolfowitz's argument for attacking Saddam and moved instead to assault Al Qaeda and its Taliban host in Afghanistan. There were no preparations or significant planning for war in Iraq until September 2002 and no point-of-no-return buildup until January 2003.

In other words, George W. Bush did not arrive in the White House determined to invade Iraq. So why did he ultimately decide to do it? Bush's struggle to vindicate his family and outdo his father predisposed him toward completing a job his dad left unfinished. But it was his broader attempt to develop a foreign policy different from his father's that led him into his biggest mistake. Succeeding at foreign policy was the last and most important way for George W. to prove himself in relation to his father. His struggle to come up with an original doctrine of his own frames not just his original mistake of launching an invasion of Iraq, but the more extensive international failure of his presidency. Act One of the Bush Tragedy is the son's struggle to be like his dad until the age of forty. Act Two is his growing success over the next fifteen years as he learned to be different. The botched search for a doctrine to clarify world affairs and the president's progressive descent into messianism constitute the conclusive third act.

IN THE YEARS AFTER Bush Senior left office, the more vocal and intellectually dominating conservatives grew ever more dismissive of his realist approach to international relations. They acknowledged George H. W. Bush and his team as temperate and skillful diplomats, whose personal relationships and persuasive skills helped them to assemble the coalition that pushed Saddam out of Kuwait and handle the peaceful collapse of the Soviet empire. But this was faint praise where it wasn't an open sneer. The hawks and neocons were contemptuous of Bush 41's diplomatic realism—in many ways more so than toward the "social work" foreign policy of Bill Clinton, who had at least stiffed the United Nations when he bombed Kosovo. The neocons had two primary emblems of 41's spinelessness: the "Chicken Kiev" speech he gave in Ukraine in 1991, which indicated his willingness to accommodate communism for the sake of stability, and his decision to leave Saddam in power at the end of the Gulf War. They also disparaged his mild reaction to the Chinese crackdown on democracy protesters at Tiananmen Square. The neoconservative alternative was a foreign policy modeled on Ronald Reagan, whose moral vision and assertion of military might they credited with winning the Cold War.

During his first presidential campaign, George W. Bush gave every indication of accepting the neocon critique of his father. Where the elder Bush was a balance-of-power realist, the younger Bush saw foreign policy as a moral exercise. Where his father had been tactical and reactive, he described himself as strategic and "forward leaning." His father was a manager and a diplomat, focused on alliances, relationships, and agreements. George W. liked being a bit of a cowboy, with little use for international law or the United Nations, when using them didn't suit American interests.

Worst of all in his view, there was no Bush 41 Doctrine. His father had left behind no grand foreign policy framework, no organizing and distinguishing idea, the way consequential presidents like Truman and Reagan did. The son wanted to develop one. Over the past eight years, there have in fact been five distinct Bush Doctrines. These conceptions have overlapped to varying degrees, with the sprouts of the new one usually appearing before the previous has been cleared away. But Bush's foreign policy doctrine has rarely been static, because none of his ideas have been workable enough to last through his presidency, let alone beyond it. Bush's search for a doctrine has driven his major foreign policy mistakes. It has also been a mistake in itself.

Bush Doctrine 1.0 was Unipolar Realism (3/7/99–9/10/01). Driven more by the refutation of Clinton's liberal internationalism than of 41's diplomatic realism, it challenged his father's worldview only obliquely. In his first major speech on the subject, at the Citadel Academy in Charleston in September 1999, George W. promised to make the military stronger by not sending it on "vague, aimless and endless deployments," the way Bill Clinton had in Bosnia and Kosovo. In his presidential debates with Al Gore a year later, W. criticized the Clinton policy of nation-building not driven by American interests and called for the United States to be "humble" in telling other countries how to govern themselves. Bush steered clear of his father's men Baker and Scowcroft, but was advised by Colin Powell and Scowcroft's protégée Condoleezza Rice, who was likewise grounded in classic "balance of power" realism. In an article in *Foreign Affairs* taken to represent the candidate's views, Rice suggested a reorientation of interest-based foreign policy, shading away from China and toward India, and taking a harder line on the emergence of Russian authoritarianism.

On the basis of such clues—what he said, who was around him, and what they thought—it appeared to most observers that George W. Bush was likely to challenge his father's foreign policy legacy only in small ways. He was a realist with a different list of things to do, a harder shell, and less use for the "smiles and scowls of diplomacy." In his first eight months he showed how much less. Bush declared his intention to abrogate the ABM treaty and move ahead with developing missile defense. He brushed off Russian outrage about this. Where his father was a sinophile, the son saw a growing military threat. He talked tough when the Chinese shot down a U.S. military plane violating their airspace and held its crew hostage. He spoke ambiguously about whether he supported continuing the long-standing policy of "strategic ambiguity" with respect to Taiwan. He repudiated the Kyoto Accords on global warming. He spurned Yassir Arafat and stood by Ariel Sharon in Israel. He broke off negotiations with North Korea. If the threat from Osama bin Laden was not a focus for Bush, that may have been because Bill Clinton emphasized it so strongly on his way out.

After Bush had been in office only a month, Charles Krauthammer was already proclaiming Bush's unilateral tendency to be a new doctrine. "Bush, like Reagan, understands that the U.S. can reshape, indeed remake, reality on its own," Krauthammer wrote in *Time,* in words that must been music to the new president's ears. The columnist described the new approach as "Don't ask. Tell." But if the first Bush Doctrine had a Walkeresque aggressiveness, it was still bounded by his father's realism. Bush was not prepared to challenge China or Iraq militarily, as the neoconservatives urged him to do. In this phase he still framed his foreign policy more in terms of interests than ideals.

UNIPOLAR REALISM SURVIVED its initial encounters with reality, but not with September 11. By the end of that day, the president had a new approach. Bush Doctrine 2.0 was With Us or Against Us (9/11/01–5/31/02). The new doctrine didn't represent a repudiation of the first one so much as an elaboration of it to deal with the previously neglected problem of terrorism. On the day of the attacks, Bush's spontaneous reaction, spoken in the auditorium of Booker Elementary School in Sarasota, Florida, was to say that "Terrorism against our nation will not stand"—an echo of his father's famous remark about Saddam's invasion of Kuwait. The next day, the president told Tony Blair that he didn't want to "pound sand" just to make himself feel better—his shorthand for Clinton's ineffectual response to the bombing of the American embassies in Kenya and Tanzania in 1998. Instead, 43 quickly formulated a sweeping strategic response: nations had to choose whether to be with or against the United States. That evening Bush articulated his version of the new doctrine from the Oval Office: "We will make no distinction between the terrorists who committed these acts and those who harbor them."

Rice appears to have been the original framer of this idea, which was refined in consultation with Bush and his speechwriters that day. Though still fundamentally realist, Bush Doctrine 2.0 represented a moral turn in Bush's conceptualization of international relations. It provided the justification for not just pursuing Al Qaeda, but for deposing the Taliban, its host in Afghanistan. If Rice first came up with the "no distinction" idea, it was Cheney who first started calling it the "Bush Doctrine" in public. In a November 2001 speech to the U.S. Chamber of Commerce, Cheney offered this definition: "We will hold those who harbor terrorists, those who provide sanctuary to terrorists, responsible for their acts."

But by the time Cheney spoke those words, a second wave of terrorism had already exposed the inadequacy of Doctrine 2.0. The anthrax attacks in New York and Washington created a sense of vulnerability that was in many respects greater than the mass murder at the World Trade Center and Pentagon. As horrific as September 11 was, it was a discrete crime, whose perpetrators were quickly identified and pursued. The anthrax letters, by contrast, killed only a few people, but remained unsolved. To this day, officials disagree about whether the sender or senders were Islamic terrorists, or Americans pretending to be Islamic terrorists. The only real consensus is that the FBI catastrophically botched the investigation.

Inside the administration, the October bioterror attacks had a greater impact than is generally appreciated—one in many ways greater than 9/11. Without the anthrax attacks, Bush probably would not have invaded Iraq.

Even before September 11, bioweapons were the vice president's territory. Cheney's fascination with the subject dated back to the Pentagon's preparations for the first Gulf War. His chief of staff, Scooter Libby, shared his boss's obsession. He used a 1903 smallpox epidemic as the backdrop for a historical novel about Japan, *The Apprentice*, which he published in 1996. In May 2001, Bush announced that Cheney would be in charge of efforts to protect the country from weapons of mass destruction, and Libby took charge of the issue within his office. President Bush was involved enough in their early discussions to give Libby the nickname "Germ Boy."

On September 11, the Cheney-Libby project became urgent. Bush now asked the vice president to assess America's vulnerability to chemical, biological, and nuclear weapons. At that point, nearly everyone involved in national security assumed there would be another wave of terrorist attacks. The daily intelligence summary substantiated this panic; "chatter" was at record levels. Cheney and Libby focused on two possibilities: a "decapitation" attack directed against the government and one directed at civilians that would cause even greater panic and larger casualties than September 11. To carry off either, terrorists would need a weapon of mass destruction. In an effort to understand the potential threat, Libby ordered up a briefing on a war game, known as "Dark Winter," which modeled a smallpox outbreak in an American city in much the way the continuity of government exercises simulated nuclear catastrophe.

According to a source close to Bush, Cheney swiftly reported back to the Oval Office with a sobering message: the United States was essentially defenseless against the most likely form of assault, a biological attack. "I sat through the most gruesome briefing in the Oval Office about anthrax, how it could spread, and how we had no defenses," Bush's first press secretary, Ari Fleischer, told me in the summer of 2007. "Dick Cheney was the strongest advocate of the possibility of attack and need to prepare for it."

In the weeks after September 11, the Secret Service began monitoring the air inside and outside the White House. The chimneys of bio-detectors were visible from the front lawn. Cheney began traveling with a full biohazard protective suit. He and Libby were already spending much of their time at the famous "secure, undisclosed location." This designation encompassed both Camp David and the nearby Site R, a national security bunker at Raven Rock Mountain, in the Blue Ridge hills near Waynesboro, Pennsylvania. Officially known as the Alternate Joint Communications Center, Site R was the location where the Joint Chiefs of Staff planned to operate during a Soviet nuclear attack and one of the primary locales used in the 1980s continuity of government exercises. Excavated under hundreds of feet of greenstone granite, the 700,000-square-foot bunker can accommodate three thousand people.

Then on October 4 the worst fears inside the White House were realized. Bush choked up as he thanked government workers in a morning speech at the State Department. Ari Fleischer reports that he had "never before and never since seen the President look as tired and as troubled as he did that morning." When they returned to the White House, Bush called Fleischer into his office and explained the reason: he had just learned that a Florida man had been stricken with anthrax. Bush feared it was the dreaded second wave. This was Cheney's assumption as well. On October 12, five days after the beginning of the Afghan War, the vice president appeared on *The NewsHour* and told Jim Lehrer: "I think the only responsible thing for us to do is to proceed on the basis that [September 11 and the anthrax attacks] could be linked. And obviously that means you've got to spend time as well, as we've known now for some time, focusing on other types of attacks besides the one that we experienced on September 11."

Anthrax letters were received at several media organizations in New York. In Washington, letters were received in two Senate offices, which shut down parts of the Capitol complex for weeks. All of the anthrax letters directed to the media and government officials were sent from the same mailbox, in Trenton, New Jersey. But they contained different grades of anthrax—the subject of much confusion in subsequent weeks. At least one—the letter sent to Judith Miller of *The New York Times*—bore the same postmark and handwriting, but contained only a harmless white powder.

Another anthrax letter, never recovered (or at least never disclosed) was apparently sent to the White House. On October 22, anthrax was found on an automated slitter used to open letters at a Secret Service facility in an undisclosed location some miles away. This meant the White House was a target of biological terrorism. "I think the seminal event of the Bush administration was the anthrax attacks," someone close to the president told me. "It was the thing that changed everything. It was the hard stare into the abyss."

Though the president refused to acknowledge it at the time, he, his wife, and much of his staff began taking the antibiotic Cipro as a precaution, as did fifty members of the mail-handling staff in the executive office buildings. With the Beltway snipers still at large, terrorist scares and threats continued to erupt, many of them withheld from the press. On October 23, the day after anthrax was found at the White House mail facility, the Department of Health and Human Services informed the president's office that a man in a Florida hospital was believed to have smallpox. A wave of relief swept through the West Wing when he turned out only to have syphilis.

That month, Cheney and Libby began spending time at HHS, which was leading the confused response to the anthrax attacks and making preparations for the possibility of something much worse. Their greatest fear was an attack involving smallpox. The smallpox virus killed an estimated 300 million people in the twentieth century. It was still taking 2 million lives a year as late as 1967, when the World Health Organization began the massive campaign that wiped out the disease a decade later. After smallpox was eradicated in 1977, only the United States and Russia were permitted to retain research samples of the virus, under closely monitored, secure conditions. But an intelligence review ordered by Cheney determined that Iraq, North Korea, and Russia were all likely to possess undeclared stocks.

Cheney and Libby believed that Iraq's potential to produce a smallpox weapon necessitated universal vaccination of the general population, something that hadn't happened in the United States since 1972. On the other side of the argument was Donald Henderson, the heroic epidemiologist who led the WHO smallpox eradication program and later became Bush 41's science adviser. After the anthrax attacks, HHS brought Henderson in as a consultant to help develop emergency plans.

When I visited him at his office at the Center for Biosecurity in Baltimore, Henderson recounted a surprise, unpublicized visit he paid to the Centers for Disease Control in Atlanta with Cheney and Libby on July 18, 2002. Henderson flew down with them on Air Force Two and spent most of the trip explaining to the vice president and his chief of staff why he and other epidemiologists thought a massive vaccination program would be a terrible idea. Henderson was skeptical of evidence that Iraq was working with smallpox. But his view was that in the unlikely event an outbreak occurred, public health officials could contain it using the "vaccination ring" technique they'd used during the eradication program.

Widespread compulsory vaccination, on the other hand, would be a calamity. Doctors no longer had experience with smallpox symptoms. Even medical professionals were horrified when they saw the range of *normal* reactions to a vaccination: grotesque scabs, lesions, and pustules. Henderson showed me a pamphlet that HHS distributed to hospitals to document the abnormal reactions: blackened limbs, uncontrolled swelling, and a reaction called progressive vaccinia, in which sores cover the body from head to toe. But worse than the panic these reactions would cause would be the predictable casualties. According to Henderson, adverse reactions to the vaccine were estimated to kill between one and two out of every million people inoculated. The question of legal liability would be a nightmare. Henderson said that Cheney and Libby didn't seem to disagree with his arguments, which he reviewed with them on the return flight. By the time their plane landed back at Andrews Air Force Base at the end of the day, Henderson assumed he had persuaded them to drop the idea of mass public vaccination. "I thought, Thank God they've finally gotten the message. Finally we've been able to get it through to them that this just does not make sense," Henderson said.

When he reached his home in Baltimore two hours later, Henderson's wife was waiting with an urgent message to call the office. "They were going to have a press release the next morning announcing that they were going to vaccinate the entire country immediately," Henderson said. "I couldn't believe it." But after girding for battle and taking a 5:00 A.M. train to HHS the next morning, Henderson was relieved to be told that the vaccination plan was off after all. Bush had overruled Cheney. Bush eventually announced a compromise: mandatory vaccination of 500,000 military personnel, and voluntary vaccination for the same number of health care workers or "first responders." After that, the government would offer the vaccine to a larger number of health care and emergency workers. But by the time the vaccine was ready for use, in early 2004, the panic was over. Saddam didn't have a smallpox weapon after all. Bush was vaccinated at the White House, but decided that members of his family and the White House staff didn't need to run the risk. Cheney himself chose not to be vaccinated.

Those who believe the vice president operates in bad faith—that he concocted evidence of Iraqi WMD to justify a war—should consider his stance on universal smallpox vaccination. By most estimates, even a safe vaccine would have killed a few hundred Americans and made thousands seriously ill. Cheney's readiness to sacrifice hundreds of civilian lives may make him sound like Dr. Strangelove. But if the idea was mad, it was sincerely mad, testifying to how seriously he took the possibility that Saddam had biological weapons and might use them, or give them to terrorists to use, against the United States. The smallpox episode punctures another myth too: that Bush blindly follows Cheney. Bush's sense of autonomy is far too sensitive for him to function as anyone's puppet—or worse, to be seen as one. He follows Cheney's advice further than anyone else's, but only so far as Cheney can sustain the president's sense that he is the one leading the way.

CHENEY'S FOCUS ON IRAQ as the likely culprit in the anthrax attacks indicated how his view of the first Gulf War had evolved. Whether or not he tacitly absorbed the neocons' moral critique about ending it prematurely, he embraced their evidentiary and strategic argument. He adopted their claims about Saddam's weapons, his connections to terrorists, and the case that a status-quo-minded intelligence community was prone to underestimate both aspects of the Iraqi threat.

After the first Gulf War, weapons inspectors from the United Nations Special Commission (UNSCOM) discovered that Saddam had been as little as eighteen months away from building a nuclear weapon, not ten years away as most analysts had believed. Libby and Wolfowitz now convinced Cheney that Saddam was not only likely to have resumed work on a bomb, but was also playing cat and mouse with the inspectors to hide his work on biological weapons. In 1995, UNSCOM found a freeze drier labeled "smallpox" at an Iraqi facility. In 1997, it found military documents indicating that Iraqi troops had been vaccinated against the disease. An Iraqi scientist admitted to inspectors that he had done research into camelpox.

According to Donald Henderson, there were benign explanations for all of these incriminating data points. The freeze drier had been used to produce smallpox vaccine, when Iraq suffered one of the last outbreaks of the disease, in 1971–72. Iraq's military vaccinations dated from that period as well. Camelpox is deadly to dromedaries, but cannot spread to humans; the research was straightforward veterinary medicine. But in trying to build a case for a new assault, Libby and Cheney tended to discount, if they even listened to, benign explanations of what they were certain was Saddam's biological weapons program.

The other claim Cheney accepted without reservations was that Saddam was a "state sponsor of terrorism." Libby and Wolfowitz had long been interested in their friend Laurie Mylroie's unified field theory of terrorism. Mylroie argued that Saddam was behind every major terrorist attack against Americans in the 1990s, including the first attack on the World Trade Center in 1993 and the Oklahoma City bombing in 1995. Mylroie's book *Study of Revenge: Saddam Hussein's Unfinished War Against America* was published by the American Enterprise Institute, where she was a fellow. On the back cover are glowing blurbs from Libby, Wolfowitz, and Richard Perle. Cheney followed these men into the tortured pathways of Mylroie's conspiracy theory, including her tantalizing suggestion that the 9/11 ringleader Mohammed Atta had met with Iraqi intelligence officers in Prague.

Libby, who had Cheney's ear, and Wolfowitz, who had Rumsfeld's, had lost the argument for making Iraq the first target after September 11. But the anthrax attacks and Mylroie's Atta-in-Prague hypothesis supported their case for making it the next one. They seized on claims that the anthrax found in the Washington letters was highly refined or "weaponized." The quality of the anthrax, they argued, pointed to a state sponsor. But even if Iraq wasn't behind the anthrax attacks, Wolfowitz and Libby argued that Saddam had the means and the motive to give biological weapons to Al Qaeda in the future. Cheney bought deeply into all of these hypotheses—that Saddam had bioweapons, that he was involved in the anthrax attacks, and that he was supporting Al Qaeda. In the fall of 2003, after his claims about Saddam's WMD had been decisively refuted, the vice president was still citing the Atta-in-Prague conspiracy theory. He used the fictitious meeting to argue that Iraq had been "the geographic base of the terrorists who have had us under assault now for many years, but most especially on 9/11."

Numerous books, studies, and articles have examined the dishonesty of the administration's Iraqi WMD and terrorism case, and of how Cheney, Libby, Rumsfeld, Wolfowitz, Perle, and Douglas Feith skewed intelligence to support it. The best examination of this episode is Michael Isikoff and David Corn's book *Hubris*. Isikoff and Corn charge the neocons and Cheney with intentional fraud. An indictment that's easier to prove—and arguably more damning—is self-deception. The logic behind the invasion of Iraq was coherent. I and many other Bush skeptics known as liberal hawks agreed that after September 11, a Saddam armed with nuclear or biological weapons became an intolerable threat. What none of us realized until it was too late was the way in which the evidence necessary to support this case was being monumentally fudged. Cheney, Rumsfeld, and the neocons saw only what they wished to see. They did think Saddam had WMD. But in the firmness of that belief, they fell short of any standard of intellectual honesty. They tried to frame a man they thought was guilty—which is not quite the same thing as framing someone you know to be innocent.

In another administration, there would have been various checks on this kind of collective delusion. A Kennedy, a Nixon, a Clinton, and a George H. W. Bush all would have considered evidence to some degree. Under another president, there would have been a real discussion about what else those aluminum tubes might be for. At some point, cognitive dissonance would have set in. But once Bush's mind was made up that Saddam was building biological and nuclear weapons, it closed to alternative explanations. He thought picking through evidence was beneath him. In 43's White House, as his communications director Dan Bartlett put it in an anonymous background briefing, "The President of the United States is not a fact checker." If the director of the CIA told him the case for Saddam's WMD was a "slam dunk," that was all Bush needed to hear.

This unchallenged groupthink pointed powerfully in the direction of war. If terrorism + WMD = intolerable threat, then the United States had to take on not just state sponsors of terrorism, such as the Taliban, but the most egregious proliferators of WMD with connections to terrorists. Cheney had already begun to make this argument to Bush by late 2001. An early glimpse of where this logic was headed came in Bush's January 2002 State of the Union address. That speech is remembered for Bush's Reaganesque denunciation of an "axis of evil"—which rounded out his threat to the top target, Iraq, with warnings to Iran and North Korea. But the most revealing line about the president's thinking came later in the speech, when Bush promised not to stand by as dangers increased. "The United States of America will not permit the world's most dangerous regimes to threaten us with the world's most destructive weapons." Everything in Cheney's worldview came together here—his Hobbesian view of geopolitics, his alarm at America's defenselessness against biological attack, Mylroie's unified field theory of terrorism, and his vision of an all-powerful executive free to bypass Congress, the United Nations, and international law.

DICK CHENEY DIDN'T SELL Bush on the invasion of Iraq directly. He first sold him the theory that justified it. This was Bush Doctrine 3.0, Preemption (6/1/02–11/5/03). The problem with the earlier idea of With Us or Against Us was that it didn't promulgate any strategy for protecting the United States in an age of biotechnology, miniaturization, nonstate actors, and porous borders. To make the country more secure, we'd have to find a way of cutting off these threats at the root, not just by taking on hosts, but by disabling known and potential WMD proliferators. Preemption was no longer a hawkish version of George H. W. Bush's realism. It was Dick Cheney's notion of prophylactic aggression Where Doctrine 2.0 justified the war in Afghanistan, which was harboring Al Qaeda, Doctrine 3.0 would provide a basis for invading Iraq, which might assist Al Qaeda in the future. As Gerson writes: "All of [Bush's] instincts tended toward a single ambition: a desire to reshape the security environment we found in the world, rather than endlessly responding to escalating dangers and attacks." Preemption was the first doctrine to satisfy this single-minded ambition.

Bush unveiled this theory, studded with Gersonian faith nuggets, at the West Point graduation in June 2002. It was in this speech, probably the most important of his presidency, that Bush first articulated his theory of "preemptive action." The president explicitly framed it as a successor to Cold War doctrine:

> When the spread of chemical and biological and nuclear weapons, along with ballistic missile technology—when that occurs, even weak states and small groups could attain a catastrophic power to strike great nations. Our enemies have declared this very intention, and have been caught seeking these terrible weapons. . . . For much of the last century, America's defense relied on the Cold War doctrines of deterrence and containment. In some cases, those strategies still apply. But new threats also require new thinking. Deterrence—the promise of massive retaliation against nations—means nothing against shadowy terrorist networks with no nation or citizens to defend. Containment is not possible when unbalanced dictators with weapons of mass destruction can deliver those weapons on missiles or secretly provide them to terrorist allies.

The administration's entire foreign policy apparatus now began to revolve around Bush's warning that "if we wait for threats to fully materialize, we will have waited too long."

There was nothing especially novel about the basic concept. As Condi Rice emphasized, preemption was based on an old idea of anticipatory self-defense, long recognized under international law. It was the justification for Israel's Six Day War against Arab nations that were preparing an attack. The only real innovation was seeking to update the idea to take in the problems of nonstate actors and high-technology weapons. Rice further fleshed out the new doctrine in the National Security Strategy of the United States issued by the

National Security Council. Quoting extensively from the West Point speech, this document further develops the justification: "The greater the threat, the greater is the risk of inaction—and the more compelling the case for taking anticipatory action to defend ourselves, even if uncertainty remains as to the time and place of the enemy's attack," the white paper proclaims. "To forestall or prevent such hostile acts by our adversaries, the United States will, if necessary, act preemptively."

By making this idea its central doctrine, the administration signaled its readiness to act on the principle at any time. It isn't clear whether the decision to invade Iraq was already made at the time of the West Point speech on June 1. But it evidently had been a month later, when Richard Haass, the State Department's director of policy planning, went to present his case against the war to Condi Rice on July 7. Rice told him to save his breath—it was already a done deal. After the meeting, Haass called Colin Powell, who told him that he had to be wrong—no decision had been made yet. Then Powell did some checking and reported back that Haass was right. On July 23, Sir Richard Dearlove, the head of British intelligence, briefed Prime Minister Tony Blair on Dearlove's visit to Washington. The decision to invade Iraq had been made, "justified by the conjunction of terrorism and WMD." The minutes of the meeting, known as the Downing Street Memo, also noted that "the intelligence and facts were being fixed around the policy."

Powell's ignorance about the decision means that it was made outside of any sort of National Security Council process. This suggests that the decision to invade Iraq followed the pattern of the Military Commissions order—a final decision made with Bush and Cheney alone together in the president's office. But when did Cheney get fully on board? And how did he move the president toward a decision?

A pivotal moment in Cheney's decision was the American Enterprise Institute World Forum meeting in Beaver Creek, Colorado, which took place from June 20 to June 23, 2002. By then, AEI had become such a proxy for neoconservative opinion that Gerald Ford was the only person at the gathering to say aloud that attacking Iraq sounded like a bad idea. Others present, including Wolfowitz, Libby, Perle, and Newt Gingrich, looked around uncomfortably, as Ford compared the idea to Vietnam—not because they feared he might be right, but because they thought the eighty-eight-year-old former president was completely past it. At that point, the neocons were embracing a proposal from Ahmed Chalabi and his Iraqi National Congress to act as an American proxy in Iraq the way that the Northern Alliance had done in Afghanistan. This, Chalabi explained in an elaborate presentation, would not require a massive American troop presence, but only a deployment of Special Forces. Cheney said little as is his wont, but was seen to nod sagely in agreement. Two attendees told me they thought Cheney made his decision in favor of war that weekend.

That would isolate Bush's decision to attack Saddam as occurring in the two-week window between June 23 and July 7, 2002. This timing also explains Cheney's surprise visit to the CDC on July 18 and his urgent push to vaccinate the country against a smallpox weapon he thought Saddam could unleash in response to, or to preempt, a preemptive American attack. It also suggests that the debate about whether to go to war with Iraq that occupied the country for the next nine months was a conversation without consequence. Some of the delay between the decision that summer and the attack in March 2003 was necessary to make a show of seeking U.N. support, and to lay the military groundwork for an invasion. But delay also served the purpose of avoiding one of Bush 41's political pitfalls. Going to war closer to the 1992 election would in all likelihood have ensured George H. W. Bush a second term. For his son, less time between invasion and election was better.

Cheney and Rumsfeld both advocated a plan that assumed Chalabi would take charge of Iraq following an American assault. They remained fixated on this scenario despite opposition from the CIA and State Department, which regarded Chalabi as a charlatan. Cheney and Rumsfeld only gave up on using the Iraqi National Congress as a proxy some months later, when more detailed military planning revealed that Chalabi had no real forces at his command. Even then they remained attached to the idea that Chalabi could lead a pro-Western Iraqi government.

Rumsfeld was a shark who swam with the neocon fish. But he wasn't one of them; like Cheney, he is better characterized as a nationalist hawk. Rumsfeld wanted to go to war with Iraq for his own reasons. He saw invading Iraq as an opportunity to demonstrate the theory of "military transformation." With new technology, the defense secretary believed the Pentagon could fight wars cheaply and easily, with many fewer troops. By proving the efficacy of new technology and tactics, Rumsfeld thought he would leave an important legacy in his second turn at the Defense Department.

He intended for the military to go in light, knock over Saddam, hand power to some plausible civilian authority, probably Chalabi, and get back out as quickly as possible. The defense secretary originally wanted an occupying force no larger than 75,000—as against the more than 400,000 troops sent to the Persian Gulf in 1990. Rumsfeld's military transformation theory held up well in the invasion itself. Deposing Saddam didn't require a larger deployment, and we might have done it as well with 75,000 troops as 140,000. But the defense secretary's insistence on preparing only for the war he wanted left him with little capacity to win the war he got.

The arguments for going in small weren't just that Rumsfeld wanted to prove his theory of military transformation and that a larger force would make the invasion harder to sell. It was that more troops were literally unavailable. Even a 200,000-strong occupation force could not be sustained for any length of time without reintroducing the draft. And a draft was not to be considered for a panoply of reasons, including the way it would undermine public support for a war and the post-Vietnam military's commitment to an all-volunteer force.

Rumsfeld's agenda—and the practical limit on a larger deployment—was the buzzsaw that General Eric Shinseki ran into when he shared with a congressional committee his view that a much larger force was needed. Shinseki was publicly contradicted by Paul Wolfowitz a few days later and forced into early retirement shortly thereafter. Rumsfeld's neoconservative deputy wasn't steeped in the military transformation debate. He hatcheted Shinseki because he understood that a lean deployment was the only kind possible, and had embraced it as the price of getting his boss on board.

The risk of a lengthy or difficult occupation similarly threatened to undermine Rumsfeld's goal by making war with Iraq seem like a big, uncertain project. That explains why officials who focused on what would come after the invasion got the Shinseki treatment as well. Contingency planning is one of the Defense Department's core functions, and there was no reason to doubt it was happening in relation to the pending invasion of Iraq. But the secretary of defense wanted no focus on the possibility that the occupation might go badly. With help from Cheney's office, Rumsfeld squashed a planning effort under way at the State Department, where Tom Warrick had supervised the Future of Iraq Project. This effort yielded a thirteen-volume study of postwar problems, covering everything from the administration of justice to protecting archaeological treasures. Rumsfeld buried the State Department plan and blacklisted the planners. Recognizing the bureaucratic imperative, Wolfowitz helped undercut elaborate postwar preparations. Pentagon officials interviewing candidates to assist with the transition in Iraq scoffed at the idea that the civilian administrators they were hiring would be overseas for as long as ten months. By that time, they'd be turning the liberated country over to the Iraqis.

THE NEOCONSERVATIVES THEMSELVES had a different motivation for going to war with Iraq. They were less focused on preventing what Saddam might do to the United States than on what getting rid of him could do *for* the United States. The neocons thought pulling the plug on his toxic regime would transform the sick political culture of the Arab Middle East.

There is considerable irony here. When they first emerged in the 1970s, the neoconservatives were anything but wide-eyed idealists. They were tough-minded skeptics about the efficacy of well-intentioned government intervention in both the domestic and international spheres. The founding document of neoconservative foreign policy is Jeane Kirkpatrick's 1979 *Commentary* essay "Dictatorships and Double Standards," which condemned Jimmy Carter's naive promotion of democracy and human rights, criticizing the pressure Carter applied against repressive regimes in Nicaragua and Iran that had been friendly to the United States. Drawing a distinction between totalitarian governments and merely authoritarian ones, Kirkpatrick argued that once governments went communist, they stayed that way.

But with the waning of the Soviet threat, neoconservatives turned around 180 degrees and called for American pressure against authoritarian regimes, on the theory that democracy was the best safeguard against communist expansion. They pushed Reagan to create the National Endowment for Democracy, an institution that encouraged the emergence of multiparty democracy in various countries. The crucial moment in the neoconservative reversal came in 1986, when Paul Wolfowitz, then assistant secretary of state for East Asia, pulled Reagan away from supporting the Marcos regime in the Philippines, which led to a peaceful revolution and a successful democratic transition. Being largely shut out of George H. W. Bush's administration solidified the neoconservative emphasis on democratic transformation in China and elsewhere as the alternative to balance-of-power realism in the post–Cold War world.

After September 11, 2001, the growing neoconservative enthusiasm for democracy was transmuted into a reverse domino theory for the Arab world. Many neocons believed that turning secularized Iraq into a third pro-Western democracy in the region would cause other authoritarian regimes to topple. As it liberalized, the Middle East would cease to provide a breeding ground for terrorism. Arabs would also come to accept the presence of Israel, something the mostly Jewish neoconservatives cared about especially. Wolfowitz has often been described as the "architect" of war in Iraq. The war could have used an architect—someone responsible for planning what would happen during the occupation. In reality, he was more like the war's theologian, coming up with a variety of theorems, arguments, and justifications for his abiding faith that the political nature of the Arab world could be transformed from without.

Wolfowitz and his protégé Scooter Libby, the other most influential neoconservative inside the administration, were driven by a particular notion about how to transform the sick political culture of the Middle East. The big thinker behind their theory was the Arab scholar Bernard Lewis, a professor emeritus at Princeton. The originator of the phrase "the clash of civilizations," Lewis believed Muslims had been engaged in a "cosmic struggle for world domination" since the time of Muhammad. Centuries of defeat, subjugation, and misrule, to which the United States contributed by supporting corrupt and incompetent dictators, prepared the way for Islamist terrorism. Cheney met Lewis when he was secretary of defense, and the two became friends. After September 11, he became interested in Lewis's argument about what had gone wrong in the Arab world.

Over a series of lunches at the vice president's residence in 2002, Lewis laid out his case for using American military power to change the regime in Iraq. Years of "anxious propitiation" had left the Muslim world convinced of our weakness. Force was what Arabs respected. A conclusive show of strength could catalyze a change in the opposite direction. Lewis's framework was heavily based on his understanding of Turkey, the Muslim country he had studied most closely. In his analogy, the exiled Chalabi would play the role of the secularizing Mustafa Kemal Ataturk, reorienting his country toward the West. Lewis's academic disciple Fouad Ajami, a Lebanese-born Shi'ite, made similar arguments to the vice president and Libby. In his August 2002 speech to the Veterans of Foreign Wars, Cheney quoted him: "the Middle East expert Professor Fouad Ajami predicts that after liberation, the streets in Basra and Baghdad are 'sure to erupt in joy in the same way the throngs in Kabul greeted the Americans.'" Many people who never read a word of Lewis's scholarly work absorbed his ideas by way of Ajami's columns in *U.S. News & World Report,*

Charles Krauthammer's in *The Washington Post,* and Thomas Friedman's in *The New York Times.*

The neoconservatives have a weakness for historical analogies—and for one analogy in particular. "Anxious propitiation" was a fancy name for appeasement, compromising with an enemy that needed confronting. In this analogy, Saddam was Hitler, who grew in strength as the West postponed challenging him. Or, if not Nazi Germany, Iraq was a Soviet-style totalitarian state, vulnerable to a combination of American moral and military pressure. It was these comparisons that led neoconservatives to assume that American forces would receive a hero's welcome when their tanks rolled into Iraq. Thinking by metaphor, they compared the coming Arab liberation to the emancipation of Western Europe from Nazism in 1944 and of Eastern Europe from communism in 1989. Why wouldn't liberated Iraqis shower the same gratitude upon their friend the United States?

But if democratic transformation was the neoconservatives' reason for war with Iraq, they recognized that more straightforward security arguments would have greater currency inside the bureaucracy and with the public. WMD and terrorist links weren't mere cover stories for the neocons. From their point of view, these were solid arguments for regime change. But Wolfowitz's tendency to give his transformational theory realist cover, and the corresponding tendency of the nationalist hawks to offer moral justifications, made the case for a war a jumble. In the summer of 2002, the neocon and non-neocon justifications were converging in an overdetermined conclusion. They all thought there were so many good reasons for regime change in Iraq that it didn't much matter which ones any particular official emphasized.

By mid-2002, Cheney had become a down-the-line ally of the neoconsevatives. But that does not mean he had turned into some sort of democratic idealist. He never cited Bernard Lewis's theory in any of his public advocacy for the war. For the congenitally pessimistic vice president, transforming the political culture of the Middle East can't have been more than a castle in the sky, a long-shot best-case scenario. But to speculate in the absence of more concrete evidence, the vice president surely recognized that the grandiosity of the neocon vision of a new Arab world would resonate with the president. Favoring the war and recognizing Bush's weakness for the big idea, Cheney would have had to be less shrewd than we know he is not to cite Lewis's arguments. For Bush, boldness had a constant allure. Remaking the Middle East via Iraq was just the kind of game-changing idea he went for.

If there was a third person in the room when Bush made his decision, it would have been Condi Rice. If she wasn't there, Rice would have been the first person Bush discussed his decision with after making it. Rice has an almost spousal antenna for what George W. Bush is thinking. She invariably manages to arrive in the same place he's going at the same moment. Based on what we know about their relationship, Rice's role in the decision to go to war was almost certainly not fervent advocacy on either side beforehand, but rather feeding the president's need to feel he was doing the right thing once he made up his mind. In the course of bolstering Bush, Rice always convinced herself as well. This was not reckless in the way Cheney's advocacy was, but it was an abdication of her fundamental responsibility as national security adviser.

Resistance from 41's cautious diplomats, especially Rice's mentor Brent Scowcroft, watered the seedling of his regime-change decision. Scowcroft and Baker, who had taken Kissinger's place as the amoral demons of neoconservative thought, both criticized the idea of democratic transformation, giving rise to the widespread assumption that George H. W. Bush disagreed with the direction in which his son was headed. Scowcroft's op-ed piece, entitled "Don't Attack Saddam," appeared in *The Wall Street Journal* on August 15, 2002, the timing suggestive of inside information about what was happening inside the Oval Office. Given their goal of getting George W. Bush to press ahead with his conclusion, the neoconservatives could hardly have chosen better antagonists. They also found themselves pushing against an open door in trying to persuade Bush to ignore objections at the U.N. Security Council. Where his father had painstakingly assembled international support for repelling Saddam's invasion of Kuwait, 43 thought ignoring the objections of a few irksome allies not only made life easier but was politically shrewd. "The more the Europeans attack me, the stronger I am in the United States," Bush told José María Aznar, when the Spanish prime minister visited his ranch in Crawford less than a month before the war began. Aznar, an ally, said the only thing that worried him was Bush's boundless confidence.

Bush's ignorance about Iraq on the eve of the invasion remains shocking. In January 2003, he invited three leading Iraqi exiles to the White House. The conversation indicated that he didn't know the difference between Sunni and Shi'ite Muslims. One of the exiles, Kanan Makiya, recalled Bush turning to Rice at the same meeting and saying, "Our preparations for rebuilding Iraq are well advanced, right?" "Yes, Mr. President," Rice replied. With the Iraqi National Congress plan that Cheney supported, Bush felt even less need than he might have otherwise to consider such minutiae. The American military would quickly crush the Iraqi army and Republican Guard, which wouldn't fight any more convincingly than they had in 1991. The exiles echoed Fouad Ajami's prediction that American forces would be greeted with "sweets and flowers." We would install a Chalabi government, and begin withdrawing in a matter of months. Had Bush confessed his feelings at that point, they might have resembled Henry V's charge to his bishops on the eve of another invasion:

Now are we well resolved; and by God's help,
And yours, the noble sinews of our power,
France being ours, we'll bend it to our awe
Or break it all to pieces.

THE CABLE CHATTERERS SWOONED at Bush's "Mission Accomplished" performance. Chris Matthews cooed about Bush's "amazing display of leadership" and macho swagger. "I think we like having a hero as our president," he declared on *Countdown with Keith Olbermann.* On an edition of Matthews's own show *Hardball,* G. Gordon Liddy noted the way the parachute harness emphasized Bush's "manly characteristic." On CNN, Laura Ingraham described Bush as "a real man."

Bathed as he was in the glow of success, it took some time for the president to recognize that the occupation was not going as planned, or more precisely that it was going as unplanned. The president remained focused on finding Saddam Hussein. But once the dictator was captured, Bush's only real source of disappointment seemed to be that the Iraqis weren't showing gratitude to their American liberators, the way people in the former Warsaw Pact countries had to Ronald Reagan after the fall of the Berlin Wall. Bush's obsession with this point is perhaps the only insight to come out of Paul Bremer's self-serving memoir of his period in charge of the Coalition Provisional Authority in Iraq. Bush repeatedly told Bremer that the first president of the new Iraqi government had to be "someone who's willing to stand up and thank the American people for their sacrifice in liberating Iraq." In discussions about who should be president of Iraq, Bush advocated an obscure Sunni businessman named Ghazi al-Yawar because, in Bremer's words, he "had been favorably impressed with his open thanks to the Coalition."

When Ayad Allawi was chosen as interim prime minister at the end of May 2004, Bush harped on the same point, noting in a Rose Garden press conference that Allawi "stood up and thanked the American people, for which I was grateful. He was speaking to the—to the mothers and dads and wives and husbands of our brave troops who have helped them become a free country and I appreciated his strong statement."

When Allawi visited Washington that fall, he made a point of voicing his overwhelming gratitude to the United States at every opportunity—including in a speech to Congress written for him at the White House. "There are no words that can express the debt of gratitude that future generations of Iraqis will owe to Americans," Allawi said. "It would have been easy to have turned your back on our plight, but this is not the tradition of this great country, nor the first time in history you stood up with your allies for freedom and democracy."

This ventriloquism reflects Bush's own view of his historic role. Liberating Iraq placed him alongside FDR, Truman, and Reagan. Bush seems never to have grasped why Iraqis might be ambivalent about liberators who replaced despotism with chaos. In early 2007, he was still fixated on the issue, telling Scott Pelley of *60 Minutes* in an interview at Camp David: "I think the Iraqi people owe the American people a huge debt of gratitude. That's the problem here in America. They wonder whether or not there is a gratitude level that's significant enough in Iraq," Bush said. But the American people weren't wondering that; only Bush was. The American people were wondering how we'd gotten into this mess, and how we might get out.

The failure to find WMD helped expose the difference between reason and rationale. In May 2003, Wolfowitz was the first to come partially clean, in an interview he gave to the journalist Sam Tanenhaus for *Vanity Fair*. "For reasons that have a lot to do with the U.S. government bureaucracy we settled on the one issue that everyone could agree on which was weapons of mass destruction as the core reason," Wolfowitz said. That's an accurate characterization of Wolfowitz's personal view. He would have wanted regime change even if he knew there were no WMD. For Cheney, however, WMD—and terrorist links—were more than an argument of convenience. He clung tenaciously to the idea that WMD would be found, long after David Kay, the head of the postwar survey group, told him it had all been a delusion. The absence of biological weapons undermined Cheney's reason for going to war, not just his rationale.

The president, on the other hand, seemed almost bizarrely untroubled. After telling Bush in January 2004 that he had not found evidence of WMD in Iraq, Kay was amazed to encounter no sign of disappointment. "I don't think he ever lost ten minutes of sleep over the failure to find WMD," Kay later commented. According to Andrew Card, Bush still believed in 2006 that Saddam had them. (Freud on Woodrow Wilson: "facts ceased to exist for him if they conflicted with his unconscious desires.") At a Washington press dinner in March of that year, Bush performed a comic riff about looking all over for WMD in the Oval Office. This was a joking matter to Bush because illegal weapons had never been his real reason for going to war. His unconscious motive was finishing his father's business. His conscious one was draining the Islamic swamp. The Lewis-Wolfowitz argument was still available, and in the summer and fall it began to take precedence over the various other rationales Bush had offered in the run-up to the invasion.

AS THE WMD MIRAGE melted away, Bush's retrospective case for the war shifted, and his theory of foreign policy along with it. Bush Doctrine 4.0 became Democracy in the Middle East (11/6/03–1/19/05). If the West Point speech expressed the justification that supported invading Iraq, Bush's November 6, 2003, speech at the National Endowment for Democracy framed a new theory of international relations around the way he now hoped to justify his war. The United States, he announced, "has adopted a new policy," which he described as "a forward strategy for freedom in the Middle East." Bush argued that excusing and accommodating tyranny over the previous sixty years hadn't made Americans safe "because in the long run stability cannot be purchased at the expense of liberty." Stability was one of Scowcroft's watchwords. Bush called liberty "the design of nature" and "the direction of history."

Here finally was the grand vision Bush had been looking for. Democratizing the Arab world was a clear, moral goal, the ambitious work of a consequential presidency. Like compassionate conservatism, it was a form of social evangelism, a mission inspired by faith but secular in application. Bush's new formulation had the added advantage of extending the term of evaluation. If we were witnessing what Rice called "the birth pangs of a new Middle East," the first report card wouldn't be in for some time.

But Bush's stirring words underscored the difficulty with his ever-changing foreign policy. The problem wasn't that he wanted to spread democracy and human rights—a goal that in other contexts unites liberal hawks and doves with many conservatives. Indeed, it is impossible to imagine a successful American foreign policy that does not draw upon ideals as well as interests. Bush's problem wasn't his broadest goal but his relentless ebb into abstraction, incompetent execution, and glaring inconsistency. In a matter of four years, the president's view had reversed itself completely. In 1999, Bush rejected the very notion of nation-building. Now he was embracing *region*-building. This implied, among other changes, a fundamental reorientation of the training and practices of America's armed forces. But the military, perhaps taking Bush at his earlier word, had not planned the second Gulf War with the goal of remaking a society in mind.

Had he been someone capable of acknowledging error, Bush's misjudgment in invading Iraq might have been mitigated by skillful improvisation. How might such a person have reacted? He would have told his secretary of defense that the spectacle of looters stripping government buildings down to their concrete skeletons wasn't the kind of untidy freedom the United States could tolerate. As the Pentagon failed to create viable structures, he might have shifted control to the State Department and devolved power to the United Nations, instead of trying to fend it off. He could have acknowledged the emergence of an insurgency, and adopted a different strategy to combat it before 2007. He should have blocked, reversed, or at least understood the significance of Paul Bremer's two first and most disastrous orders, to disband the Iraqi army and bar those with Ba'ath Party connections from serving in the government. (Bush later told Robert Draper that disbanding the army wasn't his policy, and that he wasn't sure why it had happened.) He would have fired Rumsfeld after Abu Ghraib, if not sooner. He would have taken steps to dismantle the echo chamber around him, instead of adding layers of insulation. None of that would have ensured a better outcome, but it surely would have diminished the harm from his original mistake.

Why couldn't Bush respond in a more supple fashion, even after his reelection? Partly, his inability to adjust reflects his limitations as an executive. Despite his MBA training, Bush emphasizes leadership and decision-making to the exclusion of administration and management. He delegates manfully, but doesn't solicit feedback, evaluate results, or hold people accountable, except in extraordinary circumstances. Unlike his father, he isn't comfortable entertaining inconclusive debate. Bush sees reconsidering decisions or openly changing course as evidence of weak leadership. This stubbornness was born of a success that came from not giving in to his parents' doubts about him and not listening to their advice. At a temperamental level, the president has almost no ability to accept blame or learn from mistakes. Disagreement, whether from critics or allies, sounds like his mother's nagging and his father's disappointment. Thus criticism has the opposite of its intended effect on him. Disapproval hardens Bush's conviction that he must be right and reinforces his refusal to surrender. Having earned his position in life through willpower, he feels he shouldn't have to ask anyone for permission. This obstinacy has been evident in his personnel practices as well as policy choices. The more the media demanded Bush yield up a head—CIA director George Tenet, Rumsfeld, Rove, Gonzales—the longer that person was likely to be staying around. The problem here is pretty obvious. If all criticism is discounted as whining and accepting it equates to personal weakness, how can you ever recognize that you're wrong?

Bush's inflexibility is rooted in the old family drama. It reflects not just a personality forged in opposition to his father, but an idea of leadership developed in conscious contrast to him. Where George H. W. Bush weighed options, W. sizes you up and decides. Where 41 saw shades of gray, 43 finds moral clarity. "The son prides himself on being the guy who cuts through it all, who is decisive, not wishy-washy," Brent Scowcroft told me in November 2007. "The subtleties, partly because of his inexperience, don't seem to matter as much. His father, with the background he has, knows that at best you're operating forty-nine/fifty-one—and you'd better be sure that the fifty-one is on your side and not the forty-nine."

"Resolution" is a key term for Bush 43. It is his essential metaphor for political leaders who show character in the face of difficulty and challenge: Churchill, Truman, and Reagan, all of whom were opposed fiercely but vindicated in the end. To accept negative judgments about his decision to invade Iraq or his handling of the occupation would threaten something more vulnerable than troop morale. It would vindicate his father's diplomacy, caution, and flexibility over his own hawkish certitude.

Bush makes a point of saying, whenever it comes up, that he doesn't get advice from his father about the conduct of the war. Judging from his father's roundabout efforts to influence him, this seems likely to be true. In his book about Rumsfeld, Andrew Cockburn reports a visit 43 paid to Kennebunkport during the summer of 2004. His father gave him a memo that Scowcroft had asked him to pass along about Iraq. The president glanced at it before throwing it aside, telling his dad, "I'm sick and tired of getting papers from Brent Scowcroft telling me what to do, and I never want to see another one again." With that 43 stalked out of the room and slammed the door behind him. Bush appointed Robert Gates secretary of defense only after asking Gates to assure him that he didn't agree with Scowcroft on the war.

George W. Bush found a surprising source of support in another elder statesman, Scowcroft's old patron and former business partner Henry Kissinger. Kissinger had publicly supported the war to overthrow Saddam, but privately told friends he never thought Bush would be stupid enough to try to make Iraq into a democracy. In conversations with Bush reported by Bob Woodward, however, Kissinger delivered a message of resolve that confirmed 43's abiding instinct. He told Bush and Cheney not to allow the debate to be framed around troop reductions. This, he said, would spur the enemy, undermine support for the war, and lead inevitably to defeat. Kissinger gave Mike Gerson a copy of the famous "salted peanuts" memo he had written to Nixon about Vietnam in 1969. ("Withdrawal of U.S. troops will become like salted peanuts to the American public; the more U.S. troops come home, the more will be demanded.")

Even after anything resembling near-term success in Iraq became an implausible objective, Bush continued to frame a binary choice between victory and surrender. The collapse of his preemption justification for the war (terrorism + WMD = intolerable threat) sent Bush not into any reexamination of his decision, but toward grander and grander justification. Throughout 2004, the scope of what he called his "Freedom Agenda" expanded from the goal of democracy in the Middle East to the goal of democracy everywhere. Paradoxically, Bush fully adopted the argument of the neoconservatives just as their fondest hope—the transformation of the Middle East through the invasion of Iraq—was turning to ashes.

Shortly before the election in 2004, Bush's friend and former Texas Rangers partner Tom Bernstein gave him the galley proof of *The Case for Democracy* by the former Soviet refusenik and right-wing Israeli politician Natan Sharansky. Sharansky's book portrays Bush in a heroic light, comparing the war against terrorism to the struggle against the Nazis and the Soviets. The author describes his reaction to a speech in June 2002, when Bush turned his back on Yassir Arafat and called on the Palestinians to elect leaders untainted by terror. "I re-read the speech, almost pinching myself. It was a beautiful expression of the principles I also believed should be the foundation of the peace process," Sharansky writes. "From my perspective, the president's speech was potentially no less dramatic than when, twenty years earlier, Ronald Reagan had called the Soviet Union an evil empire."

Sharansky draws a contrast to Bush's father's "notorious" Chicken Kiev speech telling the Ukrainians to avoid "suicidal nationalism," which he calls "an unmitigated disaster." "A people who were only months away from realizing their 300-year-old dream of independence were being told by the American president to forget about it," he writes. Sharansky had met the elder Bush in the White House in 1990 and was asked the disagreeable question of how the United States could help Gorbachev keep the Soviet Union together. The former dissident relates that Bush Senior told him it would be better to have the Soviet nuclear arsenal remain in reliable hands than fall under the control of unknown leaders, even if they were popularly elected. To Sharansky, Bush 41's comments typified the immoral embrace of stability over democratic aspiration.

All this was music to the son's ears. Bush 43 was so taken with Sharansky's book that he gave copies to Condi Rice and Tony Blair. He touted the book in an interview on CNN. "This is a book that . . .

summarizes how I feel. I would urge people to read it," he told John King. After the election, Bush invited Sharansky to the White House for an hour-long talk. Sharansky later recounted the conversation to Jeffrey Goldberg of *The New Yorker*:

> "At the end of the conversation, I say, 'Say hello to your mother and father.' And he said, 'My father?' He looked very surprised I would say this. So I say to the President, 'I like your father. He is very good to my wife when I am in prison.' And President Bush says, 'But what about Chicken Kiev?' "

SHARANSKYISM, THE EXFOLIATED version of the Freedom Agenda, became Bush Doctrine 5.0, Freedom Everywhere (1/20/05–11/7/06). Bush unveiled his newest foreign policy in his second inaugural address, which announced the goal of abolishing oppression on planet earth: "It is the policy of the United States to seek and support the growth of democratic movements and institutions in every nation and culture, with the ultimate goal of ending tyranny in our world." Democracy is God's gift to humanity, Bush declared, and the United States would help extend its blessings. In his second term, as the remaining neocons were exiting the administration, blaming him for the failure in Iraq and trying to salvage what remained of their own reputations, Bush was adopting a faith-flavored version of their fantasy foreign policy. "History has an ebb and flow of justice, but history also has a visible direction, set by liberty and the Author of Liberty," he proclaimed.

It is hard to believe that anyone other than Bush and his speechwriters, who seemed increasingly to be making his foreign policy, thought about the issue of democracy promotion in such shallow, utopian terms. Though his inaugural address sounded religious, there is no theological basis for democracy as God's chosen system of government. The Old Testament favors monarchy, the New Testament, communism. It was as if Bush now simply identified his democratic crusade with the will of God. (Freud on Woodrow Wilson at the Versailles peace talks: "Wilson's unconscious identification of himself with the Saviour had become so obvious that it compelled even those who had never studied the deeper psychic strata to recognize its existence.") And if the right-wing liberation theology of the speech was narcissistically askew, its foreign policy argument was equally idiosyncratic. The notion of the United States leading an eternal moral crusade for democracy did not represent the views of Rumsfeld or Cheney, let alone Powell, Scowcroft, Kissinger, or 41. Only Condi Rice, who had long since ceased to think with any independence, echoed Bush's Freedom Agenda in remarks in Paris a couple of weeks later. "Our charge is clear," Rice, the new secretary of state, told an audience of French political science students. "We on the right side of freedom's divide have an obligation to help those unlucky enough to have been born on the wrong side of that divide." The president's second inaugural address was breathtaking in part because of how completely a man who once condemned nation-building as social work had now abandoned any shred of realism, at least at a philosophic level.

The messianic language in the president's second inaugural did inspire a brief attempt to translate his Freedom Agenda into policy. In February 2005, Rice postponed a planned visit to Egypt to register a protest against the detention of the opposition leader Ayman Nour. Bush then phoned Hosni Mubarak to demand that the Egyptian president allow a freer press and let outside observers monitor the upcoming election. Lebanon's "Cedar Revolution," which brought down the pro-Syrian government, encouraged the administration to think its transformational Mideast policy was having an impact. Rice also pressed for elections in the Gaza Strip. In a burst of democratic idealism, she ignored warnings from Israel and the Palestinian Authority and insisted on participation by the terrorist organization Hamas. There may even have been a municipal election of some sort in totalitarian Saudi Arabia.

But Bush Doctrine 5.0 flopped in practice faster than any of its predecessors. Within a year, no one in the administration other than Rice wanted to talk about the Freedom Agenda. This idea did the impossible: it caused Dick Cheney and the State Department bureaucracy to agree about something, namely that the president's policy was a pipe dream. The problem was not that the message was wrong. It was the impracticality of implementing idealistic policy in a dangerous world. When Mubarak cracked down on protesters and postponed elections, the Bush administration responded as timorously as in the pre-9/11 days, lest the Egyptian president reduce his cooperation on terrorism and oil prices—or worse, become vulnerable to Islamist overthrow. The Israeli reinvasion of southern Lebanon squelched hopes for a democratic renaissance there. And the election that brought Hamas to power in Gaza in January 2006 underscored the risk Jeane Kirkpatrick once warned against: that indiscriminate pressure for democracy could produce regimes no better on human rights and far more hostile to the United States.

The dissonance between Bush's message and his cavalier attitude toward civil liberties discredited him as a moral messenger. While pressing for divinely ordained liberty in the Middle East, Bush was still taking Dick Cheney's advice on keeping Guantánamo open, allowing torture, and unconstitutionally listening in on phone conversations by American citizens. Thus did Bush's universal call for democracy not only become an exercise in futility but in many places actually prove counterproductive. From Russia to Venezuela, associating democratic opponents with Bush's foreign policy became a pretext for taking rights away. In Iran, the Nobel Peace Prize–winning human rights lawyer Shirin Ebadi complained that Bush's advocacy was setting her cause backward. Thus did the fifth Bush Doctrine recede into what the president called, in a phrase from his second inaugural, the "work of generations."

BY THE TIME CHENEY peppered Harry Whittington in early 2006, the wise heads of Washington were all saying Bush was in need of external rescue—which naturally made him resist it harder. Bush's father's friends tried to function like the tailhook that caught his plane on the USS *Lincoln*, grabbing hold lest it plop into the Pacific. James Baker—the man the Bushes call in an emergency—put together the

Iraq Study Group to make recommendations about the war. Bush naturally resisted this parental second-guessing, with Cheney's office arguing against the congressionally chartered advisory board on the basis of "unitary executive" theory.

For the Republican side, Baker picked friends and advisers including 41's former CIA director Robert Gates, his former secretary of state Lawrence Eagleburger, and former Wyoming senator Alan Simpson, another of the elder Bush's old pals. Scowcroft did not serve on the panel, but was consulted as an outside expert. Most of the participants saw their task as taking the son's car keys away. One member of the panel made this metaphor explicit, comparing the job to a family's effort to deal with an alcoholic member who can't see how much damage he is causing. Asked how Bush had reacted to being briefed on the group's conclusions, Eagleburger joked, rather cruelly: "His reaction was, 'Where's my drink?'"

Not surprisingly given the views of its participants, the Iraq Study Group prescribed the antithesis of Bush's Freedom Agenda. The report called for a return to diplomatic realism, without any reference to democratizing the Middle East or the Almighty's Gift of Freedom. It stated the goal of withdrawing a significant number of American combat units from Iraq by early 2008. It proposed renewing efforts to broker a peace agreement between Israel and the Palestinians, and argued for initiating dialogue with Iran and Syria. Many of these ideas were simply a throwback to the policies of Bush 41 and Baker's shuttle diplomacy.

Bush's reaction to the Iraq Study Group went beyond brushing off its unhelpful suggestions. At a press conference with Tony Blair, the president sarcastically told reporters that reports like Baker-Hamilton were seldom read. But he and Blair took this one so seriously that they actually did read it. Bush went on to diminish the uninvited meddling at every opportunity. The thirty-thousand-troop surge he announced in January was a direct rejection of the study group's advice, though he made a point of finding a page in the report that could be read as licensing troop increases. It was during this period, when his son was dismissing the Iraq Study Group report, that Bush Senior was continually breaking down in tears at public occasions, at the launch of the USS *Bush,* in the Florida House of Delegates, and on *Larry King Live*.

Without conceding a thing, George W. Bush was losing control over his own policy. He had to let Rumsfeld go. After the Republican defeat in 2006, diplomacy returned, with Rice pressing negotiations with Iran and North Korea over their nuclear programs. She began her own shuttle diplomacy in the Middle East. The administration tried to alter its tone in relation to European allies, even proposing an initiative on climate change.

In this context, the president's increasingly messianic rhetoric ceased to command attention. At a conference in Prague organized by Sharansky, Bush proclaimed his Freedom Agenda as a kind of global manifest destiny. "Freedom is the design of our Maker, and the longing of every soul," he declared, calling himself a "dissident President" because of his goal of ending world tyranny. But by this time even the biggest daydreamers among the neoconservatives were growing weary of Bush's fantasy. Richard Perle, speaking from the same podium an hour earlier, called on Bush "to close the gap between what he says and believes and what the machinery of our government actually does." But this was impossible, because Bush had never learned enough about the State Department bureaucracy to reorient it. As with his faith-based initiative, leaving implementation of his big idea to others meant that nothing happened.

Bush's final foreign policy (11/8/06 to date) was the absence of any functioning doctrine at all. After the Republican loss of both houses of Congress, his administration cobbled together an enfeebled hybrid based on the collapse of the previous five: a retreat from unipolarity, a moratorium on the application of preemption (though bombing Iran remained under discussion), and a general agreement to regard the Freedom Agenda as presidential hot air. Bush and his speechwriters have not acknowledged his final doctrine's demise. He has said that he will make democracy promotion his major post-presidential project, and that he intends to set up a freedom institute as part of the presidential library to be built at Southern Methodist University in Dallas.

The final irony of Bush's foreign policy crack-up was the way it vindicated his father's choices. Not "finishing the job" and taking ownership of Iraq in 1991 now looked like an act of wisdom. Not making a triumphal speech when the Berlin Wall came down appeared as shrewd management of a dicey situation, which advanced the practical cause of freedom more than a provocative speech would have. Appreciating the value of stability sounded like maturity. Avoiding needlessly bellicose rhetoric seemed like common sense. As the historian Timothy Naftali writes in his generally admiring 2007 biography of George H. W. Bush, "As the younger Bush's own presidency limped to an end, many missed the elder Bush's realism, his diplomacy, his political modesty, and, yes, even his prudence." The more the son's Walker qualities glared, the more his father's historical reputation grew.

THIS DISILLUSIONMENT with the false hero can be found in the Henriad too. Both Laurence Olivier's classic 1944 film of *Henry V* and Kenneth Branagh's 1989 version glorify the protagonist as a patriotic champion. But others have interpreted the play less nationalistically. In 2003, the director Nicholas Hytner staged *Henry V* at London's National Theatre in desert camouflage, presenting it as a parable about the recent invasion of Iraq. This sort of cynical reading has the effect of making the negative judgments about Henry within the play resonate more persuasively than the lines of celebration. To the French dauphin he challenges and later kills, the young English king is "a vain, giddy, shallow, humorous youth"—humorous having the meaning of "capricious."

While he is a resolute leader, Henry V is also a tyrant. He threatens to massacre French civilians, warning the citizens of Harfleur to surrender lest they see their daughters raped, their fathers' heads dashed against the walls, and "your naked infants spitted upon pikes." In the judgment of the great nineteenth-century essayist William Hazlitt,

> He was careless, dissolute, and ambitious; —idle, or doing mischief. In private, he seemed to have no idea of the common decencies of life, which he subjected to a kind of regal license; in public affairs, he seemed to have no idea of any rule of right or wrong, but brute force, glossed over with a little religious hypocrisy and archiepiscopal advice. His principles did not change with his situation and professions. . . . Henry, because he did not know how to govern his own kingdom, determined to make war upon his neighbors. Because his own title to the crown was doubtful, he laid claim to that of France. Because he did not know how to exercise power, which had just dropped into his hands, to any one good purpose, he immediately undertook (a cheap and obvious resource of sovereignty) to do all the mischief he could.

Change "France" to "Iraq," and this can serve as harsh judgment on the career of George W. Bush. After giving up drinking, finding God, and assuming power, he became, like Henry V, a stick figure: narrow-minded, overconfident, and mesmerized by his own might and virtue. Hazlitt's sketch presages the failure of an American president who suffered from the same aggression, arrogance, inflexibility. Like Hal, Bush let anger guide him, justifying his instincts through a shallow resort to religious sanction. In the end, both men were less transformed than they appeared.

Shakespeare's Henry V is honest, at least with himself, about his political reason for invading France. The new King hopes to remove the taint from the crown his father stole from Richard II and establish his branch of the Lancaster family as the rightful line of succession. King Henry knows that the pretext his legal advisers have cooked up for war is pretty thin. His justification is that military victory will wash the Lancaster slate clean. But the play also suggests a psychological motivation, which the monarch understands less well. Henry V has to prove that his father, and everyone else, was wrong to expect so little of him. He does this by exceeding the accomplishments of Henry IV, who talked about, but never began, his crusade to

Jerusalem. Through bold, decisive action, Henry V thinks he can show himself to be not just a worthy successor, but an improvement upon his flawed father.

The conclusion to the Bush Tragedy is supplied by Henry V—not the character in Shakespeare's drama, but Henry V the historical figure. Military transformation in the form of the longbow gave the English army an extraordinary technological advantage, to which historians credit the miraculous victory over superior numbers at Agincourt. But occupying France proved to be a larger problem for Hal's son, Henry VI. France was too big, the English didn't have enough men, and the long conflict drained the their treasury. The English yielded back more and more captured territory before finally giving up the dream of ruling France in 1453, thirty-eight years after Agincourt.

In the early nineteenth century, Hazlitt noted that the English people still loved their fictional Henry V, the hero of Shakespeare's play. "There he is a very amiable monster, a very splendid pageant," he wrote. But Hazlitt himself found it impossible to admire him.

"He was a king of England, but not a constitutional one, and we only like kings according to the law."

CHAPTER SEVEN

Dead Precedents

Look back into your mighty ancestors!

—HENRY V

IN MAY 1940, WINSTON CHURCHILL BECAME PRIME MINISTER and confronted perhaps the bleakest state of affairs in his nation's history. The Blitzkrieg had already swept across Belgium and Holland, and France was on the verge of collapse. The British fleet was trapped at Dunkirk, facing its greatest defeat in centuries. After overrunning the European continent, the Nazis were bound to invade the British Isles next.

In this moment of doom, Churchill took it upon himself to persuade Parliament that there must be no negotiation with Hitler, and to steel the country for the anticipated attack. He went about this mission with a combination of realism, hope, and eloquence that make his first few weeks in office among the most poetic passages in modern history. Through his language and his will, he bound the British people together, and prepared them for what was to come.

Churchill's words from this period never fail to give you goose bumps. They are to Anglo-American political oratory what Shakespeare is to English literature, a model and inspiration for most of what follows. And indeed, it was with the echoes of "gentlemen in England, now a-bed" from Henry V's St. Crispin's Day speech that

Churchill spoke to the nation over the BBC on May 19: "Let us therefore brace ourselves to our duties, and so bear ourselves that if the British Empire and its Commonwealth last for a thousand years, Men will still say: *This* was their finest hour."

Nearly everything Churchill said in those days was memorable. "I have nothing to offer but blood, toil, tears, and sweat," "We shall fight on the beaches," "Nay, if we fight to the end, it can only be glorious," "A long night of barbarism"—these and other indelible phrases all come from the concentrated period of a few weeks. "We shall go on and we shall fight it out, here or elsewhere," Churchill told his cabinet on May 24. "If this long island story of ours is to end at last, let it end only when each one of us lies choking in his own blood upon the ground." One understands why statesmen on both sides of the Atlantic borrow this language so often—even though comparing their situations to Churchill's invariably courts ridicule.

Such was the case in the summer of 2001, when the new American president offered some spontaneous remarks at an Oval Office ceremony in which he accepted the loan of a bronze head of Churchill from Her Majesty's government. Bush noted that Churchill "stood on principle. He was a man of great courage. He knew what he believed." Because of these qualities, Bush commented, Churchill "seemed like a Texan to me." The president went on to say that Sir Winston "wasn't afraid of public opinion polls" and "didn't need focus groups to tell him what was right."

At the ceremony, Bush explained how the head came to be there. He had "casually mentioned to the Ambassador" that there was not a proper bust of Winston Churchill for him to put in the Oval Office. Later, after he had developed a close alliance with the British prime minister, Bush adjusted his story slightly. "Tony Blair knew that I was an admirer of Churchill and he arranged for this bust to be loaned here," he told a group of British journalists.

This seems a straightforward enough explanation, with an obvious point about the president's affinity for the British hero of American conservatives. Bush often joked that with the bust in his office, "Churchill is now watching my every move." But some years later,

Newsweek reported a slightly different version of how the Churchill head, a bronze made in 1946 by the sculptor Jacob Epstein, came to reside in Bush's office. Karl Rove was having dinner at the British embassy with a man who had become his friend some years before, the ambassador, Sir Christopher Meyer. According to the magazine:

> Rove mentioned George W. Bush's fascination with Churchill. "He was a man who saved the world," Rove said of Churchill, "a wartime leader who charted his own course, and did it with wit and personal morality and courage." Meyer called Rove a few days later. "The P.M. has a spare bust or two of Churchill," Meyer said. Would the president like one? Absolutely, came the reply.

As with some of Bush's other favorite legends (like the one about *A Charge to Keep,* the painting he hung above the Churchill bust), the minor discrepancies expose a telling bit of calculation. In his first version, Bush *asks* for the bust of Churchill, indicating his veneration for the British leader. In his second version, Blair *offers* the bust, recognizing Bush's affinity for Churchill. But in Rove's version, Rove arranges the deal, underscoring his own historical role (not to mention his new social status—dinner with the ambassador).

As with Bush's religious life, his projection of himself as someone fascinated by history—and by Churchill in particular—has an element of calculation, but became more genuine as time went on. When Bush announced the air assault on the Taliban in October 2001, he declared, "We will not waver, we will not tire, we will not falter, and we will not fail"—closely echoing Sir Winston in 1941: *We shall not fail or falter; we shall not weaken or tire.* However contrived at the outset, the identification became genuine; Bush really thought he saw his qualities reflected in the saturnine British statesman. In a later speech at another ceremony, Bush said that "Churchill possessed, in one writer's words, an 'absolute refusal, unlike many good and prudent men around him, to compromise or to surrender.'" He noted that Sir Winston was "the kind of guy that stood tough when you needed to stand tough; he represented values that both countries hold dear—the value of freedom, the belief in democracy, human dignity of every person."

These are not Churchillian sentiments precisely; they are Bush's beliefs, spliced into the hero Rove recommended and explained to him. Churchill staunchly defended democracy against Nazism, to be sure, but he did not believe in it the way Bush does, as a divine gift and universal solvent. He upheld the monarchy, the hereditary House of Lords, and the British Empire. He opposed Indian independence and doubted that democracy was viable there. "The best argument against democracy is a five-minute conversation with the average voter" is one of Churchill's famous sayings. As for the "human dignity of every person," it is not a concept with which Churchill has ever been identified, even if one ignores the pro-life ring to the phrase.

In saying Churchill seems like a Texan to him, Bush is claiming to share political virtues that Churchill epitomized. When he says Churchill didn't need polls or focus groups to tell him what to think, he has found a new formulation for his favorite cliché: I don't need polls and focus groups to tell *me* what to think. The compliment is so anachronistic and solipsistic that it sounds like a joke, though it wasn't meant to be. What Bush comes to admire in Churchill is simply his own self-image projected onto a grand historical screen.

It is too early for a historical verdict on Bush. But it is not too soon for a judgment on Bush's history. Bush's exploitation of Churchill is emblematic of the way he relates to the past, finding his own reality in it and then admiring what he sees reflected in the mirror. His self-regarding appropriation of history echoes his instrumentalist approach to religion, which he uses for support and self-affirmation. Bush treats the past as a storehouse of confirmatory fables. His favorite anecdotes reflect his fantasy of resolute leadership. Identification with analogous figures from the past helps Bush resist doubt and avoid hearing criticism. His use of history justifies his impulses and shores up his stubbornness.

The first glimpse of Bush's solipsistic use of history came in a 1999 debate, when Judy Woodruff asked him what he learned from a biography of the Cold War mandarin Dean Acheson that Bush had said he was reading. "The lessons learned are that the United States must not retreat within our borders, that we must promote the peace," Bush said. His answer wasn't technically wrong. But like his various Churchill comments, it didn't earn a passing grade. The candidate had summarized his own outlook on foreign policy, not Acheson's.

Bush is not a historical ignoramus. Contrary to what many assume, he does have an appetite for books, which has grown larger during his White House years. If we take his own claims seriously, reading history has become not just a pastime, but the dominant activity of his second term. With three weeks left in 2006, Bush told one writer he had already read eighty-seven books that year, as part of a competition with Karl Rove (who was ahead at 102). This is an almost implausible load. Michiko Kakutani, the daily critic for *The New York Times,* reviewed only sixty-seven books in 2006—and Bush's list included *Mao: The Unknown Story* (801 pages), *American Prometheus,* a biography of Robert Oppenheimer (784 pages), and *The Great Influenza: The Epic Story of the Deadliest Plague in History* (546 pages). And this came on top of his daily Bible reading. The White House press office has declined to release a full list, and some of the books Bush mentioned to others were thrillers about world- and damsel-saving heroes, including the Travis McGee mysteries by John D. MacDonald and George Fraser's Flashman series. But the bulk of his reading appears to be serious popular history.

In fact, Bush's count may well have been truthful. By 2006, he was severely isolated. He didn't go out in Washington, or host friends for dinner except on rare occasions. His binge reading suggests a private quest for vindication as lonely as Johnson's or Nixon's. But whether Bush flipped all those pages or not, reading history didn't do him much good for a simple reason: he doesn't know how to think historically. All politicians tend to view history politically. But the president's approach isn't just what the British historian Herbert Butterfield called the fallacy of "present-minded" history—projecting one's own world backward onto the past. Bush's approach is narcissistic history.

It reads too many of his own verities in, and gets too few of the past's complexities out.

AFTER THE SUPREME COURT ruled in *Bush v. Gore*, 41 teased 43 by calling him "Quincy," after the only other son to succeed his father as president. George W. spent his pre-inaugural break reading *John Quincy Adams: A Public Life, a Private Life*, by Paul C. Nagel, to see what might be in the comparison. But that shoe didn't fit; he had virtually nothing in common with the dour, meditative writer-statesman at the level of policy or personality. And the Adams family was a poor precedent: a two-term father and a one-term son. George W. hoped the Bush chronicles would have it the other way around. Bush did indicate, however, that he'd found a couple of points of commonality. "The man had a domineering mother, that's for certain," he told two *New York Times* reporters visiting his Crawford ranch. He also commented in the same interview that Quincy suffered unfair accusations of nepotism, noting that the elder John Adams had written "letters [to his son] assuring him that it's not the case."

In his acceptance speech at the 2000 convention, Bush had pointed to four more conventional models for the kind of consequential president he intended to be. He described the presidency as "the office of Lincoln's conscience and Teddy Roosevelt's energy and Harry Truman's integrity and Ronald Reagan's optimism." This was the standard litany of conservative saints, which has come to include Truman as an honorary Republican—and with a fifth, Churchill, appended as an honorary American. In his years in office, Bush's historical explorations have remained largely confined to these five figures. Which shrine he ransacked at which moment reflected his shifting foreign policy doctrines and changing fortunes.

During the 2000 campaign and the first nine months of his presidency, his models were Teddy Roosevelt and Ronald Reagan, the man who built the Panama Canal and the man who refused to give it away. TR (or "Ted" as Bush nicknamed him) was, like Bush, an Eastern patrician who styled himself a cowboy, in love with action and allergic to introspection—the Walker personality type in chaps. Under Rove's tutelage, Bush learned that Ted represented the conservative way of presidential activism, combining the energetic executive that Cheney propounded with Bush's missionary zeal. Along with the Adams biography, Bush spent his pre-inaugural break leafing through *Bully Pulpit*, a collection of Teddy Roosevelt quotes. Roosevelt meant "bully" in the sense of "jolly good," a nuance Bush may have missed.

If Teddy Roosevelt was a distant model, Reagan was Bush's more immediate one. He too was a self-created cowboy, and Bush copied his persona down to the ranch refuge, where he took up Reagan's hobby of clearing brush. (Bush's Western White House was in sweltering Crawford, a place no one else even pretended to like, where Reagan's was in the glorious foothills of Santa Barbara.) Like Bush, Reagan was underestimated. Like Bush, he turned his enemies' condescension to his advantage. But if he was right to dismiss some of the liberal myths about Reagan, Bush modeled himself on the equally unreal folk hero of conservatives: the governmental minimalist, the steadfast challenger of the Soviets, the conviction politician. To Bush, Reagan was another exemplar of the qualities he saw in himself, most importantly optimism, and what he called "moral courage" and "moral clarity." From the time of his campaign, Bush championed the policies of Reagan's that his father had abandoned, including supply-side tax cuts and missile defense.

Bush's oration at Reagan's National Cathedral funeral was an exercise in solipsistic praise. Bush began by talking about Rock River, the Illinois town where Reagan grew up, using the terms he usually applied to Midland: "the kind of place you remember where you prayed side by side with your neighbors, and if things were going wrong for them, you prayed for them, and knew they'd pray for you if things went wrong with you." He praised Reagan for believing in "taking a break now and again"—riding a horse at his ranch as opposed to a mountain bike. This was a hobby Bush pursued so relentlessly that the roster of those injured trying to keep up includes former commerce secretary Don Evans (broken collarbone), media adviser Mark McKinnon (separated shoulder), former chief of staff Andrew Card (broken arm), and at least one Secret Service agent with a broken rib. But the larger point was that Reagan, like Bush, didn't care about fashion or convenience, was an optimist, and held to principles "as firm and straight as the columns of this cathedral." Those principles, according to Bush, were defending liberty wherever it was threatened and calling evil by its name. "He had the confidence that comes with conviction, the strength that comes with character," Bush said.

In trying to be like Ronnie and be like Teddy, Bush faced a conflict, because of the way in which Reagan and Roosevelt were an unstable combination. The Reagan principle, somewhat at odds with the Reagan practice, is a smaller, less active domestic government combined with the powerful projection of military strength. The Teddy Roosevelt principle is dramatic governing intervention, both at home and abroad. Like his father, Bush confronted a fundamental tension of modern conservatism: how to confront problems, including the demand for a robust national defense, in a context of governmental minimalism. Teddy Roosevelt's answer was a bigger, stronger federal government. George W. Bush's solution, publicly funded religious compassion, was a paltry answer to this quandary, and he had no deeper one. Bush would embrace the contradictions within the conservative movement by taxing like a supply-sider, spending like a liberal, and praying like an evangelical.

It remains far from clear whether Bush even appreciated the larger philosophical predicament he faced. His cartoon version of Reagan acknowledged neither his hero's departures from small-government philosophy, nor his own. There was a yawning gap between Reagan's language of principle and his often pragmatic policies. Reagan cut taxes, but then raised taxes three times to mitigate the damage. There was also a massive gap between his hawkish rhetoric and his peacemongering personal instincts. Reagan said he'd never negotiate with terrorists and denounced the Evil Empire, but traded arms for hostages and horrified his hawks by embracing Gorbachev and proposing the elimination of nuclear weapons at Reykjavik. He used a mild fog to great advantage, bridging the chasms among conservatives with his charm and humor. Bill Clinton managed a comparable Democratic divide for eight years with a different set of tools, his detailed policy knowledge and a gift for empathy.

But Bush, a man of tremendous submerged anger and no patience whatsoever, lacked any such finesse in unifying the Republican Party around the compromises it needed to make, either internally or with Democrats. In Texas Bush had wheedled and charmed. But in Washington, he demanded obedience. This didn't work very well, or for very long. Bush's mulishness made it impossible for him to maintain Democratic alliances, the way Reagan did. And it meant that when his own side turned on him, as when he nominated Harriet Miers to the Supreme Court, and again over his spending and immigration policies, it did so with a surprising vehemence.

BUSH DID RECOGNIZE that his Roosevelt-Reagan model didn't fit the historical moment he faced after September 11. Only Franklin Roosevelt and Abraham Lincoln (and, briefly, John F. Kennedy) had existential peril thrust upon them. Bush had to be careful here: Franklin Roosevelt was the other party's icon. And comparing oneself to Lincoln, America's greatest president, runs a risk of arrogance and excess. But in framing the historical moment, Bush found a Lincoln that fit. He cast himself as the reluctant warrior, who did not choose his conflict, but would pursue it with a calm vigor and resolution. Bush now cited Lincoln's "moral courage" more than Reagan's. In this way, Lincoln became the patron saint of Bush's original conception of his war presidency.

The language of Bush's speechwriters soon took on the cadences of Lincoln's "civic religion"—his manner of talking about the secular conflict he faced in terms borrowed from the King James Bible. In defense of his application of faith, Bush has often quoted Lincoln's famous comment after the Confederate victory at Bull Run in 1862 that he was driven to his knees in prayer out of the conviction that he had nowhere else to turn. At the 9/11 memorial service at the National Cathedral, Bush said, "This conflict was begun on the timing and terms of others. It will end in a way and at an hour of our choosing." This was the diction of the Gettysburg Address and Lincoln's second inaugural. A few days later, Bush was photographed getting aboard Air Force One flaunting a copy of *April 1865: The Month That Saved America* by Jay Winik. Bush's subsequent reading included *Lincoln: A Life of Purpose and Power* by Richard Carwardine, *Lincoln's Greatest Speech: The Second Inaugural* by Ronald C. White Jr., and *Team of Rivals: The Political Genius of Abraham Lincoln* by Doris Kearns Goodwin.

Lincoln—and occasionally Franklin Roosevelt—also supplied Bush with his justification for the arrogation of wartime powers urged by Cheney. In April 1861, Lincoln acted without congressional authorization in suspending the writ of habeas corpus, calling out state militias, and imposing a blockade on the rebelling states. John Yoo and David Addington, among others, pointed to this precedent for Bush's restraint of civil liberties on the basis of inherent executive authority. But as the presidential scholar Louis Fisher has argued, Lincoln acknowledged overstepping his constitutional power with his emergency measures in a way Bush never has. Lincoln recognized the authority of Congress, and sought support for his actions after the fact. Congress gave Lincoln retrospective approval for everything he had done earlier in the Civil War, including his suspension of habeas corpus. Congress explicitly declined to do the same in Bush's case.

But the planned invasion of Iraq demanded a patron more contemporary than Lincoln. As he mounted his case for war, Bush turned again to Churchill to justify his most fateful decision. Bush invited two Churchill biographers, Martin Gilbert and John Keegan, to the White House for conversations. Churchill too now became Bush's exemplar of "moral courage" and "moral clarity"—those qualities defined as whatever Bush decided he had to do to protect the country.

The president's new dominant analogy became the favorite of the neoconservatives, Neville Chamberlain's deal with Hitler at the Munich conference. In Berlin in May 2002, Bush noted that "those who seek missiles and terrible weapons are also familiar with the map of Europe. Like the threats of another era, this threat cannot be appeased [and] cannot be ignored." In his September 2002 speech to the United Nations, he used the phrase "gathering danger" to describe the threat from Saddam, echoing the title of *The Gathering Storm*, Churchill's account of how the world ignored warnings of the Nazi threat.

The appeasement narrative served as both prior rationale and posthumous justification for the invasion of Iraq. In a speech to students in Prague, on the eve of the 2002 NATO summit meeting, Bush noted that "Ignoring dangers or excusing aggression may temporarily avert conflict, but they don't bring true peace." The Czech Republic, which had fallen to the Nazis in 1938 while the world stood by, provided a perfect locale for him to make his case that Saddam was a new Hitler. In his final ultimatum on March 17, 2003, when he gave the Iraqi dictator forty-eight hours to abdicate, Bush warned: "In this century, when evil men plot chemical, biological and nuclear terror, a policy of appeasement could bring destruction of a kind never before seen on this earth."

After the original WMD justification for the Iraq War fell away, Bush found a new Nazi analogy. The danger in withdrawing prematurely from Iraq would be appeasing "Islamic fascists" as a whole. Bush warned in the fall of 2005 that Muslim militants would use victory in Mesopotamia to overthrow all the moderate governments in the Middle East and set up a new Islamic caliphate. "No act of ours invited the rage of the killers, and no conscience, bribe or act of appeasement will change or limit their plans for murder," he said. Donald Rumsfeld took up the appeasement analogy as well, invoking Churchill's famous line that it was like feeding a crocodile in the hope that it would eat you last.

With the rise of Bush's Freedom Agenda, Churchill the imperialist took a back seat while Reagan the visionary democrat and Teddy Roosevelt the civilizing benefactor returned to the fore. Reagan's death in the summer of 2004 gave Bush several opportunities to promulgate his new policy of global democratic transformation under the guise of praising the departed. At this point, Bush modeled himself on a somewhat different Reagan than he had in 2000 and 2001. Instead of Reagan the tax-cutter and hawk, Bush now focused on Reagan the apostle of democracy, quoting his predecessor as saying that freedom was "one of the deepest and noblest aspirations of the human spirit." When Bush cast Iraq as a beacon of liberty, he sounded like Roosevelt declaring in 1902 that "each inhabitant of the Philippines is now guaranteed his civil and religious rights, his rights to life, personal liberty, and the pursuit of happiness." In 2004 as in 1902, the local reality fell somewhat short of this ideal.

One can take this comparison even further. Teddy Roosevelt used "doctrine" much in the way Bush did to justify his urge for intervention. He came up with the Roosevelt Corollary to the Monroe Doctrine, asserting an American right to intervene against bad or incompetent governments in Central America, as a basis for occupying Haiti, Nicaragua, and the Dominican Republic. This was the Freedom Agenda of its day. When Bush proclaimed in his second inaugural that "America's vital interests and our deepest beliefs are now one," he was extending the Roosevelt Corollary to all hemispheres in a world shrunken by globalization. But in his second term, Bush turned utopian in a way Roosevelt and Reagan never did. The Gipper at his most misty-eyed never envisioned a world without tyranny.

IN URGING INTERVENTION in the First World War, the post-presidential Theodore Roosevelt had "come to savor unpopularity," in the phrase of biographer H. W. Brands. Brands's *T.R.: The Last Romantic* was one of the big books Bush read over the 2005 Christmas holiday, at the end of what up to that point was his most disastrous year in office. But 2006 was even worse, and as Bush's woes deepened, he found solace in the model of Harry Truman, the patron saint of unpopular presidents. One well understands the allure of this analogy. The plainspoken Truman operated from the gut and disdained what Bush derides as "process decisions." He lacked legitimacy because of the way he came into office, was mocked for his unsophistication and foreign policy inexperience, and was barely reelected in 1948. But more to the point for Bush was Truman's refusal to entertain moral qualms or listen to his critics. After he left office, Truman's

Cold War policies were vindicated. His reputation rose to the point where many historians consider him to have been a great or near-great president.

In December 2005, Bush analogized his occupation of Iraq to Truman's reconstruction of Japan and Germany after the Second World War. In a speech at the Wilson Center, the president cited the skepticism directed at Truman's belief that democracy, if planted in Japan, would spread through Asia.

> Like today, there were many skeptics and pessimists who said that the Japanese were not ready for democracy. Fortunately, President Harry Truman stuck to his guns. He believed, as I do, in freedom's power to transform an adversary into an ally. . . . The spread of freedom to Iraq and the Middle East requires the same confidence and persistence. And it will lead to the same results.

Bush developed the comparison between his presidency and Truman's more fully in May 2006 at his favorite occasion for an important address—the West Point graduation. Only in retrospect, Bush said, was it possible to see that Truman had established the key doctrines and policies of the Cold War. "President Truman made clear that the Cold War was an ideological struggle between tyranny and freedom," Bush said, continuing:

> At a time when some still wanted to wish away the Soviet threat, he brought Winston Churchill to Missouri, to deliver his famous "Iron Curtain" speech. And he issued a presidential directive called NSC-68, which declared that America faced an enemy "animated by a new fanatic faith" and determined to impose its ideology on the entire world. This directive called on the United States to accept the responsibility of world leadership, and defend the cause of freedom and democracy—and that's exactly what the United States did.

The parallel was clear, but Bush went on to make explicit that he saw himself following Truman's lead in a successor struggle: "Today, at the start of a new century, we are again engaged in a war unlike any our nation has fought before—and like Americans in Truman's day, we are laying the foundations for victory," he said.

Critics were swift to point out a host of differences: Truman had collaborated effectively with Republicans, including Arthur Vandenberg, the chairman of the Senate Foreign Relations Committee who helped forge a consensus in favor of the Marshall Plan. Despite the unparalleled postwar power of the United States, he did not give in to unilateral temptation; Truman built multinational institutions for the new era, like NATO, the International Monetary Fund, and the World Bank. And Iraq was hardly Japan or Germany. But Bush clung to this raft. After the Republican defeat in 2006, he met with the new Democratic leaders of Congress. Truman's policies had been unpopular in their time, but "history showed he was right," Bush told them. The same would go for him. In a background interview with a group of television reporters in September 2007, Bush said that the president who succeeded him would be like Eisenhower, who was critical of many of his predecessor's policies, but continued them once he was in office. But this only begged the comparison. If Bush was Truman, where were the durable institutions, the supportive alliances, the sound doctrine? Bush's contribution to the new era was an unnecessary war, an overblown conception of the terrorist threat, and a hollow rhetoric of victory.

AGAIN AND AGAIN, when asked about his legacy or the judgment of history, Bush would say he didn't worry or even think about it. In an interview with National Public Radio in January 2007, he commented, "My own view is that history will take care of itself. History has a long reach to it. I told people that last year I read three analyses of Washington's administration, and my attitude is if they are still writing about the first president, the 43rd doesn't need to worry about it." In an interview with *U.S. News & World Report*, he made the same point: "You never know what your history is going to be until long after you're gone. So presidents shouldn't worry about history. You just can't. You do what you think is right, and if you're thinking big enough, that history will eventually prove you right or wrong."

This nonchalance was belied both by what Bush said privately—that his democracy agenda and his faith-based initiative would be at the center of his legacy—and by his feverish reading. Bush kept up his pace into 2007, by which time he was in a kind of historical overdrive. In March, he invited the Tory historian Andrew Roberts to lunch at the White House to discuss his recently published *A History of the English-Speaking Peoples Since 1900*—a sequel to Winston Churchill's four earlier volumes of similar title. The author was joined by Cheney, Rove, and a group of neoconservative intellectuals. As in his book, Roberts tried to transplant Bush's head onto Churchill's body. The president's prosecution of the War on Terror, Roberts believes, is "vigorous" and "absolutely unwavering." That Bush has brought "full democracy" to Iraq is an unequivocal fact. Roberts and the neocons fed Bush's preference for the unknowable future over a problematic present by assuring him that history would vindicate him. His reputation would follow the course of Churchill and Truman, if only he continued to hold firm.

As of late 2007, Bush had yet to reach the record-low 22 percent approval rating Truman attained in 1952, his final year in office—though he was getting close. Critics, not all of them liberal, found their own analogies. They compared him not to Lincoln, but to his successor, the arrogant, ignorant Andrew Johnson. They saw in Bush not the shadow of Teddy Roosevelt but—taking their cue from Rove—a born-again William McKinley, who started the Spanish-American War on false pretenses and enmeshed the United States in a decades-long conflict in the Philippines. Lynne Olson, the author of *Troublesome Young Men*, a book about the prewar Churchill faction that Bush was reading in the summer of 2007, wrote that the president had more in common with Neville Chamberlain than with Sir Winston.

In an academic journal article, D. Jason Berggren and Nicol C. Rae considered George W.'s connection to Jimmy Carter and Woodrow Wilson, who, they argued, shared with Bush an "evangelical style." Like Bush, Carter and Wilson challenged the idea of realist foreign policy with a scripturally inspired vision of America as democratic exemplar. The missionary failures of these three presidents do have a lot in common. Carter was naive and insincerely humble, scolding about human rights while doing little to advance them. Wilson promoted peace and democracy in a way that was not only aloof and condescending but also alarmingly detached from reality. We recognize both Wilson and Bush when we read in Freud and Bullitt's study that "it was natural for him in his thinking to ignore the facts of the real outer world, even to deny they existed if they conflicted with his hopes and wishes." Where Wilson was undermined by his arrogance and Carter by his innocence, Bush's failure grew out of his incompetence and his blatant inconsistency in applying his precepts. While claiming divine mandate for the promotion of democracy abroad, he disregarded civil liberties and asserted unconstitutional authority at home.

The most powerful analogy Bush's critics have on their side is the parallel between Iraq and Vietnam. If Bush's supporters think in terms of 1938, his opponents dwell on 1968—when the United States was escalating instead of mitigating an erroneous war of choice. In this parallel, Bush stands in for LBJ—besieged by protests, blocked by Congress, but unable to acknowledge failure or reverse course. Bush had LBJ in mind from the start, and intended to avoid his mistakes. Instead of micromanaging the war by picking bombing targets, he would ask his generals what they needed and leave the strategy to them. But here too the historical cliché led him astray. Bush avoided overmanaging his war at the cost of drastically undermanaging it. Until the fall of 2006, his generals told him what he wanted to hear and he seldom challenged them. To his usual question "Do you have everything you need?" they almost always answered "Yes."

In August 2007, Bush took on the Vietnam analogy directly in a speech to the Veterans of Foreign Wars. This was perhaps Bush's most elaborate response to a historical analogy. He acknowledged that Iraq was like Vietnam in many respects, and contended that the United States shouldn't have backed away there either. Bush cited Graham Greene's 1955 novel *The Quiet American* as an early exemplar of the misguided view that America had no business in Vietnam. The Cambodian genocide and exodus of the Vietnamese boat people showed, Bush said, that things could indeed get far worse if America disengaged. Withdrawing from Vietnam had harmed American credibility in a way that led Islamic terrorists to think they could defeat us. But perhaps the more relevant Graham Greene novel was *Our Man in Havana*, in which a desperate vacuum cleaner salesman convinces the British Secret Service that a diagram of his product's circuitry is the enemy's secret weapon.

ALMOST EVERYONE WHO met with Bush in the final phase of his presidency remarked on his extraordinary assurance in the face of massive unpopularity. Bush, in the isolation of his final years, tried to establish that he did not suffer from dark nights of the soul like LBJ or Nixon, that he kept self-pity at bay. One way that Bush lacked the dimensions of a tragic figure was in his absence of introspection. He wouldn't admit the question of failure even in private. But there was something contrived about Bush's projection of confidence, which comes through in the interviews Robert Draper conducted for his White House chronicle *Dead Certain*. Bush told him:

> "And part of being a leader is: *people watch you*. I walk in that hall, I say to those commanders—well, guess what would happen if I walk in and say, 'Well, maybe it's not worth it.' When I'm out in the public, I fully understand that the enemy watches me, the Iraqis are watching me, the troops watch me, and the people watch me.
>
> "The other thing is that *you can't fake it*. You have to believe it. And I believe it. I believe we'll succeed."

Bush thought he couldn't betray any sign of uncertainty. He had to convey confidence in order to succeed. And to *seem* confident he had to *feel* confident. As Bush described it, his optimism was a kind of autohypnotism. This is the politician's technique of making himself believe what he needs to believe. But when the projection of confidence becomes so far detached from reality, it turns into something else again: willful self-delusion. This is the opposite of Churchill's mode of leadership, which did not shy away from realistic appraisal at far darker moments.

It would be foolish to answer Bush's untethered confidence with a correspondingly definitive judgment of failure. Time and competent successors could turn America's involvement in Iraq into less of a catastrophe. But Bush cannot hide his mistakes behind the unknowability of future judgment. What we can say even before he leaves office is that Bush played out his family drama in a way that had devastating consequences for his family, his country, and the world. To challenge a thoughtful, moderate, and pragmatic father, he trained himself to be hasty, extreme, and unbending. He learned to overcome all forms of doubt through the exercise of will. There was no worse preparation for the historical moment that was thrust upon him. Ambitious to accomplish great things, sure of the purity of his motives, and fundamentally unwilling to think, he squandered his chance. In the end, the analogies all fall short. There's no good model for the situation Bush faced as president, and no real precedent for the kind of gambler he was. His flawed character proved to be his destiny.

There are Churchillian echoes in George W. Bush's story, though they may not be the ones the president hears. The struggle with low expectations, the early failures, the burden of dynasty, the coping through alcohol—these are all themes of Churchill's biography as well as Bush's. Their two dramas also share a ghost, the hovering paternal phantom. Like George W., Sir Winston was obsessed with his famous and successful father. Lord Randolph Churchill was a Tory politician who was briefly leader of the House of Commons and chancellor of the exchequer. His career kept him far too busy to pay attention to his son, and the wound of his absence never really healed. Randolph Churchill died in 1895, when Winston was just twenty, but he loomed over his son's entire career as distant inspiration, warning, and terror.

Early on, neither Randolph nor Winston thought there was much chance of the younger man measuring up. Believing that his son wasn't smart enough for university, Randolph sent Winnie, who had been a poor student and something of a troublemaker at boarding school, into the army. Within a few years, Winston was attempting to follow his father's path into conservative politics. As he advanced, he developed what can only be called an obsession with avoiding his father's mistakes and exceeding his accomplishments. The son believed that his father's great fault was his impatience, and that the great error of his career was his peremptory, ill-judged resignation as chancellor in 1886, which effectively ended Lord Randolph's career. This reverses the Bush dynamic, in which the impatient son thought his father excessively cautious. But Churchill too came to see his father as a noble failure, a "grand elemental force in British politics . . . broke irrecoverably at the moment of maturity."

There is, however, a crucial difference between Sir Winston's father obsession and George W.'s. Where Bush got lost in his father's footsteps, Churchill managed to free himself psychologically and politically from his famous parent. In writing a long, admiring biography of his father in 1906, Churchill examined Lord Randolph's career and views beyond the level of cliché. Winston was able to learn from his father's mistakes without being governed by the need to do the opposite. In his book, he came to terms with Lord Randolph Churchill's legacy. He still admired his father, and was still hurt by his neglect. But from that point on, Winston was able to look at his father's career from an external perspective.

That isn't to say that the old tug ever quite went away. After being voted out as prime minister after the war, Churchill had time to reflect back on his own life and career. In Chartwell, his country home in Kent, he spent his time reading, writing, and painting watercolors. One evening, he came down to dinner and described a strange daydream to his family. He imagined that his father had come back from the dead to speak to him. Sir Winston described this reverie in a short literary piece called "The Dream." He dictated it to his secretary in 1947 and later revised it, but never published it during his lifetime.

On a foggy afternoon in November, Churchill writes, he was copying a torn portrait of his father when he felt a presence in the room, and turned around to find Lord Randolph sitting in an armchair. Son and father's ghost proceed to have a conversation. Winston describes the cataclysmic historical events that his father missed by dying in 1895, coyly failing to note his own role in them. Randolph marvels at it all and wonders how his son ever managed to earn a living. He returns to the land of beyond still assuming that Winston grew up to be a journalist and second-rate painter.

But after listening to his son speak about British and international politics, Randolph makes an important acknowledgment: he was wrong to expect so little of the boy, who turned out not to be slow-witted after all. "Old people are always impatient with the young," Lord Randolph says, apologizing. "Fathers always expect their sons to have their virtues without their faults." The ghost continues his reassessment: "Of course you are too old now to think about such things, but when I hear you talk I really wonder you didn't go into politics. You might have done a lot to help. You might even have made a name for yourself."

Here the final joke is on the father, not the son, who no longer has anything to prove to Lord Randolph or to the world in relation to his family. It is now the father who is made to appear foolish. Despite his rejection by the British public, Winston Churchill knew what his courage and candor had accomplished. Churchill had come to exemplify what George W. Bush could only project as an illusion: the autonomous identity and true confidence that allow us to accept our limitations, admit our mistakes, and improve what we can in the time that remains.

Acknowledgments

THREE PEOPLE WORKED WITH ME ON THIS PROJECT FROM BEGINNING to end: my agent, Andrew Wylie; my editor, Susan Mercandetti; and my researcher, Karen Avrich. Andrew provided superb advice and represented my interests at every stage with the fierce finesse for which he is famous. Susan was this book's first enthusiast, steady patron, and expert guide. Karen found everything I was looking for and much that I didn't know to look for with diligence and baffling speed. I am lucky to count all three as friends.

The flaws in this book would be much greater absent the keen insights and editorial suggestions of my friends and colleagues. I am deeply grateful to Tali Farhadian, Malcolm Gladwell, Michael Hirschorn, Mickey Kaus, Michael Kinsley, Nicholas Lemann, Michael Lewis, Robert McCrum, David Plotz, and Meghan O'Rourke for reading and commenting on my manuscript at various stages.

Joseph Weisberg did even more than that, improving my thinking and writing line by line. His finding time to edit me while finishing his own book was a true act of brotherly love, for which I am deeply grateful.

Donald Graham and Caroline Little, my bosses at the Washington Post Company, generously granted my request for a writing leave. The staff of *Slate* made sure no one noticed I was gone. I want to thank especially David Plotz again, Cliff Sloan, Julia Turner, Jill Pellettieri, and Zuzanna Kobrzynski, all of whom I have come to rely on in a variety of ways.

This book benefited from conversations with the shrewdest political minds I know, who in addition to those mentioned above include Kurt Andersen, Emily Bazelon, Richard M. Daley, John Dickerson, Robert Draper, Edward Jay Epstein, Noah Feldman, Henry Finder, Atul Gawande, Bart Gellman, Jack Goldsmith, David Greenberg, Richard Haass, Mark Halperin, Bruce Headlam, Christopher Hitchens, Joe Joffe, Fred Kaplan, Joe Klein, Anne Kornblut, Dahlia Lithwick, Sarah Lyall, Jon Meacham, Mark Miller, Sara Mosle, Cullen Murphy, Tim Naftali, Tim Noah, Richard Plepler, Charles Randolph, Bruce Reed, Gideon Rose, Julia Rothwax, Robert E. Rubin, William Saletan, Jack Shafer, Stephen Sherrill, Jake Siewert, June Thomas, Chuck Weinstock, Ron Wyden, and Fareed Zakaria. Thanks also to the research staffs at the George Bush Presidential Library, the Columbia University Library, and the Greenwich Library.

This was my second opportunity to work with the crack team at Random House. I want to thank particularly Gina Centrello, Laura Goldin, Jonathan Jao, Abby Plesser, Tom Perry, Steve Messina, Fred Chase, Richard Elman, Barbara Bachman, Gene Mydlowski, Barbara Fillon, Dana Maxson, and Karen Fink for their great ideas and hard work.

Joshua Liberson and Stella Bugbee are my design gurus. Chris and Sharon Davis, the Timothy Nation Foundation, and the Hoover Institute Media Fellows Program hosted me for productive writing escapes during the summer and fall of 2007.

Closer to home, I want to thank my mother, Lois Weisberg, an eternal font of inspiration, wisdom, and free child care, and my children, Nathaniel and Lily, who did their best to respect Daddy's writing time even when it took time away from them. (I almost took Lily's suggestion to call my book "Stuck in the Bushes.") My niece Aliya Ellenby, my mother-in-law, Toby Needleman, my father-in-law, Howard Needleman, and the Needleman-Cohen family all pitched in at critical moments.

Finally, there would be a Bush tragedy but no *Bush Tragedy* without the support, encouragement, and indulgence of my wife, Deborah Needleman, to whom this book is affectionately dedicated.

Notes

INTRODUCTION: PRINCE HAL IN HOUSTON

xv Yes, I flew it!: John Ritter, "Jet Co-Pilot Bush: 'Yes, I Flew It!,'" *USA Today*, March 2, 2003.

xvi *"because my father was"*: Bill Minutaglio, *First Son: George W. Bush and the Bush Family Dynasty* (New York: Three Rivers Press, 2001), 120.

xvii *Don Imus interview with George H. W. Bush*: *Imus in the Morning*, September 1, 2004, http://www.msnbc.msn.com/id/5889684/.

xvii *"like what happened in '91"*: Bill Sammon, "Bush Aims to Avoid Father's Mistakes," *Washington Times*, May 10, 2004.

xxiii *"conquered every emotion"*: Sigmund Freud and William C. Bullitt, *Thomas Woodrow Wilson: A Psychological Study* (New York: Houghton Mifflin, 1966), xiii.

CHAPTER ONE: THE BUSHES AND THE WALKERS

4 *a family secret*: Roger Hughes, "Records Show the Walker Branch of President George W. Bush's Family, Which Settled in Central Illinois, Included Slave Owners," *Illinois Times*, April 5, 2007.

8 *a female between*: Ibid.

8 *a letter to the editor*: "I'm for Lynch Law and Whipping Post, D. D. Walker Writes," *St. Louis Republic*, July 22, 1914.

9 *"I was always scared as hell of him"*: Peter Schweizer and Rochelle Schweizer, *The Bushes: Portrait of a Dynasty* (New York: Doubleday, 2004), 30.

10 *"there really wasn't a lot of love"*: Michael Kranish, "An American Dynasty," *Boston Globe*, April 22, 2001.

10 *an experienced man*: Schweizer and Schweizer, *The Bushes*, 33.

11 *James Bush resigned his parish*: James Smith Bush obituary, Yale University, http://mssa.library.yale.edu/obituary_record/1859_1924/1889-90.pdf.

12 *believing they "weren't crap":* Walt Harrington, "Born to Run: On the Privilege of Being George Bush," *Washington Post,* September 28, 1986.

13 *"3 High Military Honors":* *Ohio State Journal,* August 8, 1918; *New Haven Journal-Courier,* August 15, 1918.

15 *"lack of pride in material possessions":* Herbert S. Parmet, *George Bush: The Life of a Lone Star Yankee* (New Brunswick, N.J.: Transaction, 2001), 154.

16 *"never heard him fart":* Harrington, "Born to Run."

16 *"that kind of language":* Mickey Herskowitz, *Duty, Honor, Country: The Life and Legacy of Prescott Bush* (Nashville: Rutledge Hill, 2003), 148.

16 *"Have we come to the point":* "This President Thing," *Time,* June 14, 1963.

18 *Prescott was treasurer:* Kitty Kelley, *The Family: The Real Story of the Bush Dynasty* (New York: Doubleday, 2004), 115–16.

20 *led Howard Fineman of* Newsweek*:* Maureen Dowd, "Bushfellas," *New York Times,* June 23, 1999.

20 *"they would never have their Ted Sorensen":* Schweizer and Schweizer, *The Bushes,* 328.

21 *"It's not that this is John F. Kennedy's father":* Hugh Sidey, "A Dad Reflects on His Family," *Time,* November 20, 2000.

21 *"They never had to work":* Patricia Kilday Hart, "Don't Call Him Junior," *Texas Monthly,* April 1989.

22 *house on Perkins Road:* Mary Walker interview, 1991, Greenwich Library Oral History Project, 10.

23 *"big shots" at everything:* Schweizer and Schweizer, *The Bushes,* 93.

24 *"a very aggressive person":* Mary Walker interview, 19.

24 *"hero worship":* Kelley, *The Family,* 133.

27 *an "inspiration":* letter to C. Fred Chambers, George H. W. Bush, *All the Best, George Bush: My Life in Letters and Other Writings* (New York: Scribner, 1999), 162.

27 *calling his uncle "father":* Michael Kranish, "An American Dynasty," *Boston Globe,* April 22, 2001.

28 *"He loves all the natives":* Mary Walker interview, 23.

28 *"I see the brides":* Schweizer and Schweizer, *The Bushes,* 301.

CHAPTER TWO: FATHER AND SONS

32 *"something on my own":* Herskowitz, *Duty, Honor, Country,* 87.

32 *"capitalize completely" letter to Gerry Bemiss:* Bush, *All the Best,* 62.

33 *restricted his business opportunities:* S. V. Dáte, *Jeb, America's Next Bush: His Florida Years and What They Mean for the Nation* (New York: Tarcher/Penguin, 2007), 81.

33 *"I didn't have a red Studebaker":* Margaret Carlson, "It's a Family Affair," *Time,* July 23, 1990.

34 *the structure of his family was "matriarchal":* R. W. Apple Jr., "The Family Ties: Dad Was President (but Please, No Dynasty Talk)," *New York Times,* January 31, 2000.

35 *Barbara Bush's autobiography:* Barbara Bush, *Barbara Bush: A Memoir* (New York: Scribner, 1994).

36 *their five children:* Herskowitz, *Duty, Honor, Country,* 148.

37 *"she kind of smothered me":* Timothy Naftali, *George H. W. Bush* (New York: Times Books, 2007), 11.

38 *"before you have more children?":* George Lardner Jr. and Lois Romano, "Tragedy Created Bush Mother-Son Bond," *Washington Post,* July 26, 1999.

38 *some form of dyslexia:* Justin A. Frank, *Bush on the Couch: Inside the Mind of the President* (New York: Harper Perennial, 2005), 24.

39 *"little wieners, line up":* Michael Duffy and Nancy Gibbs, "The Quiet Dynasty," *Time,* August 7, 2000.

40 *legacies could no longer expect:* Geoffrey Kabaservice, "The Birth of a New Institution: How Two Yale Presidents and Their Admissions Directors Tore Up the 'Old Blueprint' to Create a Modern Yale," *Yale Alumni Magazine,* December 1999.

40 *unlikely Bush would have been admitted:* Carter Wiseman, "In the Days of DKE and S.D.S.," *Yale Alumni Magazine,* February 2001.

40 *"There were really two Yales":* Charles McGrath, "My Classmate George W.," *Slate,* August 17, 2000.

41 *"only a cigarette burn":* "Branding Rite Laid to Yale Fraternity," *New York Times,* November 8, 1967.

41 *Skull and Bones:* Minutaglio, *First Son,* 104.

42 *East Coast snobs and elitists:* Kelley, *The Family,* 267.

42 *"didn't learn a damn thing":* Schweizer and Schweizer, *The Bushes,* 166.

45 *"Big ole Daddy":* Kelley, *The Family,* 217.

46 *"I regret it":* Parmet, *George Bush,* 114.

46 *"stupid coat and tie job":* Kenneth T. Walsh, "The Lost Years of Al and Dubya," *U.S. News & World Report,* November 1, 1999.

47 *"the harshest words":* George Bush with Doug Wead, *George Bush: Man of Integrity* (Eugene, Ore.: Harvest House, 1988), 118.

48 *"do anything for the cause":* Richard Reeves, *President Nixon: Alone in the White House* (New York: Simon & Schuster, 2001), 547.

48 *privileged and soft Ivy Leaguer:* Bush, *All the Best,* 181.

48 *suicidal thoughts:* Bush, *Barbara Bush,* 135.

51 *"riding his daddy's coattails":* Lois Romano and George Lardner Jr., "Young Bush, a Political Natural, Revs Up," *Washington Post,* July 29, 1999.

52 *"never be out-Texaned again":* Kevin Phillips, *American Dynasty: Aristocracy, Fortune, and the Politics of Deceit in the House of Bush* (New York: Viking, 2004), 140.

52 *about once a month:* Brit Hume interview with President George W. Bush, Fox News Channel, September 23, 2003.

53 *"I'm the serious one":* Bush and Wead, *Man of Integrity,* 121.

54 *"money didn't excite me":* Dáte, *Jeb,* 1.

55 *"hang-'em-by-the-neck conservative":* Kelley, *The Family,* 408.

56 *"my own identity":* David Maraniss, "The Bush Bunch," *Washington Post,* January 22, 1989.

56 *"the roman candle of the family":* Richard Ben Cramer, *What It Takes: The Way to the White House* (New York: Random House, 1992), 17.

58 *worst piece of press:* Margaret Warner, "Fighting the Wimp Factor," *Newsweek,* October 1987.

59 *"leftover competition":* Schweizer and Schweizer, *The Bushes,* 341.

61 *"I'm the businessman who came to town":* Kevin Sherrington, "Dallasite Won't Be 'Passive,' " *Dallas Morning News,* February 25, 1989.

61 *"You tell George not to run!":* Interview with Doug Wead, May 2007.

61 *"I'm rather hoping he won't":* "People in the News," Associated Press, April 28, 1989.

61 *"You've been giving me advice":* Elizabeth Mitchell, *W: Revenge of the Bush Dynasty* (New York: Hyperion, 2000), 252.

62 *"because I'm Barbara and Jenna's dad":* Maureen Dowd, "New Races (Their Own) for 2 Bush Sons," *New York Times,* November 30, 1993.

63 *"the son of George Bush":* Skip Hollandsworth, "Born to Run," *Texas Monthly,* May 1994.

63 *"One big difference":* Robert Suro, "President's Family; One of Bush's Campaign Advisors Is Also His Son," *New York Times,* April 26, 1992.

63 *"what you can learn from a failed presidency":* James Moore and Wayne Slater, *The Architect: Karl Rove and the Master Plan for Absolute Power* (New York: Crown, 2006), 24.

63 *"Why don't you feel good about me?":* Schweizer and Schweizer, *The Bushes,* xi–xii.

64 *He had also converted:* Dáte, *Jeb,* 305.

64 *"I am the little guy":* Alexandra Pelosi, *Journeys with George,* HBO Films, 2003.

67 *the wisdom of not finishing off Saddam:* George Bush and Brent Scowcroft, *A World Transformed* (New York: Knopf, 1998).

68 *"Being George Bush's son":* "A Son of a Famous Name," *Newsweek,* January 24, 2000.

69 *argued in a* Wall Street Journal *op-ed:* Brent Scowcroft, "Don't Attack Saddam," *Wall Street Journal,* August 15, 2002.

69 *Bush reacted against Scowcroft:* Schweizer and Schweizer, *The Bushes,* 535.

70 *"Feels good":* Martin Metzer, Ron Hutcheson, and Drew Brown, "War Begins with Strikes Aimed at 'Leadership Targets,' " Knight Ridder, March 19, 2003.

70 *"wrong father to appeal to":* Bob Woodward, *Plan of Attack* (New York: Simon & Schuster, 2004), 421.

70 *George H. W. Bush weeping: Larry King Live,* CNN, October 5, 2006.

71 *"The true measure of a man":* "First President Bush sobs while talking of Jeb," AP, December 5, 2006. NBC video at www.msnbc.com/id/16053170/.

71 *"some small defeat":* Peggy Noonan, "A Father's Tears," *Wall Street Journal,* December 8, 2006.

CHAPTER THREE: THE GOSPEL OF GEORGE

73 *"the mustard seed":* Mary Leonard, "George W. Bush: A Legacy Reclaimed," *Boston Globe,* January 23, 2000.

75 *"toward a national campaign":* George W. Bush, *A Charge to Keep: My Journey to the White House* (New York: William Morrow, 1999), 13.

75 *on Billy Graham:* Bush and Wead, *Man of Integrity,* 45–46.

76 *"A good and powerful day":* Arthur Blessitt, "The Day I Prayed with George W. Bush to Receive Jesus!," http://www.blessitt.com/bush.html.

77 *"our walk on the beach":* Nancy Gibbs and Michael Duffy, *The Preacher and the Presidents: Billy Graham in the White House* (New York: Center Street, 2007), 330.

78 *a ministry–coffee house–nightclub:* http://www.blessitt.com/books/turned3.html.

78 *"naturally stoned/ on Jesus!":* http://www.planetdan.net/junk/blessitt/index.htm.

79 *he did use this language:* David Aikman, *Man of Faith: The Spiritual Journey of George W. Bush* (Nashville: W Publishing Group, 2004), 75.

82 *"some kind of heavy doctrinal difference":* Ken Herman, "The Candidates and the Higher Authority," *Houston Post,* October 2, 1994.

82 *"Faith gives us purpose":* Terry Mattingly, "George W. Bush Not Yet Putting His Beliefs into Specifics," *Knoxville News Sentinel,* March 20, 1999.

82 *"easier to understand and clearer":* "We Are All Sinners," Beliefnet.com, Fall 2000, http://www.beliefnet.com/story/47/story_4703_1.html.

82 *"we'll be great partners":* Bill Keller, "God and George W. Bush," *New York Times,* May 17, 2003.

83 *"The President doesn't care what faith it is":* Jeffrey Goldberg, "George W. Bush's Loyal Speechwriter," *The New Yorker,* February 13, 2006.

85 *George W. Bush citing mote and beam parable:* "We Are All Sinners."

85 *Neil Bush referred to evangelical Christians:* Thomas B. Edsall, "Once Derided Christian Right Is Now Key for GOP," *Washington Post,* September 8, 1995.

86 Mere Christianity *by C. S. Lewis:* "The Vice President and the Evangelicals: A Strategy," unpublished memo, December 18, 1985, 12. Much of the material in this chapter is drawn from a series of interviews with Doug Wead in May 2007 and copies of memos provided by Wead.

86 *"we haven't been inclined":* Bush and Wead, *Man of Integrity,* 46.

89 *Bush told visitors:* Richard E. Smalley, "Future Global Energy Prosperity: The Terawatt Challenge," Symposium X—Frontiers of Materials Research, December 2004, http://cohesion.rice.edu/NaturalSciences/Smalley/emplibrary/120204%20MRS%20Boston.pdf.

89 *Bush memo to his staff:* http://www.pbs.org/wgbh/pages/frontline/shows/jesus/readings/chargetokeepmemo.html.

90 *"the message of Charles Wesley":* Bush, *A Charge to Keep,* 45.

90 *The artist, W. H. D. Koerner:* Sidney Blumenthal, "From Norman Rockwell to Abu Ghraib," *Salon,* April 26, 2007.

90 *Western short story:* "The Slipper Tongue," *Saturday Evening Post,* June 3, 1916.

90 *"Bandits Move About from Town to Town":* *Saturday Evening Post,* April 14, 1917.

90 *story in* The Country Gentleman: January 26, 1918.

91 *dressed as Mahatma Gandhi:* Bush, *A Charge to Keep,* 135.

91 *"I'm only one bottle away":* Aikman, *Man of Faith,* 108.

92 *he privately called "wackos":* Moore and Slater, *The Architect,* 32.

97 *Bush can be profane:* Michael Isikoff and David Corn, *Hubris: The Inside Story of Spin, Scandal, and the Selling of the Iraq War* (New York: Crown, 2006), 3.

100 *"Just get me a damn faith bill.":* David Kuo, *Tempting Faith: An Inside Story of Political Seduction* (New York: Free Press, 2006), 166.

100 *John DiIulio interview:* Ron Suskind, "Why Are These Men Laughing?," *Esquire,* January 2003.

100 *$30 million "compassion fund":* Kuo, *Tempting Faith,* 214.

101 *Kay Coles James:* Garry Wills, "A Country Ruled by Faith," *The New York Review of Books,* November 16, 2006.

102 *the sense of equanimity:* David Frum, *The Right Man: An Inside Account of the Bush White House* (New York: Random House, 2003).

102 *"God wants you here":* Michael Gerson, *Heroic Conservatism: Why Republicans Need to Embrace America's Ideals (and Why They Deserve to Fail if They Don't)* (New York: HarperOne, 2007), 79.

102 *a comparison Gerson makes explicit:* Ibid., 73.

103 *"a job to do":* Remarks by President Bush, South Lawn, White House, September 16, 2001.

103 *"the hand of a just and faithful God":* Remarks by President Bush at the National Prayer Breakfast, Washington Hilton, February 6, 2003.

103 *"a shift in Bush's theology":* Deborah Caldwell, "George Bush's Theology: Does the President Believe He Has a Divine Mandate?," *National Catholic Reporter,* February 21, 2003.

CHAPTER FOUR: THE SHADOW

110 *"He was exuding more charisma":* Nicholas Lemann, "The Controller," *The New Yorker,* May 12, 2003.

110 *"Huge amounts of charisma":* Frank Bruni, "Behind Bush Juggernaut, an Aide's Labor of Loyalty," *New York Times,* January 11, 2000.

112 *he had trouble shuffling cards:* Letter from Rove to Wayne Slater citing errors in James Moore and Wayne Slater, *Bush's Brain: How Karl Rove Made George W. Bush Presidential* (New York: Wiley, 2003), given to author by Slater, January 27, 2003.

112 *"I was definitely uncool":* Lee Davidson, "Triumph of the Underdog," *Deseret Morning News,* December 8, 2002.

113 *"moved to Reno":* Thomas B. Edsall, "Party Hardy," *The New Republic,* September 25, 2006.

114 *"elite, effete snobs": The Rush Limbaugh Show,* August 15, 2007.

114 *became embroiled in a bitter dispute:* Moore and Slater, *Bush's Brain,* 254.

115 *spy into his bedroom:* Letter from Rove to Wayne Slater, January 27, 2003.

117 *"I'm more of a nerd":* Carl M. Cannon, Lou Dubose, and Jan Reid, *Boy Genius: Karl Rove, The Architect of George W. Bush's Remarkable Political Triumphs* (New York: PublicAffairs, 2005), 11.

117 *a personality conflict with Fitzgerald:* Mark Halperin and John F. Harris, *The Way to Win: Taking the White House in 2008* (New York: Random House, 2006), 194.

118 *hiring James Baker:* Melinda Henneberger, "Driving W.," *New York Times Magazine,* May 14, 2000.

118 *"the Rove bullshit":* S. C. Gwynne, "Genius," *Texas Monthly,* March 2003.

119 *conduits for rumors:* Joshua Green, "Karl Rove in a Corner," *The Atlantic Monthly,* November 2004.

120 *"political hacks like me":* Louis Dubose, "Bush's Hit Man," *The Nation,* March 5, 2001.

121 *"I might run":* Sam Attlesey and Cathy Harasta, "Likely Buyers Accustomed to Big Deals," *Dallas Morning News,* February 24, 1989.

121 *Rove was suspected of leaking negative information:* Elisabeth Bumiller, "C.I.A. Leak Case Recalls Texas Incident in '92 Race," *New York Times,* August 6, 2005.

122 *his father had allowed others to define him:* Lemann, "The Controller."

125 *"mother substitute":* Frum, *The Right Man,* 41.

125 *harshly reprimanding his political guru:* Moore and Slater, *Bush's Brain,* 223.

126 *repeating it to Tucker Carlson:* Tucker Carlson, "George W. Bush Doesn't Give a Damn What You Think of Him. That May Be Why You'll Vote for Him for President," *Talk,* September 1999.

127 *the ethical choice:* Moore and Slater, *Bush's Brain,* 222.

128 *"create somebody like him":* Henneberger, "Driving W."

129 *refocus his research:* Interview with Lewis Gould, May 2007.

131 *McKinley "saw that the issues":* Dan Balz, "The Governor's 'Iron Triangle' Points the Way to Washington," *Washington Post,* July 23, 1999.

132 *"on the [media's] time frame":* Miriam Rozen, "The Nerd Behind the Throne," *Dallas Observer,* May 13, 1999.

132 *"the 1896 election":* Moore and Slater, *The Architect,* 104.

133 *"no persona other than Bush's guy":* Ken Herman, "Select Few Earn Spots on Bush's First Team," *Austin American-Statesman,* February 28, 1999.

134 *govern as a divider:* Edsall, "Party Hardy."

136 *completely dominated by the political arm:* Suskind, "Why Are These Men Laughing?"

136 *he quoted Sam Houston:* Matt Bai, "Rove's Way," *New York Times Magazine,* October 20, 2002.

138 *"We can also go to the country":* Richard L. Berke, "Bush Adviser Suggests War as Campaign Theme," *New York Times,* January 19, 2002.

143 *Bush was beginning to recognize:* Robert Draper, *Dead Certain: The Presidency of George W. Bush* (New York: Free Press, 2007), 309.

143 *Laura Bush on Karl Rove:* Chris Wallace interview with Laura Bush, *Fox News Sunday,* May 14, 2006.

143 *he e-mailed a reporter:* Todd S. Purdum, "Karl Rove's Split Personality," *Vanity Fair,* December 2006.

143 *the loss had been a fluke:* Wayne Slater, "Rove Saw Rise, Fall of GOP Dream," *Dallas Morning News,* August 14, 2007.

CHAPTER FIVE: THE FOREMOST HAND

146 *whether Germany was in NATO:* Interview with Kenneth Adelman, May 2007.

148 *Karl Rove opposed the choice:* Draper, *Dead Certain,* 90.

150 *"Dick Cheney I don't know anymore":* Jeffrey Goldberg, "Breaking Ranks: What Turned Brent Scowcroft Against the Bush Administration?," *The New Yorker,* October 31, 2005.

151 *described Cheney as a "moderate":* Todd Purdum, "A Face Only a President Could Love," *Vanity Fair,* June 2006.

152 *"But he is even quieter now":* Michael R. Gordon, "Cracking the Whip," *New York Times Magazine,* January 27, 1991.

153 *campus unrest:* Nicholas Lemann, "The Quiet Man: Dick Cheney's Discreet Rise to Unprecedented Power," *The New Yorker,* May 7, 2001.

154 *they would cease speaking:* Interview with Kenneth Adelman, May 2007.

157 *"She took off her dress":* Lynne Cheney, *Sisters* (New York: Signet, 1981).

158 *I have a right to confidentiality:* Lynne Cheney, *Executive Privilege* (New York: Simon & Schuster, 1979), 46–49.

160 *a study of eight speakers of the house:* Richard B. Cheney and Lynne Cheney, *Kings of the Hill: Power and Personality in the House of Representatives* (New York: Continuum, 1983).

162 *"exercise the powers the Framers intended":* Iran-contra Committee Minority Report, 1987, 450.

162 *"monarchical notions of prerogative":* Frederick A. O. Schwarz Jr. and Aziz Z. Haq, *Unchecked and Unbalanced* (New York: New Press, 2007), 1.

163 *Congress's vacillation and indecision:* Richard Cheney, "Congressional Overreaching in Foreign Policy," *American Enterprise Institute Studies* 507, 1990, 121.

163 *These tasks included diplomacy:* Ibid., 119.

163 *Cheney's view of the legislative branch:* Ibid., 121.

164 *"the scope of the inviolable powers":* Ibid., 112.

165 *secure, undisclosed locations:* James Mann, *Rise of the Vulcans: The History of Bush's War Cabinet* (New York: Viking, 2004), 138–42.

165 *"the dark side":* Tim Russert interview with Vice President Richard Cheney, *Meet the Press,* September 16, 2001.

166 *a resolution to push Saddam:* Mann, *Rise of the Vulcans,* 191.

166 *"premature to relax Cold-War style pressure":* Bush and Scowcroft, *A World Transformed,* 154.

166 *the internal debate:* Mann, *Rise of the Vulcans,* 206.

168 *a policy document:* Richard Cheney, *Defense Strategy for the 1990s: The Regional Defense Strategy,* January 1993.

168 *he embraced the notion of a Pax Americana:* Mann, *Rise of the Vulcans,* 211.

169 *"a Reaganite policy":* Statement of Principles, Project for the New American Century, June 3, 1997.

169 *the removal of Saddam:* letter to President Clinton, Project for the New American Century, January 26, 1998.

171 *present an idea:* Draper, *Dead Certain,* 283.

173 *an executive order at a private lunch:* Barton Gellman and Jo Becker, " 'A Different Understanding with the President,' " *Washington Post,* June 24, 2007.

173 *Cheney requested an all-access pass:* Ibid.

174 *"I have a right":* Lynne Cheney, *Executive Privilege,* 47.

175 *"any means at our disposal":* Tim Russert interview with Vice President Richard Cheney, *Meet the Press,* September 16, 2001.

175 *Cheney and his legal team:* Jack Goldsmith, *The Terror Presidency: Law and Judgment Inside the Bush Administration* (New York: W. W. Norton, 2007).

178 *Yes, I do have the view:* Vice President's Remarks to the Traveling Press, December 20, 2005.

179 *thirty yards away:* Paul Burka, "Full of Holes: The Gossip About Cheney's Bad Shot," *Slate,* February 14, 2006.

181 *Opinion of Aharon Barak:* http://hei.unige.ch/~clapham/hrdoc/docs/terror israeljudgment.pdf.

CHAPTER SIX: AN AMIABLE MONSTER

184 *Paul O'Neill claimed that getting rid of Saddam:* Ron Suskind, *The Price of Loyalty: George W. Bush, the White House, and the Education of Paul O'Neill* (New York: Simon & Schuster, 2004).

184 *dig Saddam out of power:* Frum, *The Right Man,* 26.

184 *"see if Saddam was involved":* Richard A. Clarke, *Against All Enemies: Inside America's War on Terror* (New York: Free Press, 2004), 32.

184 *"I believe that Iraq was involved":* Bob Woodward, *Bush at War* (New York: Simon & Schuster, 2002), 99.

184 *reforming the existing policy of sanctions:* Mann, *Rise of the Vulcans,* 301.

187 *Rice suggested a reorientation:* Condoleezza Rice, "Promoting the National Interest," *Foreign Affairs,* January/February 2000.

187 *"smiles and scowls of diplomacy":* Bush speech at the Reagan Library, November 19, 1999.

187 *Bush's unilateral tendency:* Charles Krauthammer, "The Bush Doctrine: In American Foreign Policy, a New Motto: Don't Ask. Tell," *Time,* March 5, 2001.

188 *didn't want to "pound sand":* Dan Balz and Bob Woodward, "We Will Rally the World: Bush and His Advisers Set Objectives, but Struggled with How to Achieve Them," *Washington Post,* January 28, 2002.

188 *Rice appears to have been the original framer:* Dan Balz and Bob Woodward, "America's Chaotic Road to War: Bush's Global Strategy Began to Take Shape in First Frantic Hours After Attack," *Washington Post,* January 27, 2002.

189 *a historical novel about Japan:* Lewis Libby, *The Apprentice* (St. Paul, Minn.: Graywolf Press, 1996).

189 *Cheney would be in charge:* Statement by President Bush, "Domestic Preparedness Against Weapons of Mass Destruction," White House, May 8, 2001.

190 *"Dick Cheney was the strongest":* Author interview with Ari Fleischer, August 2007.

190 *chimneys of bio-detectors:* Evan Thomas and Daniel Klaidman, "Full Speed Ahead," *Newsweek,* January 9, 2006.

190 *a national security bunker:* Steve Goldstein, " 'Undisclosed Location' Disclosed: A Visit Offers Some Insight into Cheney Hide-out," Knight Ridder, July 20, 2004.

190 *"as tired and as troubled":* Ari Fleischer, *Taking Heat: The President, the Press, and My Years in the White House* (New York: William Morrow, 2005), 189.

191 *"the only responsible thing for us to do":* Jim Lehrer interview with Vice President Richard Cheney, *NewsHour,* PBS, October 12, 2001.

191 *he turned out only to have syphilis:* Fleischer, *Taking Heat,* 200.

193 *mandatory vaccination:* Remarks by President Bush on Smallpox Vaccination, December 13, 2002.

195 *Mohammed Atta had met with Iraqi intelligence:* Laurie Mylroie, *Study of Revenge: Saddam Hussein's Unfinished War Against America* (Washington: AEI Press, 2000).

196 *"the geographic base of the terrorists":* Tim Russert interview with Vice President Richard Cheney, *Meet the Press,* September 14, 2003.

196 *"not a fact checker":* Background Briefing on Iraq WMD, White House, July 18, 2003.

197 *"All of [Bush's] instincts":* Gerson, *Heroic Conservatism,* 122.

198 *Bush unveiled this theory:* President Bush Delivers Graduation Speech at West Point, United States Military Academy, West Point, New York, June 1, 2002.

198 *the new doctrine:* "Prevent Our Enemies from Threatening Us, Our Allies, and Our Friends with Weapons of Mass Destruction," The National Security Strategy of the United States of America, September 2002.

203 *The founding document of neoconservative foreign policy:* Jeane J. Kirkpatrick, "Dictatorships and Double Standards," *Commentary,* November 1979.

207 *"The more the Europeans attack me":* Transcript published in *El País,* November 25, 2007.

207 *"Our preparations for rebuilding Iraq":* Dexter Filkins, "Regrets Only," *New York Times Magazine,* October 7, 2007.

208 *"someone who's willing to stand up":* Fred Kaplan, "A Debt of Gratitude: Why Is Bush So Obsessed with Ungrateful Foreigners?," *Slate,* March 13, 2007.

208 *Allawi "stood up and thanked the American people":* Remarks by President Bush on the Iraqi Interim Government, White House, June 1, 2004.

208 *he made a point of voicing his overwhelming gratitude:* Ayad Allawi Address to Congress, September 23, 2004.

209 *"a gratitude level that's significant enough in Iraq":* Scott Pelley interview with President George W. Bush, *60 Minutes,* January 14, 2007.

209 *"we settled on the one issue":* Sam Tanenhaus, "Bush's Brain Trust," *Vanity Fair,* July 2003.

209 *no sign of disappointment:* Isikoff and Corn, *Hubris,* 349.

209 *Bush still believed in 2006:* Draper, *Dead Certain,* 388.

210 *"a forward strategy":* Remarks by President Bush on freedom in Iraq and the Middle East, 20th Anniversary of the National Endowment for Democracy, U.S. Chamber of Commerce, November 6, 2003.

211 *disbanding the army wasn't his policy:* Draper, *Dead Certain,* 211.

212 *"The son prides himself":* Interview with Brent Scowcroft, November 2007.

213 *"I'm sick and tired":* Andrew Cockburn, *Rumsfeld: His Rise, Fall, and Catastrophic Legacy* (New York: Scribner, 2007), 219.

213 *a surprising source of support:* Bob Woodward, "Secret Reports Dispute White House Optimism," *Washington Post,* October 1, 2006.

213 *Kissinger gave Mike Gerson a copy:* Bob Woodward, *State of Denial: Bush at War, Part III* (New York: Simon & Schuster, 2006), 406–9.

214 *"potentially no less dramatic":* Natan Sharansky, *The Case for Democracy: The Power of Freedom to Overcome Tyranny and Terror* (New York: PublicAffairs, 2004), 244.

214 *Chicken Kiev speech:* Ibid., 67–68.

215 *"summarizes how I feel":* John King interview with President Bush, *Paula Zahn Now,* CNN, January 18, 2005.

215 *" 'But what about Chicken Kiev?' ":* Goldberg, "Breaking Ranks."

218 *an alcoholic member:* Robert Dreyfuss, "A Higher Power: James Baker Puts Bush's Iraq Policy into Rehab," *Washington Monthly,* September 2006.

218 *" 'Where's my drink?' ":* Dana Milbank, "In Theater of War, It's Iraq Study Group's Turn to Take the Stage," *Washington Post,* December 7, 2006.

219 *a "dissident President":* President Bush's speech in Prague, Czernin Palace, Czech Republic, June 5, 2007.

219 *"close the gap":* Tod Lindberg, "Dissident in Chief," *The Weekly Standard,* June 18, 2007.

220 *"many missed the elder Bush's realism":* Timothy Naftali, *George H. W. Bush: The American Presidents Series: The 41st President, 1989–1993* (New York: Times Books, 2007), 176.

221 *He was careless, dissolute, and ambitious:* William Hazlitt, *Lectures on the Literature of the Age of Elizabeth and Characters of Shakespear's Plays* (London, 1817).

CHAPTER SEVEN: DEAD PRECEDENTS

224 *"this long island story of ours":* Martin Gilbert, *Churchill: A Life* (New York: Owl, 1992), 651.

224 *the loan of a bronze head of Churchill:* "President Bush Accepts a Bust of Winston Churchill," Oval Office, July 16, 2001.

224 *"Tony Blair knew":* Roundtable Interview of the President by British Print Journalists, November 12, 2003.

225 *"a spare bust or two of Churchill":* Jon Meacham, "D-Day's Real Lessons," *Newsweek,* May 31, 2004.

225 *"Churchill possessed":* President Bush Discusses Importance of Democracy in Middle East, Library of Congress, February 4, 2004.

227 *Bush's list included:* Kenneth T. Walsh, "Bush's Reading List: Heavy on Bios and Baseball," *U.S. News & World Report,* October 9, 2007.

228 *"The man had a domineering mother":* Frank Bruni and David E. Sanger, "From the Ranch, President-Elect Gazes Back and Looks to Future," *New York Times,* January 14, 2001.

229 *"moral clarity":* Remarks by President Bush at Congressional Gold Medal Ceremony Honoring President Ronald Reagan and Nancy Reagan, United States Capitol, May 16, 2002.

229 *"they'd pray for you":* Remarks by President Bush at the National Funeral Service for Former President Ronald Wilson Reagan, National Cathedral, Washington, D.C., June 11, 2004.

229 *roster of those injured:* Draper, *Dead Certain,* 305.

233 *"No act of ours":* President Bush Discusses the War on Terror, Chrysler Hall, Norfolk, Virginia, October 28, 2005.

233 *like feeding a crocodile:* Secretary of Defense Donald H. Rumsfeld, Address at the 88th Annual American Legion National Convention, Salt Lake City, Utah, August 29, 2006.

234 *"aspirations of the human spirit":* Ronald Reagan Presidential Library, October 21, 2005.

234 *"each inhabitant of the Philippines":* Theodore Roosevelt, Hartford, Connecticut, August 22, 1902.

234 *had "come to savor unpopularity":* H. W. Brands, *T. R.: The Last Romantic* (New York: Basic Books, 1997).

235 *President Harry Truman stuck to his guns:* President Bush at the Woodrow Wilson Center, Ronald Reagan Building, December 14, 2005.

235 *the responsibility of world leadership:* President Bush Delivers the Commencement Address, United States Military Academy, West Point, New York, May 27, 2006.

236 *"history showed he was right":* Holly Bailey, Richard Wolffe, and Evan Thomas, "Bush's Truman Show," *Newsweek,* February 12, 2007.

236 *"history will take care of itself":* National Public Radio interview with President George W. Bush, January 29, 2007.

237 *"You do what you think is right":* Kenneth T. Walsh, "History's Verdict," *U.S. News & World Report,* January 21, 2007.

237 *center of his legacy:* Gerson, *Heroic Conservatism,* 171.

237 *Bush's head onto Churchill's body:* Jacob Weisberg, "George Bush's Favorite Historian," *Slate,* March 28, 2007, http://www.slate.com/id/2162837/.

237 *the president had more in common with Neville Chamberlain:* Lynne Olson, "Why Winston Wouldn't Stand for W.," *Washington Post,* July 1, 2007.

238 *an "evangelical style":* D. Jason Berggren and Nicol C. Rae, "Jimmy Carter and George W. Bush: Faith, Foreign Policy and an Evangelical Presidential Style," *Presidential Studies Quarterly* 36 (4), 2006, 606–32.

238 *"natural for him in his thinking":* Freud and Bullitt, *Thomas Woodrow Wilson,* xii.

238 *Bush took on the Vietnam analogy:* President Bush at the Veterans of Foreign Wars National Convention, Kansas City, Missouri, August 22, 2007.

239 *"You have to believe it":* Draper, *Dead Certain,* x–xi.

241 *his father's great fault:* Winston S. Churchill, *Lord Randolph Churchill* (London: Macmillan, 1906), Vol. 2, 244.

242 *"you are too old now":* Winston S. Churchill, "The Dream," in *The Norton Book of Personal Essays,* edited by Joseph Epstein (New York: W. W. Norton, 1997), 62–71.

Index

ABOUT THE AUTHOR

JACOB WEISBERG is the editor in chief of *Slate*. He previously worked for *The New Republic* and was a contributing writer for *The New York Times Magazine*, a contributing editor to *Vanity Fair,* and a columnist for the *Financial Times.* Weisberg is the inventor of the "Bushisms" series. He is also the author, with Robert E. Rubin, of *In an Uncertain World.* Weisberg's first book, *In Defense of Government*, was published in 1996.

ABOUT THE TYPE

This book was set in Requiem, a typeface designed by the Hoefler Type Foundry. It is a modern typeface inspired by inscriptional capitals in Ludovico Vicentino degli Arrighi's 1523 writing manual, *Il modo de temperare le penne*. An original lowercase, a set of figures, and an italic in the "chancery" style that Arrighi helped popularize were created to make this adaptation of a classical design into a complete font family.